The Power of Praying® Through the Bible

STORMIE OMARTIAN

HARVEST HOUSE PUBLISHERS

EUGENE, OREGON

THE POWER OF PRAYING® THROUGH THE BIBLE
Copyright © 2008 by Stormie Omartian
Published by Harvest House Publishers
Eugene, Oregon 97402
www.harvesthousepublishers.com

Library of Congress Cataloging-in-Publication Data
Omartian, Stormie.
The power of praying through the Bible / Stormie Omartian.
p. cm.
ISBN-13: 978-0-7369-2358-3 (pbk.)

1. Bible—Devotional use. I. Title.
BS617.8.O43 2008
242'.5—dc22
                2008014663

Printed in the United States of America

09 10 11 12 13 14 15 16 / BP-SK / 11 10 9 8 7 6 5 4

INTRODUCTION

❦

I love reading the Word of God. I especially love it when the Scriptures I am reading inspire me to pray. And they always do. In this book I want to share with you certain verses I have chosen throughout the Bible, and how they have impressed my heart and mind and led me to pray specifically. I hope that as you read each one of these short Bible studies and devotional prayers, they will encourage you to see every verse of God's Word as a source of inspiration to draw you into a closer walk with the Lord through ongoing prayer.

I pray that each Scripture presented here will lead you to read it in your own Bible so you can go deeper into the rest of that passage or chapter. While I have written out only a verse or two here, I have also included the Bible reference for the entire passage so you can check it out more thoroughly if you would like to. There is much to be gleaned from reading Scripture in context of its surrounding material when you have the time or inclination to do so.

From the first chapter of Genesis through the Bible to the book of Revelation, you will find examples of how to pray for your life and the lives of those around you, as well as for your world and the things you care about most. You will see examples of the way great men and women of Bible history prayed and how God responded to their prayers. You will learn what God asks us to do with regard to prayer and how we should respond to His direction. You will be reminded of the ways God wants you to pray and why.

May each devotional Bible study and prayer encourage you to go deeper into God's Word to find the treasures God has for you there, and to pray in ways you might not otherwise have thought to pray. It is my prayer that each time you read in this book, it will bring inspiration for your day and hope for your future.

Stormie Omartian

God's Connection *with* Us

❧ Read and Consider ❧

Genesis 1:26–2:7

"The LORD God formed the man from the dust of the
ground and breathed into his nostrils the breath of life,
and the man became a living being" (Genesis 2:7).

God created the universe with a word. He spoke stars and planets into existence. He formed the world with simple commands. God started the creation process without any preexisting things. He began with nothing. With the presence of the Holy Spirit and the entrance of His Word, creation happened. He brought order, light, life, and beauty out of chaos and darkness. He said, "Let there be…" and it happened.

Then He became personally involved with making humans. Other places in Scripture describe God as a "potter" and human beings as the "clay" (Isaiah 64:8), making us think of our heavenly Father bent over a potter's wheel, forming mud figures into the design He had in mind for us. The finishing touch was to breathe into us His breath of life. God got personal, right from the start.

But He didn't stop there. God's action in giving us breath also gave us the ability to speak. The act of breathing that keeps us alive is the same act that we use to communicate. We breathe out to speak (and some languages in the world even breathe in to speak). We are God's image bearers (1:26-27). We breathe and speak because of His breath given to us.

We should be in awe of the privilege we have to use the breath of life to speak to our Creator. We were made to communicate with our Maker. Even though we may not start out doing it very well, He still wants to hear us speak to Him. Just as we are delighted when

5

our babies make their first tiny sounds, so our heavenly Father is delighted when He hears the sound of one of His children speaking words intended for His ears.

So breathe a prayer to God often. If words don't come to mind right away, start by saying, "Thank You." As you say those two words slowly, begin to add "for..." until different ways to end the sentence begin to flow. Once you do this a while, you will realize that you can use your inspiration (breathing in) as time to think of the next words and your expiration (breathing out) to express your gratitude. All the way back to the first breath of the first person, you and I were made for this. Giving us the "breath of life" is God's connection with us, and prayer is our connection with Him.

❧

*Lord, I thank You for the breath of life You have
given me. I pray You will breathe new life into me
today. Just as You spoke and brought about life in Your
magnificent world, help me to speak words that bring
life into my own small world as well. How grateful
I am to be closely connected to You in every way.*

A Walk *in the* Garden

"Then the man and his wife heard the sound of the
LORD God as he was walking in the garden in the cool
of the day, and they hid from the LORD God among
the trees of the garden. But the LORD God called
to the man, 'Where are you?'" (Genesis 3:8-9).

Certain places just feel like this first garden. Something about the lush vegetation, the time of day, or the sounds of nature all provoke an almost overwhelming longing in us to experience what Adam and Eve enjoyed every day—a walk with God.

The world is still a wonderful setting in which to know God, but something has changed. It changed way back there, in the garden. The first two people gave up the pleasure of God's company for their own interests. They heard the sound of God walking in the garden, looking for them, wanting to enjoy their usual walk. But they had sinned. Guilt overwhelmed them. They were ashamed to see God. They lost the close relationship they had with Him, and we've struggled to recapture that closeness ever since.

God didn't hide from man; it was the other way around. Adam and Eve ducked into the bushes in shame, fear, and rebellion. But God came looking. He knew where they were, but He wanted them to know He was willing to seek their company. He was aware of their disobedience, but kept His appointment with them anyway.

What amazing fellowship they forfeited! What peace they lost! And yet, before we criticize them, remember how easily and how often we repeat their mistake. We make choices that draw us away from God. We experience overwhelming moments of His presence that we wish we could wrap up and keep; yet hours later we turn our backs on Him, trying to shut His gentle whisper out of our lives.

The power in our prayer life flows out of God's presence with us. It's not *our* power; it's *His*. We don't experience or witness that power if we insist on our agenda and our schedules. We have to plan and hold sacred the places and times when we meet God. If we don't deliberately build our lives around these "garden walks" with the Lord, the world will rapidly and relentlessly fill our hours with other commitments. As He did with Adam and Eve, God will come looking for us. But how much better would it be if He found us waiting expectantly? I don't want Him to have to call out, "Where are you?" to me. What about you?

❦

*Lord, I want more than anything to have a close
walk with You. Help me not to forfeit that wonderful
intimacy by being drawn toward the distractions of
this world. Enable me to hear Your voice calling me
so that I will answer without even a moment's delay.
Help me to never hide from You for any reason.*

POWERFUL LISTENING

*"Noah was a righteous man, blameless among the people
of his time, and he walked with God" (Genesis 6:9).*

Noah listened well. When God spoke to him, he paid attention. Genesis tells us that Noah "walked with God." What a beautiful way to say that Noah lived each day with an awareness of God's presence. Beyond that, however, Noah also obeyed. What God told him to do, he did.

Noah obeyed even though God directed him to do something outlandish: "Make yourself an ark" (6:14). And Noah did. What a monstrosity he constructed on dry land, miles from the nearest body of water! How many insults, jokes, and sarcastic questions he must have endured. Yet he kept on task, obeying God's instructions. Hebrews 11:7 lists Noah among the heroes of faith. The picture that develops out of the phrase "walked with God" reveals a person who depended on God's faithfulness across the decades, through times of doubt, against the corruption that surrounded him.

With the exception of his family, Noah stood alone for God in his culture. The memory of God in the world had shrunk to a single man and his household. Many centuries later, Jesus described the people in Noah's day: "For in the days before the flood, people were eating and drinking, marrying and giving in marriage, up to the day Noah entered the ark; and they knew nothing about what would happen until the flood came and took them all away. That is how it will be at the coming of the Son of Man" (Matthew 24:38-39). In Noah's day, as in ours, the noises of busyness can drown out the voice of God. (Little did they know that a different kind of drowning would

9

soon overtake them.) Jesus warned about any time when people are oblivious to the danger of going about life without stopping long enough to listen to God.

Prayer is more than talking to God. While that is vital, too many of us give God our list of requests and then dash off to our next task. What would our lives be like if we took the time not only to talk to God but to listen to Him as well? What if we then determined to obey what He tells us to do—no matter how much our society might scoff at us?

Do you want to walk with God? Then in your prayer time, *listen* carefully for His voice. You may hear Him leading you in a new direction, with a new purpose, and with courage you never knew you had!

❧

> *Dear God, help me to live each day with a deep sense*
> *of Your presence. I don't want to go through life without*
> *taking time to be with You. I want my relationship*
> *with You to be so strong that other people recognize*
> *Your Spirit in me. Whenever I draw near to You in*
> *prayer, help me to hear Your voice speaking to my*
> *heart so that I will always follow Your leading.*

The POWER of GOD'S PROMISE

*"Whenever the rainbow appears in the clouds, I will see it
and remember the everlasting covenant between God and
all living creatures of every kind on the earth" (Genesis 9:16).*

When the clouds part after a thundershower revealing a stunning arc of colors, how many times have you stopped to look—and even called to others to join you? "Look at the rainbow!" Never ceasing to be objects of wonder, rainbows are those amazing creations that disappear as quickly as they appear, yet bring joy to our hearts when they surprise us by parting the gray with their luminescence.

That arc of color ties us right back to our ancestor Noah, to the moment after the flood when God made a promise, a covenant, that He would never again destroy the earth with a flood. Many scholars believe that the people of Noah's day had never even seen rain—that instead, the earth had been watered from springs deep in the ground. The flood occurred when "the springs of the great deep burst forth, and the floodgates of the heavens were opened" (7:11). Rain fell from heaven—and would continue to fall for the rest of the ages. But Noah did not need to fear the next time rain clouds gathered because God had made a promise. The rain would subside and the rainbow would appear. That visual sign would be a constant reminder that God always keeps His promises.

What does that have to do with prayer? Everything! When we pray, we reassert our faith that God keeps His promises. What we say out loud, or silently in our hearts, proclaims the truth of God's promises that we have read or heard in His Word. Have you ever noticed that if you are feeling bad and you keep saying negative thoughts out loud, you tend to feel them even stronger? The same is true in believing God's promises. When we speak the truth about God and about what He has promised us, while refusing to believe the lies of the enemy, it causes us to believe God stronger than before. That is not to say we should deny we have real problems or struggles, but the way we interpret them may be different. Satan wants us to believe that God has abandoned us and reneged on His promises, but God wants us to know that His promises are always true in spite of what we can see from our limited human perspective. By asserting our belief in His promises in prayer, we put ourselves in a position to see a lot more from God's perspective and a lot less from the enemy's.

So the next time you stand in wonder at the appearance of a rainbow in the clouds, breathe a prayer of thanks to God that He will always keep His promises.

❧

Lord, I thank You that You always keep Your promises
to me. Help me to understand and remember exactly
what Your promises are so that I can recall them in my
mind, keep them in my heart, and speak them out loud
whenever I need to push doubt away from me. Help
me to remember that Jesus is the ultimate proof that
You have already kept Your greatest promise to us.

WHEN WE HAVE *to* WAIT

❧ Read and Consider ☙

―――――――――――――
Genesis 15:1-6

"After this, the word of the LORD came to Abram in a vision:
'Do not be afraid, Abram. I am your shield, your very great
reward.' But Abram said, 'O Sovereign LORD, what can
you give me since I remain childless and the one who will
inherit my estate is Eliezer of Damascus?'" (Genesis 15:1-2).

Can't you just hear the exasperation in Abram's voice? "God, I appreciate that You're my shield and reward. That's great and all. Don't think I don't appreciate it, but…what I *really* want is for You to fulfill Your promise of descendants. Let's get on with that promise about becoming a 'great nation.' I want a SON!"

Abram had been waiting a long time. God had promised many descendants to Abram back when he was a mere 75 years old (12:4). He would be 100 years old when Isaac was finally born (21:5). That means Abram and Sarai waited 25 years for God to fulfill His promise.

We don't know how long Abram had already been waiting at this point in the story, but the Bible tells us he was 86 when Ishmael was born (16:16), so we can guess that this exchange between God and Abram occurred sometime in the first decade after God had made the promise.

How long do you patiently wait for answers to your prayers? Does a week seem too long to wait? What about a month? Waiting for a year seems to be beyond our ability. To see that Abram waited for a quarter of a century for an answer should give us hope to wait for our own prayers to be answered.

Abram could have given up. He could have decided that he didn't want to wait on God anymore. (He *did* eventually make a mess of things when he tried to fulfill God's promise on his own by having a child with Hagar.) At this point in the story, however, he chose to believe. If only he had continued to hang on to that belief.

What answer from God are you waiting for? Is it the answer to a prayer for the return of a rebellious child? Is it the answer to a prayer for the salvation of a family member? Is it the answer to a prayer for restoration in your marriage? For a job? For healing? For provision? Whatever it is, keep on praying and waiting. Release it into God's hands and let Him do it in His way and His time. His answer will be worth the wait.

❧

Dear God, help me to have faith enough to believe
You will answer my prayers. Give me the patience to
wait for the answers to appear. Keep me from giving
up and taking matters into my own hands. Instead,
enable me to trust that You have heard my prayers
and will answer in Your perfect way and time. Help
me to rest in peace during times of waiting.

MAKING SACRIFICES

❧ Read and Consider ❧

Genesis 22:1-19

*"Some time later God tested Abraham. He said to
him, 'Abraham!' 'Here I am,' he replied. Then God
said, 'Take your son, your only son, Isaac, whom you
love, and go to the region of Moriah. Sacrifice him
there as a burnt offering on one of the mountains I
will tell you about.' Early the next morning Abraham
got up and saddled his donkey." (Genesis 22:1-3).*

Sometimes God asks the strangest things. Noah had to build an
ark miles away from any body of water and put in stalls that
would somehow be filled with animals. (Surely he wondered how
he was going to round up the lions and keep them away from the
zebras!)

But nothing quite matches the task given to Abraham. Not only
did God ask him to kill his son, God was taking away from Abraham
that answer to the promise he had waited 25 years to receive. Isaac
was Abraham's heir, the child promised to Abraham and Sarah,
the child born in their old age. For Isaac to die would also kill the
dream.

Or would it?

It seems that Abraham didn't waste time worrying about it. He
got up early the next morning, saddled his donkey, roused the sleepy
boy and two servants, cut some wood (he would need kindling to
start the fire), and set out for the three-day journey. What went
through his mind during those three long days? I imagine that
Abraham talked to God *a lot*. And such was Abraham's relationship with God that he trusted God. He didn't understand; he knew
that obeying God would hurt him to the core, but he kept right

on walking. He kept right on obeying. When he got to the place, he built an altar, bound his son, laid him on the altar, and raised the knife.

Could any of us trust God that much?

Our hearts wince at the thought of sacrificing a human being. But we would be wise to consider how this story gives an astounding picture of what God Himself would one day do for us. As Isaac carried the wood for the burnt offering, so Jesus carried His own cross to Golgotha. As Abraham placed Isaac on the altar, so God placed His Son on the cross. As Abraham raised his knife in order to kill his son in obedience to God, so God allowed Jesus to be put to death so that sin could be punished and forgiveness could be given. Abraham knew that God would provide the lamb for the offering (22:8). Many centuries later, He did. John the Baptist pointed this out to his followers: "Look, the Lamb of God, who takes away the sin of the world!" (John 1:29). How much do you trust God—*really?* Enough to die for Him? Enough to let a dream in your life die?

How about enough to live for Him?

❧

Lord, I know You always ask me to surrender everything to You—including the dream in my heart. And even when that dream is from You, You still ask me to let go of my hold on it. So I surrender every dream in my heart to You right now. I don't want to cling to something You will not bless, or give up on something that is Your will for my life.

A PRAYER *for* SUCCESS

*"Then he prayed, 'O LORD, God of my master
Abraham, give me success today, and show kindness
to my master Abraham'" (Genesis 24:12).*

When you face a big job or an important responsibility, you want to succeed. The best way to see success is to go directly to God, who wants the very best for your life, and ask for His guidance. That's what Eliezer did.

Abraham had asked his servant to find the right bride for his son Isaac. This was most likely Eliezer, Abraham's trusted servant for many years. Eliezer realized the great weight of the responsibility he carried, so he submitted the matter directly to God rather than depend solely on his own wisdom or on pure luck. He asked God for a sign, and God granted his request almost instantly. Before Eliezer had even finished praying, Rebekah arrived and offered to give him water for both himself and his camels. What a remarkable answer to prayer!

But let's go a little deeper. Who was Eliezer? If we go back to where he is named in Genesis 15:2-3, we discover that not only was he Abraham's trusted servant, but at that point, he stood to inherit all of Abraham's wealth if Abraham had no son. So not only did he lose out when Isaac was born, but Eliezer also had to find a suitable bride for Isaac. A lesser man might have been bitter about all he had lost. A lesser man might have defined "success" as doing whatever it might take to get back into that place of honor in order to gain the inheritance. A lesser man might not have cared what kind of bride he brought back to Isaac. Not Eliezer. He was determined to do the job well, so he prayed for success in the task.

God cares about your responsibilities. He wants to see you do well, to succeed. So don't be afraid to ask for success. Always keep in mind, however, that He may define success very differently than you do. Like Eliezer, walk so close to God that you're able to put aside what you might want for yourself in order to succeed at what God wants for you.

❦

Heavenly Father, I pray for success in all I do. Guide me in everything. Show me where I have proceeded with something without first inquiring of You. Enable me to understand Your measure of success and not try to impose my own. My goal is to serve You, knowing that any success I have will be achieved only by walking perfectly in Your will.

CALL *on the* NAME *of the* LORD

*"Isaac built an altar there and called on the name
of the LORD. There he pitched his tent, and there
his servants dug a well" (Genesis 26:25).*

I saac was having a difficult time. It seems that everywhere he
turned he got into trouble. Abimelech got after him for lying;
the Philistines stopped up his wells in order to force him to move
away; and even after he moved and dug a new well, someone argued
with him about *that* one. He couldn't win.

With each situation, however, he avoided conflict and worked for
peace for everyone involved. Finally, when it seemed that everything
was peaceful, the Lord appeared, describing Himself as the God of
Isaac's father, Abraham. "Do not be afraid, for I am with you; I will
bless you and will increase the number of your descendants for the
sake of my servant Abraham" (26:24).

This surely must have caused Isaac to flash back to the many
times when his dear father had talked about the Lord. What had
Abraham taught him? What did Isaac feel about this God who had
stopped his father's knife and sent a ram instead as a sacrifice? Did
he have memories of being untied and taken back home—and how
joyful his dad had looked on that return trip? This God was not to
be taken lightly. This God introduced Himself to Isaac, giving him
a wonderful promise of future blessing. Isaac acknowledged that
promise and "called on the name of the Lord."

What does it mean to call on the name of the Lord? It means to
acknowledge who He is and the power of His very existence to do
more than we can ask or think. It means to place our trust in Him

and praise Him for all He does. When you call on the Lord's name, you give Him the praise that He deserves by recognizing Him in all of His holiness, authority, and glory. In doing so, you open yourself to the power and blessing He wants to bring into your life.

Praise God every day for all the ways that He is sufficient for every need you have, and, like Isaac, declare your faithfulness to Him by calling on His name in prayer.

❧

Lord, You are the God of the universe and Lord of my
life. I worship You and give glory to Your name. You are
holy and wonderful—amazing and awesome—and I
thank You for all You have done for me. Because Your
Word says You are able to do beyond what I can even
think of to ask for, I call on You to meet all of my needs
in ways more wonderful than I can even imagine.

STRUGGLING *in* PRAYER

❧ Read and Consider ❧
Genesis 32:1-32

"Jacob was left alone, and a man wrestled with him till daybreak. When the man saw that he could not overpower him, he touched the socket of Jacob's hip so that his hip was wrenched as he wrestled with the man. Then the man said, 'Let me go, for it is daybreak.' But Jacob replied, 'I will not let you go unless you bless me'" (Genesis 32:24-26).

Does prayer ever seem like a struggle to you? Often our prayer times may seem more like wrestling matches than conversations, but this passage lets us know that amazing transformations can come out of the struggles we experience in prayer.

Up until this particular encounter with God, Jacob's life had been characterized by his attempts to get ahead on his own, his deceitful plots to obtain blessings, and his manipulations to make his life work out the way he wanted it to. He had not given God control and had not trusted the Lord to carry out His plans.

However, when the stranger came along and wrestled with him, Jacob was at a point in his life when he was alone and genuinely fearful about what was going to happen to him and to his family. He was about to meet his brother again, who had every right to hate him. Jacob had no idea what his brother's plans might be. During the struggle with the stranger (who turned out to be God, 32:30), Jacob told the stranger his name—the equivalent of a confession, because his name literally meant "supplanter" or "usurper." This confession led to transformation. Jacob received the blessing from his opponent—a new name and a new future. He had been changed by the confrontation. He also received an injury that resulted in a lifetime limp—an ever-present reminder of what had happened.

If you want to experience life-changing prayer, be honest with God about who you are and confess it. For example, say, "Lord, I have been fearful," or "Lord, I have been a doubter." Then say, "Lord, help me to rise above who I am now to who You have called me to be." Despite Jacob's past, God's plans prevailed in his life, but not without a struggle. Don't be afraid to struggle in prayer, knowing that God will use any measures necessary in order to carry out His plans for your life. Like Jacob, hang on and don't give up until you get the blessing that will change you forever.

❦

Lord, I desire to know You better so that I can experience
all the blessings You have for me. I confess I don't pray
as much as I would like to, and I have times of fear and
doubt, but I commit this day to trust You more and to pray
without ceasing—even if it feels like a struggle—because
I know I will find transformation in Your presence.

The POWER of PRAISE

Genesis 35:1-15

"Then come, let us go up to Bethel, where I will build an altar to God, who answered me in the day of my distress and who has been with me wherever I have gone" (Genesis 35:3).

How often do you take the time to remember what God has done for you and thank Him for it? Too often we are so busy that we accept the blessings God gives us as we rush through our hectic days without even stopping to notice them. Deadlines, meetings, and family commitments all crowd out the time we have to praise God. So often we only stop to talk to Him when we need something or when circumstances bring us face-to-face with our own inadequacy.

In this passage, however, Jacob was deliberately taking the time to slow down, stop, and build an altar to the Lord—not to ask for something—but to remember what God had done for him. And this kind of praise has power in it. When we praise God, He renews our strength and reminds us of the truth about who He is and what He wants to do in our lives. When we remember how He has been faithful in the past, it gives us confidence that we can put our trust in Him for our future. When you look back and see His hand guiding your life up to this point, it gives you faith to believe that even though the future is unclear, you can trust that He will not leave you.

It is so important to take time to reflect upon what God has done in your life and how He has been faithful to you. Then you will not fear the future, but anticipate it with the knowledge that God will be with you wherever you go.

❧

*Almighty God, I worship You for who You are. I thank
You for all You have done for me. You have given me
strength, power, provision, and purpose. I know I need
not fear the future because I see how You have blessed
me and protected me in the past. I pray You will always
be with me to guide me in the way I should go.*

PRAYING *for* YOUR CHILDREN

❧ Read and Consider ☙
Genesis 48:1-22

"Then he blessed Joseph and said, 'May the God before whom my fathers Abraham and Isaac walked, the God who has been my shepherd all my life to this day, the Angel who has delivered me from all harm—may he bless these boys. May they be called by my name and the names of my fathers Abraham and Isaac, and may they increase greatly upon the earth'"(Genesis 48:15-16).

If you are a parent (or a grandparent), God has given you the authority to pray for your children. You know your children better than anyone else. You know their hopes, their fears, their secret worries, their insecurities, their dreams, their gifts, and their abilities. You love them more than life itself. No one has a heart for their well-being and their future more than you do.

God has not only entrusted you to care for your children's physical, emotional, and spiritual needs, but He has given you a way to bless them as well. Through prayer. The most important thing you can do as a parent is bring your children daily before the Lord and pray for His protection, guidance, wisdom, and love to be infused into every part of their lives. And even though you can't always be with your children every moment, God can. And you can trust that He will be with them in power when you pray.

Each time you intercede for your children, pray that God will bless their lives and give them wisdom and discernment in the choices they face. Pray that He will protect them from the traps the enemy sets for them and that they will follow God and reject evil. Pray that they will love learning and discover the gifts and abilities that God has given them. And pray that their lives will bring glory to God and hope and healing to those around them.

Prayer is the most important gift you can give to your children. They will thrive under the care and power of a praying parent.

❦

Heavenly Father, teach me to pray for my children and grandchildren and any children You put in my life. Bless each child with a knowledge of who You are and help them to live Your way so they can stay on the path You have for their lives. Enable each child to recognize the gifts and talents You have put in them, and to follow Your leading as they develop and use them for Your glory.

CRYING OUT *to* GOD

❧ Read and Consider ☙

Exodus 1:1-14; 2:23-25

*"During that long period, the king of Egypt
died. The Israelites groaned in their slavery and
cried out, and their cry for help because of their
slavery went up to God" (Exodus 2:23).*

Have you ever felt like the Israelites in this passage? Perhaps
you too have endured a long season of repeatedly crying out
for deliverance. You might even now be in a difficult situation that
seems to offer no apparent means of escape. Perhaps you are hurting,
or someone you love is suffering, and you wonder if God can hear
your pleas for His help.

When the Israelites cried out, God not only heard them, He
answered them far beyond just helping them find relief. He totally
liberated them. But it happened God's way—the way that would
serve to teach both the Egyptians and the Israelites exactly who
He was. God raised up a leader in Moses—two leaders, actually,
because He also sent his brother, Aaron. Their first attempt to free
the people appeared to fail because the Egyptians ended up giving
Israel even more work than they had before. Even when Moses and
Aaron performed miracles, Pharaoh hardened his heart. The situation
looked more hopeless than ever. But in the midst of situations that
are dark and hopeless, God does His greatest work. Even though
the children of Israel were in bondage for nearly 400 years, "God
heard their groaning and he remembered his covenant...God looked
on the Israelites and was concerned about them." He will do the
same for you. When you cry out to God, your prayers will reach
His heart. Just remember that being set free from the past or from

a difficult situation may happen quickly or it can be a step-by-step process, depending on what God is wanting to teach you. You can't make it happen on your timetable, so be patient and continue to pray for as long as it takes. Don't ever stop believing that the Lord is a God of miracles.

❧

Lord, I cry out to You for deliverance from anything that keeps me from becoming all You created me to be. Set me free from everything that separates me from You. Lord, I know that even in the midst of what seems to be the most hopeless situation, You can do Your greatest work. Thank You that You are a God of miracles. I pray You will do a miracle in my life today.

Praying *on* Behalf *of* Others

"Pharaoh quickly summoned Moses and Aaron and
said, 'I have sinned against the LORD your God
and against you. Now forgive my sin once more
and pray to the LORD your God to take this deadly
plague away from me'" (Exodus 10:16-17).

Have you ever tried to share your faith with an unbelieving friend, coworker, or employer, only to have that person demonstrate disinterest or even downright hostility? Those around you may reject your concern for them and ignore their own need for a Savior. However, if a crisis comes, those same people will allow you to pray for them. They may even seek you out—asking for your prayers, knowing you have a "hotline" to heaven.

This becomes extremely difficult when we are called to pray for those who have hurt us. In the Sermon on the Mount, Jesus instructed His followers to disregard the conventional wisdom of the time regarding enemies and practice love through intercession instead. "You have heard that it was said, 'Love your neighbor and hate your enemy.' But I tell you: Love your enemies and pray for those who persecute you, that you may be sons of your Father in heaven" (Matthew 5:43-45).

Pharaoh put all his faith in the ability of his wise men, sorcerers, and magicians to use their secret arts to perform miracles. But when the plagues were clearly "the finger of God," Pharaoh turned to Moses for help, the one man he knew could truly intercede.

The unbelievers in your world should be able to tell by your life that you are a praying person and that they can depend on you to intercede for them with the only One who can truly make a difference.

❦

God, help me to learn to pray in power. Increase my faith to believe for the answers to my prayers. Enable me to become an intercessor for others—especially those who do not know You. I pray that everyone around me will be able to recognize by my life that I am a person of great faith and power in prayer, and that they can trust in the God to whom I pray.

STOP PRAYING *and* START MOVING

❧ Read and Consider ❧
Exodus 14

*"Then the LORD said to Moses, 'Why are you crying out
to me? Tell the Israelites to move on'" (Exodus 14:15).*

Many passages of Scripture speak of the importance of crying out to God in times of distress. In Lamentations we read, "Arise, cry out in the night…pour out your heart like water in the presence of the Lord" (Lamentations 2:19). There comes a point, however, when the time for crying out is past and our clear instruction from the Lord is to take action.

That's what God said to Moses. The Israelites didn't need to worry about the details; God would take care of everything. He would help His people by obstructing the sight of the Egyptians with clouds and darkness. He would give the Israelites light. He would cause the wind to dry up the sea bottom. They didn't need more desperate prayer. They needed to get moving!

They may have been tempted to just wait. "This can't be what God wants us to do! It's too dangerous! It's too frightening! How do we know we'll make it? Let's just keep praying about this."

Sometimes prayer is an excuse for inaction.

Famed missionary Amy Carmichael once wrote a simple rhyme to illustrate the importance of following through with action once we have thoroughly prayed over a matter:

> *A centipede was happy till*
> *One day, a toad in fun*
> *Said, "Pray, which leg goes after which?"*
> *Which strained his mind to such a pitch*

He lay distracted in a ditch,
Considering how to run.

When you hear God telling you to move in a certain direction, take two words of advice: *Do it!*

If you delay, you may well find yourself "distracted in a ditch, considering how to run." When the way is clear, remember the Lord's instruction to the Israelites through Moses—"Move on!"

❧

Holy Father, help me to understand, as I am in prayer and waiting for a leading from You, when it is time to take action. Help me to be wise enough to recognize the answers to my prayers when they come in ways I was not expecting. Give me the knowledge of Your will that lets me know when it is time to stand up and take steps of faith.

GOING DIRECTLY *to* GOD

❧ Read and Consider ❧
Exodus 19:3-8

*"So Moses went back and summoned the elders of the
people and set before them all the words the LORD
had commanded him to speak" (Exodus 19:7).*

An intermediary is someone who acts as an agent between two
different parties: a go-between, a mediator. As this passage
reveals, mediation in the form of intercession was clearly a big part
of Moses' role as leader of the nation of Israel. God specifically told
him what to say to the people of Israel, and in turn, Moses brought
their answer back to the Lord.

Throughout history, various religions have taught that people can
only approach God through the intervention of a human mediator.
This was also true for the Jewish people during the times recorded
in the Old Testament. The people could not approach God directly.
Prophets such as Elijah and Elisha arose to speak for the Lord. Kings
wouldn't go off to war without consulting a prophet, who also func-
tioned as a mediator or intercessor. This veil between God and
humanity was symbolized by the thick, heavy curtain that hung in
the Most Holy Place in the tabernacle and later in the temple—a
barrier between a holy God and sinful human beings that only priests
especially anointed for the task could pass through.

With the crucifixion of Jesus Christ, however, all that changed.
At the moment of Christ's death, the curtain in the temple was torn
in two (Mark 15:38), representing the dramatic reality that there
was no longer any obstruction between God and mankind. When
you fully grasp this truth, it will change your life. You do not need
the presence of a human intermediary to take your prayers and

concerns to your heavenly Father. Instead, the book of Hebrews tells us that we can "approach the throne of grace with confidence, so that we may receive mercy and find grace to help us in our time of need" (Hebrews 4:16).

Jesus is your great High Priest—the only mediator you will ever need. "For there is one God and one mediator between God and men, the man Christ Jesus, who gave himself as a ransom for all men" (1 Timothy 2:5-6).

Nothing is wrong with asking others to pray for and with you, but don't hesitate to take the concerns of your heart directly to God. He is waiting!

❧

Thank You, Lord, that I can come to You with my
prayers. Thank You, Jesus, that because You gave
Your life in sacrifice for mine, the veil has been torn
in two and in Your name I can go directly to God in
intercession. Help me to remember that I can confidently
come to Your throne feeling assured that I will receive
Your grace and mercy to help me in my times of need.

The POWER of LITTLE by LITTLE

Exodus 23:20-30

*"Little by little I will drive them out before
you, until you have increased enough to take
possession of the land" (Exodus 23:30).*

Have you ever asked God to do something major in your life,
and then experienced disappointment when He appeared to
be working little by little rather than all at once?

Perhaps you have a lifestyle habit that you know is unhealthy.
You've asked God to remove those persistent physical urges, but you
grow discouraged when the progress you're making seems insignificant. Or maybe, like the Israelites, you are coming under attack
from adversaries who seem intent on your personal or professional
destruction. Why doesn't God, who certainly has the power, give
us victory instantaneously or wipe out the enemies that cause so
much harm?

There are no simple answers, but this passage provides an important clue about the nature of God's activity on our behalf: He is
going by His timetable, not ours, and His will for us is determined
by what is ultimately best for us. Scripture tells us that "with the
Lord a day is like a thousand years, and a thousand years are like a
day. The Lord is not slow in keeping his promise, as some understand
slowness. He is patient with you" (2 Peter 3:8-9). Our loving heavenly
Father is working for our eternal good, but He is accomplishing
His purpose in our lives in His own perfect way and in His own
time. God knows that these little steps are better for us now. He
doesn't want us to be overtaken by the things that could happen if
we experience victory too quickly.

Be encouraged when your prayers reveal progress that can be measured even in the tiniest increments. God is at work in your life and in the lives of those around you, and before long, little by little will add up to major change.

❦

God, help me to have the patience to wait on You for the answers to my prayers. I confess I want all the answers to manifest now, but I know Your timing is perfect. Help me to understand the things that are happening in response to my prayers that I cannot see. Enable me to envision the step-by-step progress that is being made.

The POWER of INTERCESSION

❧ Read and Consider ❧
Exodus 32:1-14

"Then the LORD relented and did not bring on his people the disaster he had threatened" (Exodus 32:14).

Can prayer change God's mind? God was angry with the Israelite's disobedience, corruption, and rebellion, and He spoke to Moses of His intent to destroy them. Moses, however, sought God's favor and pleaded with the Lord to spare the very people He had miraculously brought out of Egypt. Exodus 32:14 says the Lord "relented," which means He decided not to do as He had planned. Did Moses actually change the mind of God?

Scripture speaks again and again of the power of intercession. The power is not in us as human beings, of course, or in the order or frequency of the words we speak. The power comes solely from God, the One who hears us. "The prayer of a righteous man [or woman] is powerful" (James 5:16).

Intercession is empowered when it is based on the promises of God. You can pray for another person, but if what you're asking is not consistent with or contradicts His promises, your prayers won't be effective. When your prayers for another are in line with His Word, God *will* respond. This is another good reason to read the Bible daily.

Base your prayers on the truth of God's Word. As Moses did, you can pray God's Word back to Him, reminding Him of what He has promised. You can stand before God "in the gap" (Ezekiel 22:30) and intercede for the lives of others, and for your nation. Intercession is a precious privilege. Who knows what a difference your prayers can make?

❧

*Lord, help me to have a greater knowledge of Your
Word so that I will always pray in alignment with
Your will. I know the power I have in prayer is Your
power working through me. Help me to never get in
the way of what You want to do in response to my
prayers. Help me to make a major difference in the lives
of my family, friends, and neighbors when I pray.*

The COST of FORGIVENESS

"He is to lay his hand on the head of the burnt
offering, and it will be accepted on his behalf to
make atonement for him" (Leviticus 1:4).

I n the Old Testament system of sacrifices, forgiveness came at a price—a literal, hands-on, obvious price.

Today we understand forgiveness as we look at Christ's sacrifice. He was our once-and-for-all payment for sin. In the Old Testament, under the law of Moses, the people looked ahead to Christ's salvation. With the Old Testament sacrifices and offerings, they actually *pre-enacted* the provision that was to come through Jesus. The sacrifices were symbols—the lives of innocent animals were offered as payment for the sins of the people. But the people didn't simply drop a suitable animal to be sacrificed at the door of the tabernacle. They took part in the death of the animal. Leviticus 1:4 says that the worshiper put his hand on the head of the animal that was to be killed. Once the animal was slaughtered, *then* the priests handled the rest. The animal's death symbolized the penalty for sin and the people's need for forgiveness in order to be in a relationship with God.

When you go before God to confess your sins and accept His forgiveness, is the price Jesus paid real to you? Is it as real as if you put your hand on Jesus' head as He bore the cross to Golgotha? Today, forgiveness can seem so sanitized, like the meat we buy at the market, wrapped and labeled. We can easily forget that a death occurred in order for us to have the provision.

Keep in mind that the price for your forgiveness was paid out of Jesus' sacrifice. The old sacrificial system gives us an effective reminder that the price was life itself.

❧

Dear Lord, help me to never forget the great price You
paid so that I could be forgiven. I don't want to ever
take for granted the sacrifice You made on my behalf so
that no further sacrifice of life needs to be made. Now
the sacrifice I want to make is one of thanksgiving
and praise to You for all that You have done to set
me free from the consequences of my own sin.

WHY WE DO WHAT WE DO

Leviticus 10:1-7

*"Aaron's sons Nadab and Abihu took their censers, put fire
in them and added incense; and they offered unauthorized
fire before the LORD, contrary to his command. So fire
came out from the presence of the LORD and consumed
them, and they died before the LORD" (Leviticus 10:1-2).*

Things you do over and over can become very routine. For example, if you perform a ritual enough times, even a sacred one, you can easily forget to honor the full significance of it. What's surprising, however, is to find that even when these Old Testament spiritual rituals were relatively new, some worshipers still struggled to keep the significance of their actions fresh in their minds. Nadab and Abihu were prime examples. They took lightly something that should have been holy, and they paid the ultimate price for their mistake.

From the description given to us at the opening of Leviticus 10, we know that Nadab and Abihu had disregarded instructions they'd been given. This disregard was not simply a mistake—it was an act of disrespect toward God, who had given the instructions. Their disregard seems completely out of place when you consider who these brothers were—the sons of Aaron, the nephews of Moses. They had seen miracles, walked across dry land in the middle of the Red Sea, and eaten manna. They were first-generation eyewitnesses. Their father had become the first high priest of the Israelite nation, and they, as his sons, had been welcomed into the priesthood. Exodus 24:9-10 even tells us that Nadab and Abihu were among 74 men who had climbed the mountain with Moses and had actually *seen* God.

Yet, when the time came to honor God with obedience, they just didn't think it was important enough to do what God wanted.

Have you ever become lax in that way? Do you pray as often as God wants you to? Are you spending time daily in His Word? Are those two spiritual disciplines as fresh and alive as they should be? If not, ask God to give you new excitement about spending time with Him. Ask Him to take away any apathy or carelessness on your part. Do whatever it takes to keep yourself from just going through the motions. Reconnect to the passion and meaning of being in God's presence.

❧

Holy Father, help me to never be careless about Your ways or Your Word. Enable me to not allow anything that has to do with my worship of You to become lifeless or like ritual that has lost its depth of meaning. Keep the disciplines of prayer, praise, and reading in Your Word fresh and alive in my heart so that I will always have a passionate hunger for Your presence.

Your Day *of* Atonement

✤ Read and Consider ✤
Leviticus 16:1-34

*"On this day atonement will be made for you, to
cleanse you. Then, before the LORD, you will be
clean from all your sins" (Leviticus 16:30).*

The Day of Atonement, Yom Kippur, was perhaps the most important annual holy day for the ancient Jews. It was the day when the high priest entered the innermost chamber of the tabernacle (and later, the temple) to offer a sacrifice for the sins of the whole nation. The purpose of this sacrifice? The reconciliation of God and His people.

The ritual described in Leviticus 16 had several steps. It included the sacrifice of a bull and the dripping of that bull's blood onto the cover of Israel's most sacred relic—the ark of the covenant. It also included the selection of two goats. One was to be sacrificed, symbolizing the necessary payment for sin. The other goat, the scapegoat, was set free, symbolizing the sins of the people being carried into the desert.

Because of Christ's sacrifice for our sins, every day is our day of atonement. Every day we accept that His death paid for our sins. Every day our sins are carried into a desert that we will never have to enter.

In light of that reality, how do you approach God in prayer? Do you sit before God as someone God values and loves? Or do you hang your head as if you still have to earn the acceptance you've already been given? Do you rush into His presence, or do you hesitate, hoping that what the Bible teaches about His forgiveness is true. If you tend toward the latter, claim today as your day of atonement.

Go to God with a heart of gratitude and thank Him that nothing stands between you and Him.

❧

Thank You, Jesus, for paying the price for my sins
so that I don't have to. Because of You I have been
reconciled to God, and I will never be separated from
Him again. Help me to extend to others the love and
forgiveness You've given to me. Teach me ways I can
show my gratitude to You for all You have done.

How Can I Be Holy?

> *"Speak to the entire assembly of Israel and
> say to them: 'Be holy because I, the LORD
> your God, am holy'" (Leviticus 19:2).*

What do you think about when you think of holiness? Do you think of someone who is perfect and untouchable? What do you think about your own holiness? Do you ever wonder, *How can I be holy?* Throughout Israel's history, holiness was a major issue. As the people's holiness went, so went the state of the nation. Their spiritual strength and their political strength seemed to go hand in hand. In the days of the good King Jehoshaphat, Judah actually won a battle because the people marched before the army singing and praising God for the "splendor of his holiness" (2 Chronicles 20:1-27).

When you think about how to be holy as God is holy, consider this good news: God wants to share His holiness with you. He doesn't stand over you, wagging an index finger in your face like a judgmental teacher saying, "You be holy right now!" Instead, He offers His own holiness to you. He asks you to partake of His holiness.

In Psalm 29, David encouraged us to offer praise to God for His strength and glory and holiness. When we do that, amazing things happen. Because we take the time and attention to see the splendor and beauty of God's holiness, we take on that beauty. The more we lift our heads and hearts to God in praise, the more God is reflected in our faces and in our behavior.

Remember how Moses' face was radiant when he came down from being in the presence of God (Exodus 34:29-35)? When you worship God, you are coming in contact with the beauty of His holiness and allowing that to make you beautifully holy and wonderfully whole.

That's why your time in prayer shouldn't always be squeezed in between running from one thing to the next. You need time with God to really engage and bask in His presence, allowing Him to conform you and remold you in His image. Each time you do that, you become more holy, more like Him.

❧

Dear God, I worship You for Your greatness and goodness. I praise You for Your holiness. As I worship You, I pray Your holiness will rub off on me. Help me to take on the beauty of Your holiness as I spend time in Your presence. Enable me to become more like You so that Your holiness will make me whole.

The ACT of CELEBRATION

Leviticus 23:1-36

"Speak to the Israelites and say to them: 'These are my appointed feasts, the appointed feasts of the LORD, which you are to proclaim as sacred assemblies'" (Leviticus 23:2).

In the Old Testament world, festivals marked the changing of the seasons, the bringing of the harvest, the shearing of the sheep, and so on. For the Israelite nation, these feast days were also spiritual markers of the journey the people had taken under God's care.

The most basic feast was the Sabbath, a day set aside every week to rest as God had in creation. Another frequent feast was the monthly new moon festival. This was a celebration of God's faithfulness to His people and to the covenant He had made with their ancestors.

Then there were the annual feasts. These celebrations commemorated significant historical events in which God had shown Himself in a mighty way. The Feast of Trumpets commemorated the giving of the Ten Commandments. The Passover was a reminder of the final plague by which God freed the people from Egypt. The Feast of Tabernacles memorialized the journey of the Israelites to their promised land.

Some of our holidays commemorate spiritual events as well: Easter, Christmas, Lent, and others. We use these holidays to join as communities of faith and remember together what God has done in us and among us.

We can each establish our own times of celebration. What has God done specifically in your life that might be cause for celebration? Part of the celebration of Old Testament feasts involved seeing old friends and returning to old places. Are there people with whom you can connect in order to encourage one another spiritually? Is there someone in your life who led you into a relationship with Jesus or who has had a special impact in your walk with God? Ask God to show you how to best celebrate those special events and show your appreciation to those involved. Praying for that person would be a great way to celebrate. Sending a note of thanks would be another. Invite God to help you build these kinds of living monuments that remind you of your journey with Him.

❦

Dear Lord, I celebrate the moment when I came to know You as my Lord. I celebrate the times You have healed me and blessed me. I celebrate Your answers to my prayers and the times You saved me from my own mistakes. I celebrate the wonderful people You have put in my life—especially the ones who have led me to You and taught me to live Your way. I celebrate my life with You.

The IMPORTANCE of RESTITUTION

❧ Read and Consider ❧

Numbers 5:5-10

*"When a man or woman wrongs another in any way and
so is unfaithful to the LORD, that person is guilty and
must confess the sin he has committed. He must make
full restitution for his wrong, add one fifth to it and give
it all to the person he has wronged" (Numbers 5:6-7).*

Most of us have experienced the pain of being wronged at
some point in life. We may have had personal possessions
damaged or stolen. Worse yet, we may have lost someone we loved
due to the carelessness or callousness of another individual. There
is often no adequate compensation for the pain we suffer, but this
passage speaks of God's provision of the concept of restitution as part
of His law for the people of Israel. "To make restitution" means to
provide compensation or remuneration for the losses someone has
experienced due to the actions of another. This passage makes it clear
that to simply say "I'm sorry; please forgive me" was not sufficient.
Instead, God put into place the stipulation that the guilty party not
only had to restore what had been taken but also pay an additional
interest penalty as well. Confession included restitution.

We need to accept the fact that justice is not always served in
our imperfect world. For example, many crimes are committed for
which adequate compensation is impossible. It is usually not within
our power to demand and receive remuneration for harm done at
the hands of another. However, one avenue of justice is open to all:
a heavenly Father who sees each wrongful act committed here on
earth. In the life to come we will experience perfect justice, and in
the words of Isaiah, "Every valley shall be raised up, every mountain

and hill made low; the rough ground shall become level, the rugged places a plain" (Isaiah 40:4).

Until that day comes, we need to be sure that we have not intentionally wronged another. Ask the Lord if you need to apologize and make restitution for anything in your past. The joy and freedom that come from having a clean conscience will lead you to a new level of intimacy with God. Don't put it off; take that first step today.

❧

God, I pray You would show me if I have hurt anyone in any way. If I have, show me how I can make it up to them so that things are right between us. Help me to apologize and to ask for that person's forgiveness. I want to always have a clear conscience so that nothing will undermine the closeness I have with You.

GUIDANCE *for the* JOURNEY

❧ Read and Consider ❧

Numbers 9:15-23

*"Whenever the cloud lifted from above the Tent, the
Israelites set out; wherever the cloud settled, the
Israelites encamped...At the LORD's command they
encamped, and at the LORD's command they set
out. They obeyed the LORD's order, in accordance with
his command through Moses" (Numbers 9:17,23).*

We all struggle on occasion with the weight of making a big
decision. Should we take this job or that one? Say yes or
no to our children when it comes to certain activities? Relocate our
family to a different location or stay put? Wouldn't it be wonderful
if we had a continual manifestation of God's presence to guide us
like the cloud He provided for His children in the desert?

Despite this constant visual reminder of guidance, however, the
Israelites still struggled with following and obeying. Learning to
walk with God is a process. Just when we think we have it all figured
out, God leads us into a new place where our old tricks won't work.
In fact, we may feel as if we're learning to walk all over again. And in
a way we are. We enter unfamiliar territory and are soon reminded
that, on our own, we stumble. Yet when we take His hand, we walk
with confidence. God wants us to soar far above the limitations of
our circumstances and ourselves. He wants to take us to a place we
have never been before and can't get to without His help. When
God used Moses to lead the Israelites out of Egypt, they had to
learn to depend on the Lord for every step of their journey to the
promised land. When they did not do that, they got into trouble.
It's the same for us today.

If you are at a place in your life where you feel as if you can't take one step without the Lord's help, be glad. He has you where He wants you. If you're wondering, *Have I done something wrong?* the answer is most likely that you've done something right. God has you on this path, regardless of how difficult and impossible it may seem right now, because you are willing to follow Him. He wants to accomplish great things through you that can only come out of a life of faith. He wants your undivided attention because you can't do these things on your own. The path is not a punishment; it's a privilege. It's not a restriction; it's a reward.

❧

Lord, guide me on my journey through life. Help me to understand and recognize Your leading in every decision I make. Give me clear direction so that I can stay on the path You have for me. I know following You doesn't mean everything will be easy. Help me to not lose faith when the road gets rough. I want to always arrive at the place You want me to be.

WHEN YOU'RE FEELING OVERWHELMED

❦ Read and Consider ❦
Numbers 11:10-17

"I will come down and speak with you there, and I will take of the Spirit that is on you and put the Spirit on them. They will help you carry the burden of the people so that you will not have to carry it alone" (Numbers 11:17).

Have you ever been asked to take on a job that you knew was much too big or too difficult for you, possibly one that did not involve any kind of tangible reward? Perhaps it's a volunteer position at a church or in your community, or you may have even found yourself in the position of raising someone else's child.

Overwhelming as the task might seem, it grows even more challenging when those you are serving don't seem to appreciate your efforts. In return for sacrifice, you get selfishness; your efforts at caretaking are met with complaining. At times like these you may be tempted to cry out to the Lord as Moses did, "Why have you brought this trouble on me? This burden is too heavy for me."

The Israelites were wallowing in the darkness of bitterness, casting blame upon God and His chosen leader. Instead of choosing to see God's hand in the moment, they blamed Moses and God for everything that disappointed them. As a result, their suffering was prolonged.

There is a crucial difference between the complaining that the Israelites did in the desert and the complaints Moses expressed: The people groused to one another, but Moses took his concerns to the only One who could do something about them—God.

As a result of Moses' plea for help, God promised to send

additional leaders who would help Moses carry the burden of the needs of the people. Never hesitate to take your troubles to God when you are feeling overwhelmed; He has promised that you do not have to carry them alone.

❧

God, I lift up to You the areas of my life that are overwhelming and burdensome. I have not come to You to complain, but rather to seek Your help. Where I have tried to handle everything in my own strength instead of depending on You, I ask Your forgiveness. I pray You will take each burden of my heart and enable me to rise above every challenging situation in my life.

PRAYING *for* THOSE WHO
HAVE HURT YOU

✤ Read and Consider ✤
Numbers 12:13

*"So Moses cried out to the LORD, 'O God,
please heal her!'" (Numbers 12:13).*

The two people God gave to Moses to help him lead the Israelites out of slavery were his own sister and brother, Miriam and Aaron (see Micah 6:4). You'd think they would be Moses' most ardent supporters. Ironically, however, the opening verse of Numbers 12 tells us that these two family members who should have been most loyal to Moses were speaking out against him.

Family divisions wound us deeply. Friends or colleagues may hurt us, but when betrayal arises from within our own family, the pain is profound. But Moses didn't hang on to any hurt he may have felt. Instead he prayed for his sister.

God confronted both Miriam and Aaron at the Tent of Meeting, but it was upon Miriam that the discipline fell. Since Miriam's name appears before Aaron's, we can assume that she was older and that God was holding her responsible for the division she and Aaron were spreading in the camp because of their critical tongues. As a result, she was afflicted with leprosy, a horrible contagious skin disease that would cause her to be separated from the rest of the camp—perhaps for the remainder of her life. Her younger brother Aaron was horrified when he witnessed the result of their disobedience and disloyalty; he asked Moses to forgive them for their foolishness and sin.

Moses did not hesitate but immediately cried out to the Lord on behalf of his sister: "O God, please heal her!" Though Miriam still had to face the consequence of displeasing the Lord, she was restored to the people after a seven-day time-out. God responded to Moses' plea on behalf of the very one who had wronged him.

Do you have a family member who has hurt you? Have you been able to forgive that person? If not, ask God to help you forgive completely. Then pray for that person because prayer has great power to restore broken family relationships. In the process of praying, you'll begin to sense love growing in your heart for the one who hurt you. God will still hold that person accountable for the sins he or she has committed, but forgiving and praying for that person has the power to free you from all pain and bitterness. Try it and discover the wonderful freedom waiting for you when you forgive.

❧

Lord, I pray You would help me to forgive anyone who has hurt me. Enable me to forgive them so completely that I don't hesitate to pray for their greatest blessing. Deliver me from any bitterness, and help me to live in the freedom of a forgiving heart so that there is complete reconciliation between us. I don't want to experience the terrible consequences of unforgiveness in my life.

JUST ENOUGH LIGHT *for* *the* STEP YOU'RE ON

❧ Read and Consider ☙
─────────────────
Numbers 14:19-23

" 'In accordance with your great love, forgive the sin of
these people, just as you have pardoned them from the
time they left Egypt until now.' The LORD replied, 'I have
forgiven them, as you asked' " (Numbers 14:19-20).

The history of the Israelites in the desert was checkered with times of eager obedience and great joy along with times of stubborn disobedience and great punishment. God had performed many miracles to deliver His people from Egypt, yet they still continued to doubt Him. He then took them into the desert and tested them.

One test involved water: He let them go without it for three days. God knew the people needed water, and He could easily have provided it for them. But they didn't ask. They didn't pray. They complained. And that was part of the test. God wanted them to ask. He wanted them to be dependent on Him for everything. When Moses cried out to God on their behalf, God said that if the people would listen to Him and do what He commanded, He would meet all their needs. So they listened and obeyed. They got their water and were content.

Until the next crisis.

Instead of learning something from the water situation, the Israelites complained again about their lack of food. God was not trying to starve them. He knew they needed food, and He wanted to provide it for them. But He wanted them to come to Him and rely on Him for it. Once more, Moses prayed and God provided. But this time, God provided only what was needed for each day, one day at a time. God desired that they trust Him for each day's provision. He wanted them to learn to walk with just enough light for the step they were on.

Does this sound at all familiar? Can you think of anyone you know who wants to get to the "promised land" but doesn't want to do what's necessary to make the trip? Are you aware of a person who desires to have everything he or she needs but is not willing to give up anything to get it? Have you ever felt that you should have already arrived, without having to trust God for every step to get there?

This passage illustrates that God's capacity for forgiving the sin and foolishness of His people is unlimited. We need only confess, and He is faithful and just to forgive us (1 John 1:9). At the same time, results follow our rebellious behavior. God will forgive us, but sometimes we have to experience the consequences of our sin. In this case, the people would eventually die in the desert, and of those then alive, only Joshua and Caleb would ever see the promised land.

God often provides just enough light for the step we're on, but we have to trust Him and walk in obedience to His leading. Then He will illuminate the next step we are to take.

❧

Dear God, just as You walked with Your people in the
desert after You delivered them out of Egypt, and You
forgave them and provided what they needed every
step of the way, I turn to You for deliverance and
forgiveness and ask that You would provide for my
needs every day. Help me to never doubt that You will
always give me the light I need for each step I take.

The POWER of FAITH

> *"The people came to Moses and said, 'We sinned when*
> *we spoke against the LORD and against you. Pray that*
> *the LORD will take the snakes away from us.' So Moses*
> *prayed for the people. The LORD said to Moses, 'Make*
> *a snake and put it up on a pole; anyone who is bitten*
> *can look at it and live'"* (Numbers 21:7-8).

When you read this passage, do you find yourself becoming frustrated with the stubborn ingratitude of the Israelites? In response to their plea, God had granted them victory over their enemies, the Canaanites. We don't know for certain how long the travels mentioned here lasted, but we do know that "the people grew impatient on the way; they spoke against God and against Moses" and were discontent with the food God provided for them.

Once again we're reminded of the vital importance of the confession of sin. Once again we witness the privilege of intercession, as Moses represented the Israelites' contrition before God. But this passage also bears witness to one of the most compelling principles in Scripture: The power of prayer is most clearly seen in the presence of faith.

Why would God give Moses such a seemingly strange command—to fashion an imitation snake out of bronze metal and put it up on a pole? What's more, God added this promise: Anyone who was bitten by a real snake could simply *look* at the bronze snake and live.

Of course, the artificial snake had no power, but Moses' obedience to the unusual instruction is recorded as well as the result that any person who followed God's command was saved. It was that simple, yet apparently some did not look at the snake. In their stubbornness and rebellion, many refused to believe that something so simple could save them.

It's still that way today. Jesus died on the cross to save us from the venom that infects us and leads to death—which is sin. Yet millions of people are wandering in the desert of their own sin because they refuse to lift their eyes to the cross. They refuse to believe that something so simple could save them.

The bronze snake on the pole is a type or picture of Jesus. Jesus even refers to this imagery in His conversation with Nicodemus recorded in John 3: "Just as Moses lifted up the snake in the desert, so the Son of Man must be lifted up, that everyone who believes in him may have eternal life" (John 3:14-15). In both instances, it takes a willingness to look up and believe.

Christ is our mediator, and He loves us so much that He paid the penalty for our sin with His death. That means that those of us who look to Jesus as our Savior will live eternally with Him.

❧

Lord Jesus, I look to You as my Savior and to what
You accomplished on the cross as the guarantee of my
salvation. Thank You for paying the price for my
sin. Forgive me if I have ever spoken against You in
any way, or have been motivated by fear and doubt. I
come to You in faith, believing that You hear me and
will answer my prayer. Help me to always obey You.

Do Not Be Afraid

Deuteronomy 1:19-30

"See, the LORD your God has given you the land. Go up and take possession of it as the LORD, the God of your fathers, told you. Do not be afraid; do not be discouraged" (Deuteronomy 1:21).

M any of the people listening to these words had spent 40 long years in the desert. Their parents had stood at this very spot decades earlier, but they had let their fears overwhelm them. In punishment for that blatant lack of faith, God gave that generation a death sentence: "Not one of the men who saw my glory and the miraculous signs I performed in Egypt and in the desert but who disobeyed me and tested me ten times—not one of them will ever see the land I promised on oath to their forefathers" (Numbers 14:22-23). The nation wandered until all the rebellious people died.

That rebellious generation's children now stood poised in the same spot. And what was Moses' message to them? He recounted what had gone before. He told the story of their parents' rebellion and lack of faith. They needed to hear and understand. Would they be prone to the same fear and rebellion, or would they be different? Would they enter and possess the land in full confidence of God's promises? God said to them what He had said to their parents, "Do not be afraid; do not be discouraged."

Walking into a closer relationship with God can be like entering your own personal promised land. You know it's a good place, but it's still filled with unknowns. Following Jesus doesn't mean life is going to be easy. You'll still have giants to battle, territory to claim, and work to do. But God says regarding your journey with

Him, "Do not be afraid; do not be discouraged." And the reason is because "the LORD your God, who is going before you, will fight for you" (1:30).

You see, He already knows the unknowns. He knows about the giants. He has the battle plan. All you need to do is continually look to Him in prayer and follow His lead.

❧

> *Thank You, Lord, for all the wonderful things You have done for me in the past, that You are doing for me today, and that You will do for me in the future. Keep me from fear and discouragement as I look at the challenges ahead. Thank You that You go before me with a plan for battle. I look to You for guidance so I may possess all You have for me.*

GOD IS NEAR WHEN WE PRAY

❧ Read and Consider ❧
Deuteronomy 4:1-14

"What other nation is so great as to have their gods near them the way the LORD our God is near us whenever we pray to him?" (Deuteronomy 4:7).

It is comforting to know that whenever we pray to our God, He is present with us. The truths that Moses was teaching to the Israelites still hold true for believers today. Our God is alive, He is close, He is responsive. The Lord is here to listen and to bring wisdom, insight, and transformation into hopeless situations. He is here to protect and guide His people on the paths He desires them to walk.

Moses reassured the Israelites about their privileged status as the people of God. He reminded them that they were not like the people of foreign lands whose gods could not respond to them. Their God would remain with them at all times and would hear their prayers whenever they called on Him.

What does this mean for us? Does it mean that God isn't close to us unless we are praying? No. He is always with us, just as His presence traveled constantly with the Israelites to guide them. However, when we pray, we are drawn into a deeper awareness of His presence and a clearer understanding of His nature. Prayer reminds us of who we are in relationship to Him. Prayer puts us in a place where we can hear from Him and be changed by Him. No amount of prayer to a lifeless idol could ever accomplish that. We pray to a living and responsive God who loves us and wants to be an active part of our lives. When we don't pray, we miss out on the benefits of a close walk with Him. Draw near to Him in prayer right now and sense His presence in and around you.

❖

*Lord, I thank You for being close to me when I pray.
Thank You that You hear and will answer me. Thank
You that in Your presence there is transformation for my
soul and my life. I draw close to You now and ask for
an ever-increasing sense of Your presence. I ask that You
would help me to pray more and more every day and
give me increasing faith to believe for the answers.*

Prayers *of* Intercession

*"I feared the anger and wrath of the LORD, for he was
angry enough with you to destroy you. But again
the LORD listened to me. And the LORD was angry
enough with Aaron to destroy him, but at that time
I prayed for Aaron too" (Deuteronomy 9:19-20).*

When we step in on behalf of others in prayer, amazing things
can happen. This is proven over and over again throughout
Scripture, and the example in these verses is one of the most powerful
in the Bible. In this passage, Moses recounts to the new generation
of Israelites the story recorded in Exodus 32.

Picture the scene: Moses was away, meeting with the Lord to
receive instruction and guidance for the Israelites from their true and
faithful God. During Moses' long absence on the mountain, however,
the Israelites grew restless and impatient. They decided that they
needed an idol—a golden calf—to worship. And Aaron went along
with the plan. God's wrath was stirred toward the people, and in spite
of his own anger toward them, Moses intervened on their behalf to
prevent God from destroying them. And since Aaron had succumbed
to the people's demands and fashioned the idol, he was ultimately
responsible. Yet Moses interceded for his brother as well.

Our intercessions for others may be far less dramatic than this
example, but the extreme nature of this situation shows how powerful
our prayers can be. We may be praying for another's healing,
encouragement, guidance, salvation, protection, or strengthening.
The Lord's response to Moses reveals that He listens to us and that
our prayers matter to Him. We can make a powerful impact on the

lives of those around us through our intercessions for them. Take
the time to pray diligently for those whom the Spirit puts on your
heart. Then watch what God does in their lives.

❦

*God, help me to be one of Your faithful and powerful
intercessors. Help me to not be so focused on myself and my
situation that I don't see how to pray for the needs of others.
Give me strong faith to believe that my prayers can make a
big difference in their lives. Show me the people I need to
pray for today and how I should specifically pray for them.*

GOD IS *with* YOU

*"When you go to war against your enemies and see horses
and chariots and an army greater than yours, do not be
afraid of them, because the LORD your God, who brought
you up out of Egypt, will be with you" (Deuteronomy 20:1).*

Prayer is one of your strongest weapons against fear. Imagine
how the Israelites must have felt every time they faced nation
after nation as they made their way toward the promised land. God
required that they rely on His strength, not on their numbers or
weapons or skills or any other human power they had. He seemed
to delight in making sure that they were weaker than the nations
they faced so that His power could be revealed in their victories.
And when the Israelites believed Him and followed His instructions,
God's power was always revealed.

What "wars" are you facing right now? What impossible circumstances are making you draw back in fear? Take them to the
Lord in prayer. Think of all the times in your life when God has
been faithful to you. It will reinforce your confidence that God
will take you through the next "battle" just as He has seen you
through past difficulties. When the Israelites thought back on their
dramatic rescue from Egypt and remembered God's faithfulness
to them, they renewed their strength to face the challenges ahead.
Pray that God will open your eyes to all the ways He has upheld
you in the past. Ask Him to give you fresh faith to fearlessly face
the next battle.

❧

*Almighty God, I rely on You to lead me through every
challenge and battle in my life. Help me to never
operate out of fear in the face of what seems like
impossible circumstances. Just as You have helped me
in the past, I know You will continue to help me in the
future. I praise You for the great things You will do, and
thank You that Your presence is always with me.*

PRAISE GOD *for* HIS GREATNESS

❧ Read and Consider ☙

Deuteronomy 32:1-43

"I will proclaim the name of the LORD. Oh, praise the greatness of our God! He is the Rock, his works are perfect, and all his ways are just. A faithful God who does no wrong, upright and just is he" (Deuteronomy 32:3-4).

Nothing we do is more powerful or life changing than praising God. It is one of the means by which God transforms us. Every time we praise and worship Him, His presence changes our hearts and allows the Holy Spirit to soften and mold us into whatever He wants us to be.

Because our flesh does not naturally praise and worship God, we have to *will* ourselves to do it. And because it's not the first thing we think to do, we have to decide to do it regardless of our circumstances. We have to say, "I *will* praise the Lord." Of course, the more we get to know God, the easier praise becomes. When we get to the point where we can't keep from praising Him, then we are at the place we are supposed to be.

Pause many times a day to praise God for the many blessings He's given you. Praise Him that He is your Rock, that His works are perfect, that His ways are just. Praise Him that He is a faithful and good God. Praise Him for how much He loves you and for all the ways He shows it.

Do you want a transformed life? Do you want to be more like Jesus? Do you want to be molded into all that God wants you to be? Then praise Him often. When you think of all He has done for you, praise and worship will come easily.

❧

God, I praise You for Your greatness and goodness. I worship You as the God of creation and the Lord of my life. I praise You in the good times and in the difficult times as well. Thank You that You show Your love for me by protecting me, providing for me, delivering me, and giving me Your peace and power.

GOD IS YOUR REFUGE

❖ Read and Consider ❖
Deuteronomy 33

"There is no one like the God of Jeshurun, who rides on the heavens to help you and on the clouds in his majesty. The eternal God is your refuge, and underneath are the everlasting arms...Blessed are you, O Israel! Who is like you, a people saved by the LORD? He is your shield and helper and your glorious sword" (Deuteronomy 33:26-27,29).

What an amazing picture! God rides on the heavens to help you. He is your refuge. His arms are holding you up, no matter how heavy your load, how difficult your circumstances, or how strong your fears. God not only fights for you but also provides you with a safe refuge. He actually fights *in your place* while you rest in the safety He gives. He shields you, saves you, and gains victory for you.

As you pray, ask God to show you how this passage applies to your life right now. Think of the specific challenges you face. Picture yourself in His loving protection as He fights your battles for you. Don't try to face your challenges alone. God doesn't want that. Whenever you try to go out on your own strength, He is grieved because you are not allowing Him to do for you all that He longs to do. He is grieved because you make yourself more vulnerable to Satan's attack. Every time you ask God for help, He will rush to your side, and the enemy will be forced to flee from you.

❖

Lord, You are great and there is no other God but You. You are my safe refuge from the storm. Help me to find my rest in You as You go to battle against all that opposes me. No matter whether my battles are with finances, relationships, health, or obedience, I know that because of Your presence in my life, I will never face those challenges alone. I depend on Your strength and not mine.

LOOKING *for* GOD'S WILL

*"Do not let this Book of the Law depart from your
mouth; meditate on it day and night, so that you may
be careful to do everything written in it. Then you
will be prosperous and successful" (Joshua 1:8).*

Who doesn't want to know God's will for their life? And God wants to reveal it. So why does God's will often seem to be such a mystery to us? In order to know what God wants, you need to be aware of four important aspects of His will:

First, God's will is most often found through reading the Bible and letting it sink into your heart. Joshua was commanded to know the Book of the Law backward and forward, to meditate and reflect on it. Then God promised to prosper him. The Bible declares clearly that God will direct and lead us. Psalm 37:23 says, "If the LORD delights in a man's way, he makes his steps firm." And in Psalm 32:8, God promises, "I will instruct you and teach you in the way you should go; I will counsel you and watch over you." He speaks to us through His Word, the Scriptures.

Second, God's will is ongoing in our lives. From the time we are infants until the day we die, God has a will for us—as children, young people, adults, and senior citizens. Isaiah 58:11 says, "The LORD will guide you always; he will satisfy your needs in a sun-scorched land and will strengthen your frame. You will be like a well-watered garden, like a spring whose waters never fail."

Third, God's will is specific. The prophet Isaiah heard the Lord promising His children, "Whether you turn to the right or to the left, your ears will hear a voice behind you, saying, 'This is the way; walk in it'" (Isaiah 30:21).

Fourth, God's will is profitable. The Lord told Joshua, who was to lead the Israelites into the promised land, "Do not let this Book of the Law depart from your mouth...be careful to do everything written in it. *Then you will be prosperous and successful*" (Joshua 1:8, emphasis added).

Looking for God's will may be simpler than you ever imagined. It doesn't matter what your situation is at the moment. As you read the Word and prayerfully ask for guidance, then all you have to do is take the next step that the Lord is showing you. As you take one step at a time, you will begin to see a solid way of following after God. As long as you are walking with Him continually in prayer and living His way according to His Word, you are not likely to get off the path of His will. And if by chance you do, He will get you right back on. That's because when you're always listening for God's voice, you will sense in your heart when you violate His directions. Each small step of obedience will turn into a life of obedience lived in the will of God.

❧

Dear Lord, I pray that every time I read Your Word, You will teach me all I need to know. Help me to understand Your truth and speak to me specifically about how each passage I have read relates to my life and to the lives of others. Help me to meditate on Your Word and take steps of obedience so that I can live in Your perfect will and prosper as You have promised.

LOOKING *for a* BREAKTHROUGH?

❧ Read and Consider ❧

Joshua 6:1-20

*"When the trumpets sounded, the people shouted, and
at the sound of the trumpet, when the people gave a
loud shout, the wall collapsed; so every man charged
straight in, and they took the city" (Joshua 6:20).*

Have you ever needed a breakthrough in your life? Or some
kind of deliverance? Perhaps you or your situation needed
to be transformed, but you were facing a wall as high as the one
surrounding Jericho. As far as you could see, there seemed to be no
way through it.

The good thing about knowing that you need much more than
your own strength in order to break down the walls in your life is
that it forces you to rely on the power of God to set you free. And His
deliverance and freedom are always far beyond what we can imagine.
God wants you to depend on Him and His power whenever you
face obstacles in your life. So each time you find that you can't seem
to move beyond something you are facing, determine to go deeper
into God's Word. Commit to even more fervent prayer. Decide to
give God heartfelt worship regardless of what is happening.

Those three steps of obedience are powerful and will destroy
whatever is standing in the way of your moving into all God has
for you.

The Israelites walked around the city of Jericho 13 times in one
week. So don't just stand looking at the walls that are obstructing
you. Start encircling them with shouts of praise today and every day
for as long as it takes.

❧

*Father God, I depend on You to help me overcome the
obstacles in my life. Teach me to speak Your Word in power
as I cover each situation in prayer. I lift up praise to You in
the face of impossible circumstances because You are the God
of the impossible. No matter what comes against me, Your
power is more than enough to break through it to victory.*

ROADBLOCKS *to* PRAYER

❧ Read and Consider ☙
Joshua 7:1-13

*"The LORD said to Joshua, 'Stand up! What
are you doing down on your face? Israel has
sinned; they have violated my covenant, which I
commanded them to keep'" (Joshua 7:10-11).*

At least Joshua had come to the right place. In despair over
the nation's recent defeat by the little city of Ai, Joshua and
the nation's elders performed the proper rituals of repentance and
remained there till evening. But the Lord was not impressed with
their weeping and wailing. "Stand up!" God commanded. The
problem was sin, and once the sinner was found out and the sin
removed from the camp, the problem would be solved. God didn't
need Joshua on his face at that moment; He needed Joshua to rout
out the sin so the nation could move forward.

When you pray, you've come to the right place. But that's just
the beginning. As part of your conversation with God, you will
"hear" His words speaking to your heart. He will reveal sins to
confess, actions to take, changes to make. As you read His Word,
He'll make you aware of what He wants you to do. While it's good
to keep reading, keep praying, and keep seeking—we still have to
take action, especially where sin is concerned. When God reveals
sin to you, "stand up," confess it, and take immediate steps to make
any necessary changes. After all, you've got more battles ahead, and
you need to be ready.

❧

Lord, I know my prayers have no effect if I have sin in my life for which I have not repented or confessed. Reveal to me any sin I am harboring, and I will confess it so that nothing comes between You and me. I don't want to give place to any hindrances to my prayers, and I don't want to put up a roadblock to all You want to do in my life.

INQUIRE *of the* LORD

*"The men of Israel sampled their provisions but
did not inquire of the LORD" (Joshua 9:14).*

This sentence is so brief that it can be easily missed, but it is the key to the entire story: The men of Israel "did not inquire of the LORD."

Joshua should have known better—they were in a war. The Israelites were in the middle of a divine takeover of an entire region. They would need God's guidance every step of the way. But this time the travelers had come a long way. Their food was moldy, their wineskins were old and cracked, and their clothes and sandals were worn out. It didn't occur to Israel's leaders that they were being set up. The Israelites were fooled because they didn't ask for God's guidance in deciding what to do.

Does this sound familiar? Do you ever get yourself into trouble because you fail to ask for God's wisdom and direction? Could you have made a better decision if you had "inquired of the Lord" right there in that office, in the classroom, at the doctor's office, or on that date? The passage implies that if the Israelites *had* asked for God's direction, they would have figured out what was really going on.

God wants to be part of your decisions, big and small. No issue is too insignificant to bring to God. He can see the big picture; you can't. He sees the future; you don't. He wants you to ask Him for guidance in all your daily decisions because He cares about everything that concerns you. He is your heavenly Father, and He wants to be involved in every aspect of your life. He wants to help you avoid the pitfalls that come when you don't consult Him before taking action. Pray every day that His Spirit will guide you in each decision you make.

❧

Father, I pray You would help me to not run off on my own, trying to do what I think is right instead of inquiring of You about everything so that I will do what I know is right. Help me to not fall into the traps the enemy has laid for me by forgetting to consult You about everything—even the things I may think I can handle on my own.

GET PERSONAL *with* GOD

"Therefore the LORD was very angry with Israel and
said, 'Because this nation has violated the covenant that
I laid down for their forefathers and has not listened
to me, I will no longer drive out before them any of the
nations Joshua left when he died'" (Judges 2:20-21).

After years of struggle to get to the promised land, the nation of Israel fell away from the Lord who had led them there. Why? Because they did not maintain their own personal connection to Him. Relying on the faith of their fathers wasn't enough to sustain them, and they turned to other gods.

The same principle holds true for us. We cannot rely on other people's faith, or even our own past experiences with God, to sustain our current relationship with Him. We must maintain a living, dynamic, active relationship with Him through our prayer life and Scripture reading in order to know Him at an intimate level.

Prayer is about so much more than just making requests or getting advice. It is our avenue to knowing and being known by the God of the universe. Although He already knows us completely, we don't have any way of experiencing that reality if we do not connect with Him in a personal way.

God created you, and He desires to be part of your life. He doesn't want you to fall into temptations and dangers as the Israelites did. Make sure that you maintain a consistent prayer life and guard against riding on past experiences with Him. Doing so can get you into dangerous territory.

❧

*Father God, I don't want to ever fall away from You
by neglecting to spend time in Your Word and in
prayer. I want to always be gaining a closer walk
with You. Help me to know You better and to become
more and more like You. I don't want to fall away in
temptation, sin, or laziness. I want, instead, to have
a new and deeper experience with You every day.*

God Delivers

*"But when they cried out to the LORD, he raised up for them
a deliverer, Othniel son of Kenaz, Caleb's younger brother,
who saved them...Again the Israelites cried out to the
LORD, and he gave them a deliverer—Ehud, a left-handed
man, the son of Gera the Benjamite" (Judges 3:9,15).*

The Israelite's sinful ways put them into a place of bondage to foreign nations and foreign gods. But every time they cried out to the Lord, He was faithful to rescue them.

We all need deliverance at one time or another. That's because regardless of how spiritual we may be, we're still made of flesh. And no matter how good we may think we are, we have an enemy who is trying to erect strongholds of evil in our lives. Jesus taught us to pray, "Deliver us from the evil one" (Matthew 6:13). He would not have instructed us in that manner if we didn't need to be delivered. But so often we don't pray that way. So often we live our lives as if we don't realize Jesus paid an enormous price so we could be free. God wants to free us from everything that binds, holds, or separates us from Him. He wants to *continue* to set us free every day of our lives.

Do you feel enslaved to finances, illness, addictions, unhealthy relationships, immorality, or resentments? Do you struggle to be close to God or to believe that He hears your prayers and will answer them? Do you fear that you never have victory over the areas you struggle with, and so you are more discouraged than joyful? God wants to set you free. He wants you to remember that He is the Deliverer. He says, "Call upon me in the day of trouble; I will deliver you, and you will honor me" (Psalm 50:15).

Deliverance is found by praying for it yourself (Psalm 72:12), by having someone else who is a strong believer pray with you for it (Psalm 34:17), by reading the truth of God's Word with great understanding and clarity (John 8:32), and by spending time in the Lord's presence. The most effective and powerful way to spend time in the Lord's presence is in praise and worship. Every time you worship God, something happens to break the power of evil. That's because God inhabits your praises, and this means you are in His presence.

Remember that deliverance is an ongoing process. God wants you whole and will see that process through to the end. Don't give up. "He who began a good work in you will carry it on to completion until the day of Christ Jesus" (Philippians 1:6).

❧

*Dear Lord, I pray that wherever the enemy has erected
a stronghold in my life for my destruction, You would
deliver me from it. Thank You that You paid the price for
my freedom and You continue to set me free every day. I
lift You up, exalt You, and praise You as my Savior and
Deliverer. I am grateful Your presence inhabits my praise.*

CONFESSION *and* REPENTANCE

Judges 10:6-18

"But the Israelites said to the LORD, 'We have sinned.
Do with us whatever you think best, but please
rescue us now.' Then they got rid of the foreign gods
among them and served the LORD. And he could
bear Israel's misery no longer" (Judges 10:15-16).

Sin separates us from God. It is a simple truth. This passage demonstrates the process we all need to go through in order to remove that barrier and come into right relationship with Him again. The first part of the process involves confession—telling God what you have done wrong. The second part involves repentance—turning away from the wrongdoing. The Israelites confessed that they had worshiped foreign gods; then they got rid of their idols and served the Lord.

When we don't confess our sins, we end up trying to hide from God. Just like Adam and Eve in the garden, we feel we can't face Him. But the problem with attempting to hide from God is that it's impossible. The Bible says that everything we do will be made known—even the things we say and think in secret.

Nothing is heavier and more destructive than sin. We don't realize how heavy it is until we feel its crushing weight in our relationships; we don't see how destructive it is until we hit the wall it has put up between God and us. And, as the Israelites experienced, nothing is more freeing and marvelous than God's compassion and grace. When you confess your sin, you're not informing God of something He doesn't already know. God wants to know that *you* know you've sinned and that you are ready to turn away from it.

✤

Dear God, I don't want anything to separate me from
You. Nothing is worth that. I want to confess to You
anything I have done wrong and anything that is not
pleasing in Your eyes. Wherever I have worshiped other
gods or harbored what You would consider an idol
in my life, reveal it to me and I will confess it, repent
of it, and get rid of it. I want to serve only You.

KNOW *the* SOURCE

❧ Read and Consider ☙
Judges 18

"He told them what Micah had done for him and said, 'He has hired me and I am his priest.' Then they said to him, 'Please inquire of God to learn whether our journey will be successful.' The priest answered them, 'Go in peace. Your journey has the LORD's approval'" (Judges 18:4-6).

Looking to other people for counsel can be a very wise thing to do—that is, when we seek wisdom from the right sources. In this case, however, the five warriors from the tribe of Dan looked to a priest who inquired of "god" by using idols and other images, not the true God of Israel. Later in the story, this priest proved to be fickle and disloyal as he abandoned his former master in a time of distress for a better offer. Not exactly a trustworthy source of information!

When you are seeking God's guidance, you might want to ask everyone you know for their opinions—thinking that the more counselors the better. But instead of rushing to get a quick word, stop and pray first. Ask God to give you real discernment. Test the source before you follow any advice. Ask only those who can offer true wisdom from the Lord.

The men from Dan had the right idea—they inquired about God's will. But they stopped inquiring when they heard the priest's word. Take everything you hear and make sure that it is consistent with God's Word. That is the most trustworthy source and one you can always count on.

❧

Lord, I turn to You for all wisdom, direction, and
guidance. Where I must seek advice from another
person, help me to know when that person speaks from
godly knowledge and when this is not the case. Help
me to always test the input of others with Your Word. I
want You to be my ultimate source for all knowledge.

BE CAREFUL WHAT
YOU ASK FOR

❧ Read and Consider ❧
1 Samuel 8

*"So all the elders of Israel gathered together and came to
Samuel at Ramah. They said to him, 'You are old, and your
sons do not walk in your ways; now appoint a king to lead
us, such as all the other nations have'" (1 Samuel 8:4-5).*

You can probably recall times in your life when you have prayed
for something that, looking back, could have led to disaster.
Although we think we know what is best for our lives and our
futures, often we pray for the very things that would lead to our own
destruction. God knows this; He sees the big picture. He wants us
to bring our prayers into alignment with His will. In the case of the
Israelites, no amount of instruction—even from the Lord Himself
through Samuel—could convince them that they were praying amiss.
So the Lord finally gave them the king they begged for, though He
knew he would eventually be a burden to them.

Today you have the Holy Spirit to guide you, even in your praying.
So always ask the Lord to help you pray according to His will for your
life. Also seek wisdom from the Bible so you can pray in alignment
with His will. Just as Jesus did in the garden of Gethsemane, pray
"not my will, but yours be done" (Luke 22:42). This allows God to
work in your heart so you can accept His will, even if it is not what
you thought you wanted.

❧

Help me, Holy Spirit of God, to pray according to Your will. Speak to me as I read Your Word so that I can grow in understanding. Enable me to pray in power and alignment with what pleases You. Thank You for the times I prayed for something and You didn't give it to me because it would not have been good. I can see that now, and I am grateful.

GIVE *the* GIFT *of* PRAYER

*"As for me, far be it from me that I should sin against
the LORD by failing to pray for you. And I will teach
you the way that is good and right" (1 Samuel 12:23).*

You might not think of a failure to pray for others as a sin against
God, but Samuel clearly considered it so. God calls us to support
one another, love one another, and pray for one another. When we
don't do these acts, we are not living in the unity and fellowship that
He desires us to have, and we cannot experience all the blessings
that He wants to give us. Samuel knew this and proclaimed that he
would be faithful in prayer for the Israelites—in spite of all of the
evil they had done in God's eyes.

Prayer is the greatest gift we can give to anyone. Of course, if
someone needs food, clothes, and a place to live, those needs must
be met too. But in giving that way, we also should not neglect to
pray for that person as well. Material things are temporary, but our
prayers for another person can affect him or her for a lifetime.

We can never move into all God has for us until we first move into
intercessory prayer. This is one part of our calling that all Christians
have in common because we are *all* called to intercede for others.
God wants us to love others enough to lay down our lives for them
in prayer.

❖

*Lord, I pray for each member of my family and for all of
my friends and acquaintances to be blessed with peace, good
health, provision, and a greater knowledge of You and Your*

Word. Help me to not be selfish or lazy in my praying. Show me whom else to pray for. May I never sin against You by failing to pray for other people according to Your will.

God Sees Our
Heart Toward Him

❧ Read and Consider ❧

1 Samuel 14:24-45

*"Then Saul built an altar to the Lord; it was the
first time he had done this" (1 Samuel 14:35).*

What is your relationship with God *really* like?

That question needs to be answered because some people *appear* to have it all together spiritually. They serve in the church and do all the right things, but they don't have a true personal and life-giving relationship with Jesus.

Take Saul, for example. Handsome and strong. King of Israel. Chosen by God. Yet the Bible records here that Saul made an oath to not eat until he avenged his enemies. This may have looked God-honoring, but it was unwise and impulsive and left his army stranded without sustenance. Later, he built an altar to God, but this was the first time Saul had done this—the first time the king of God's people had done the most basic act of honoring God!

The next chapter takes us even deeper, for it tells how Saul imploded as a leader, becoming completely unable to follow God's explicit instructions. In the end, Samuel tells Saul: "Does the Lord delight in burnt offerings and sacrifices as much as in obeying the voice of the Lord? To obey is better than sacrifice, and to heed is better than the fat of rams" (1 Samuel 15:22).

We don't want to be the kind of people who love God with our words only. We don't want to obey Him just because we have to or because our church says we have to. We want to have hearts so full of love for God that we can't contain it. We want to obey God because we can't bear the thought of disappointing Him. We don't want to be the kind of people who pray only when things are rough. We want to eagerly anticipate time with God each day because we love Him and enjoy His presence. God knows the difference.

Always remember that God's love for you is far beyond what you can even imagine. Ask Him to fill your heart with that kind of love for Him in return.

❧

> *Dear God, I pray I would have a heart of love for You and Your ways that is always pleasing in Your sight. I don't want to be a person who shows love for You with only words. I want to show it with my actions, my obedience to Your laws, and the way I live my life. Thank You that You love me at all times—even when I don't do everything right.*

GOD LOOKS *on* YOUR HEART

❧ Read and Consider ☙
1 Samuel 16:1-13

"But the LORD said to Samuel, 'Do not consider
his appearance or his height, for I have rejected
him. The LORD does not look at the things man
looks at. Man looks at the outward appearance, but
the LORD looks at the heart'" (1 Samuel 16:7).

I sn't it comforting to know that God does not judge us in the
same way that other people often judge us? Or even in the harsh
way in which we sometimes judge ourselves? God is concerned with
what is in our hearts. That means He cares about our thoughts, pas-
sions, attitudes, and whether we trust in Him and love His ways. He
does not place value on our outward looks, social status, financial
standing, or any other external measure that the world considers
so important.

God's selection of David—someone known as a man after God's
own heart—demonstrates God's emphasis on internal rather than
external characteristics. David's status in his family was so low that
he wasn't even called in to meet with Samuel. He was merely the
youngest son, out in the fields tending the sheep. However, David
was God's choice to be the king of Israel, to perform great deeds, and
to be part of the family line that would produce the Savior whom
God would provide for Israel. Clearly, God did not see David in the
same way that even his own family saw him.

What is God seeing in your heart today? Take a heart inventory
right now. First, pray that God would reveal and then remove anything in your heart that doesn't belong there—resentments, anger,
sinful thoughts. Second, pray for big things, knowing that if God

can use a young shepherd boy, He can use anyone in a big way! Make your heart available to God's power and see what amazing things He will do through you.

※

Dear Lord, I am so grateful that You do not judge me the way people do. Thank You that You look on my heart to see my thoughts, attitudes, and love for You, and not how successful or attractive I am. Show me anything in my heart that should not be there, and I will confess it before You. Remove all sinful desires and fill my heart with Your love, peace, and joy.

WHEN GOD DOESN'T ANSWER

❧ Read and Consider ❧
1 Samuel 28

"He inquired of the LORD, but the LORD did not answer
him by dreams or Urim or prophets" (1 Samuel 28:6).

Sometimes God does not answer our prayers immediately. He may be telling us to wait; He may have another purpose in not giving a direct answer. Whatever the reason, it is always a good idea to "inquire of the Lord," and it is always a bad idea to take matters into our own hands. This is what King Saul did. So desperate was he for some kind of response that he just couldn't wait, so he went to a medium to get an answer.

When God does not answer your prayers, step back and wait. He is giving you an opportunity to trust Him in the midst of the uncertainty and ambiguity you may be feeling. The fact that Saul immediately consulted a medium—something he knew was directly forbidden by God and that he himself had outlawed—showed the shallowness of his trust in the Lord and his lack of commitment to God's ways.

What answer to prayer are you waiting for today? Have you become discouraged about it? Are you tempted to think that God is not listening to your prayers or that He doesn't care about your request? Are you thinking that maybe you need to step in and deal with the problem on your own since you haven't seen any response from God?

If so, ask God to help you to trust Him even when it is hard to do so. Ask Him to help you release the situation into His hands so He can handle it *His way* and in *His time*. Tell Him you are thankful that He knows what to do better than you do.

❧

God, I thank You that You always hear my prayers. Give me patience to wait for the answers to come in Your way and in Your perfect timing. Give me peace to accept Your answer—even if it is no. Help me to never take matters into my own hands to try and make something happen that is not Your will. I trust You know what is best for me at all times.

WHEN GOD GIVES SPECIFIC INSTRUCTIONS

❧ Read and Consider ☙

2 Samuel 5:17-25

"So David inquired of the LORD, 'Shall I go and attack the Philistines? Will you hand them over to me?' The LORD answered him, 'Go, for I will surely hand the Philistines over to you'" (2 Samuel 5:19).

God isn't always this direct, but He does occasionally give us very specific instructions in answer to our prayers. If we ask for guidance and depend on Him, He promises to lead us in the direction that we should go (Proverbs 3:5-6). That is what He did for David in this passage, directing him when and how to attack and assuring him of the outcome. So often we do not think to ask God for this kind of specific direction because we don't expect that He will answer us. But He wants to guide our lives—even in the small details—and the more we get in the habit of asking, the more we will learn how to listen for His voice and discern what He is telling us to do.

Don't be afraid to pray for guidance in specific areas of your life, and don't get discouraged if you don't hear answers right away. It may take some time to learn how to hear God's voice leading you. But you *will* learn, and you will enjoy greater intimacy in your relationship with God. He longs to have this closeness with you, so take Him up on it and start asking questions!

❧

Lord, I don't want to take one step or make any decision without Your leading. I know You care about even the smallest details of my life and want to guide me in the way I should go. Take away my peace if I should decide to step off the path of Your greatest blessing for my life. Help me to never stray from Your perfect will.

WHEN GOD SAYS NO

2 Samuel 7

*"Go and tell my servant David, 'This is what the LORD says:
Are you the one to build me a house to dwell in?...When
your days are over and you rest with your fathers, I will raise
up your offspring to succeed you, who will come from your
own body, and I will establish his kingdom. He is the one
who will build a house for my Name, and I will establish
the throne of his kingdom forever'" (2 Samuel 7:5,12-13).*

Sometimes, God says no.

None of us like to hear no for an answer. We don't want to be told no when we ask for help, or no when we ask someone for something, or no when we want to buy something new. We want to hear yes, yes, yes!

David fully expected a yes from God—and so did Nathan the prophet. After all, David wanted to honor God greatly by building a majestic place of worship. What could be wrong with that? In fact, Nathan was so certain of God's yes that he told David to go ahead and follow his heart. It seemed to him like a good plan with good motivation.

Then God stepped in. "That night the word of the LORD came to Nathan" (7:4). And Nathan realized he had to tell King David that even though the plan seemed good, it wasn't *God's* plan.

When God says no, it doesn't mean He doesn't care for us. In fact, quite the opposite. It means He has a greater purpose, and He knows the outcome. What you asked for might be dangerous, or unwise, or second-best. Or what you asked for may be wrong—perhaps your motivation or attitude was wrong. God wisely says no. So when you hear a no from God, trust His wisdom. It may even be signaling a *yes* in another direction! David received a disappointing no from God, but he also saw a future yes. David's son, Solomon, would build the temple with more glorious resources at his disposal than anyone ever before him.

When God says no to some of your prayer requests, thank Him for His wisdom and revelation, and tell Him you look forward to the good that He will send your way instead.

❧

Dear Lord, I trust You and accept Your answers to my prayers, even when the answer is not what I want. Help me to always understand Your will, especially when the answers to my prayers are not what I expected or thought they would be. I am grateful You know what is best for me and will not allow me to seek after things I shouldn't.

The QUICKSAND of TEMPTATION

*"One evening David got up from his bed and walked around
on the roof of the palace. From the roof he saw a woman
bathing. The woman was very beautiful, and David
sent someone to find out about her" (2 Samuel 11:2-3).*

King David was a good man. A man after God's own heart. But one night he wasn't where he was supposed to be, and he wasn't doing what he was supposed to be doing. He was supposed to be fighting with his army. Instead, he was up on his roof watching the *married* lady next door take a bath. Then he sent for her to come to his palace...and the story goes downhill from there.

You're probably familiar with it. The beautiful woman, Bathsheba, ended up pregnant, and her husband ended up conveniently dead on the front line of David's battle, being sent there specifically for that purpose by David. The king married Bathsheba, but they lost their baby. And, amazingly, had it not been for a confrontation with the prophet Nathan, David may have come out of the situation thinking he had pulled one over on God just because he had covered his tracks. But that's not how it works.

What could have saved David from the temptation to involve himself with another man's wife? Instead of feasting his eyes on that naked woman, he should have turned his eyes away, admitted his temptation to God *immediately,* and gone right into the privacy of his own room. There he could have done what he had done in the midst of so many other battles or personal struggles—fallen on his face before God in prayer, praise, and worship. If he had stayed there before the Lord until the grip of temptation had released him, these tragedies would have never happened.

But he didn't. David "sent someone to find out about her." He stuck his toe into the quicksand of temptation, and before he knew it, he was in over his head.

All of us face temptation at one time or another. It may not be the same kind that David faced, but anything that draws us away from God and entices us to do what is against God's laws is temptation. Whenever that happens to you, immediately get before God and confess it. Ask Him to set you free from it and help you do the right thing. Then worship God until you feel the temptation broken over you.

The ability to withstand temptation begins the moment you look to your Savior and Deliverer for help.

✤

Dear God, I pray You will help me to always successfully
resist temptation from the moment I am confronted with it.
Help me to draw closer to You when anything tries to draw
me away from You. Deliver me from the trap of temptation
before I fall into it. Give me the strength, wisdom, and
knowledge I need to fully resist temptation at all times.

The IMPORTANCE *of* CONFESSION

♣ Read and Consider ♣

2 Samuel 24

"David was conscience-stricken after he had counted the fighting men, and he said to the LORD, 'I have sinned greatly in what I have done. Now, O LORD, I beg you, take away the guilt of your servant. I have done a very foolish thing'" (2 Samuel 24:10).

No one had to say anything—David just *knew* it. The number came back and his conscience immediately pricked him. He realized that he had wanted to count his fighting men because it would make him feel proud, make him feel powerful and in control. But when his arrogance and illusion were revealed, David confessed his sin to God.

When we do something we know is wrong, our conscience usually lets us know. We feel ashamed, tortured, and terrible. But we must be careful that Satan doesn't make us feel so condemned about our sin that we are too ashamed to come before God. The enemy wants us to struggle with guilt to the point that we can't even pray. But the Lord has given us a way out of that kind of condemnation. It's called confession.

Confessing is more than just apologizing. Anyone can do that. We all know people who are good apologizers. The reason they are so good at it is that they get so much practice. They have to say "I'm sorry" over and over again because they never change their ways. In fact, they sometimes say "I'm sorry" without ever actually admitting to any fault. Those are the professional apologizers, and their confessions don't mean anything. But *true* confession means admitting in full detail what you have done, and then fully *repenting* of it. Repentance means being so deeply sorry for what you have done that you will do whatever it takes to keep it from happening again. Confession means *recognizing* we have done wrong and *admitting* our sin. Repentance means being *sorry* about our sin to the point of grief, and so we *turn* and *walk away* from that sin.

Confession and repentance do not negate consequences, however. David went to the right place and did the right thing, but he still had to pay the price. Sometimes our sin sets in motion consequences that we must handle with the Lord's help.

Anytime you feel convicted about something and you need to confess it before God, don't hesitate. The sooner you do it, the better you will feel. Also, ask God to show you any sin in your life that *needs* to be confessed. (Too often we don't even see it.) You will be amazed at how quickly God answers that prayer.

❧

Lord, I pray You would show me any sin in my life so that I can confess it before You. I don't want guilt in my conscience to dilute my walk with You or inhibit my prayers because I am ashamed to come before You in confidence. Help me to always have a repentant heart before You so that I will quickly turn away from sin.

HUMBLED *in* HIS PRESENCE

❧ Read and Consider ❧

1 Kings 8:22-30,56-61

*"But will God really dwell on earth? The heavens, even
the highest heaven, cannot contain you. How much
less this temple I have built!" (1 Kings 8:27).*

The magnificent temple was finally complete. All the furnishings had been installed. The ark of the Lord was in the Most Holy Place. Then, before the ribbon cutting celebration could proceed, God's presence in the form of a dark cloud filled the temple. The huge crowd must have been awestruck.

Solomon raised his arms toward heaven, silencing the assembly, and began his prayer. After a brief acknowledgment of his father, David's, (and his) role within God's plan, Solomon asked a wonderful rhetorical question: "How can this temple hold You?" He knew that despite its glory, the temple could not contain God, since even the highest heaven could not contain Him. It was one of the most magnificent structures any human had ever created to honor God, yet the true glory of the temple did not lie in the skill of the builders but in the *presence of God*.

When you come before God in prayer, one way you know you're in His presence is your sense of humility before Him. You can't be full of yourself and filled with His Spirit at the same time. You will always be humbled whenever you realize that this awesome God—whom the heavens cannot contain—is willing to come and live *inside you* through His Holy Spirit.

❧

*Dear Lord, I thank You for Your presence in my
life. I am thankful and humbled that You—through
Your Holy Spirit—live inside me. Help me to never
be full of myself, but rather to always be freshly filled
with more of You each day. Help me to have a sense
of Your presence, especially as I read Your Word
and pray and live in obedience to Your ways.*

Putting God Above All Else

*"As Solomon grew old, his wives turned his heart
after other gods, and his heart was not fully
devoted to the LORD his God, as the heart of
David his father had been" (1 Kings 11:4).*

With all God had given him, how could someone as wise as Solomon get so far off of the narrow path of obedience and so far away from the Lord's ways? Could it be that his wisdom turned out to be a point of pride? Did he think that *he* was the one responsible for all his wealth and blessings, and not God?

For half of his 40-year reign, Solomon seems to have exercised his wisdom in ways that pleased God. But little mention is made of Solomon's prayer life during these years. He presented sacrifices at the temple three times a year, but there is no record of his conversations with God during those visits. Perhaps the temple visits became merely a formality.

At the 20-year mark, cracks began to form in the structure of Solomon's reign. The first indication of a problem can be seen in the way he treated a friend (Hiram) by giving him a cheap gift (9:10-14). The queen of Sheba arrived and heaped praise on Solomon for his wisdom, though she was careful to give God the credit for Solomon's successes. Despite this foreign leader's enthusiastic words about the God of Israel, there's no hint in the passage that Solomon agreed with her or encouraged her interest in the God who had blessed his kingdom.

Solomon's reputation led to great riches. He accumulated things: ships, horses, gold, chariots, palaces, and women—lots of women.

He filled his life with treasures, and that's where his heart ended up. "King Solomon was greater in riches and wisdom than all the other kings of the earth" (10:23). God had promised this. After Solomon had asked for wisdom to rule the nation, God had responded, "I will give you what you have not asked for—both riches and honor—so that in your lifetime you will have no equal among kings" (3:13). With all that wisdom, the riches should not have gone to his head. But they did.

Jesus said, "Where your treasure is, there your heart will be also" (Matthew 6:21). Once Solomon's heart was focused on his material wealth, it was easy for his foreign wives to turn his heart away from the God who had so richly blessed him.

Any one of us can be tempted to put the things of this world above our relationship with God. That's why we have to regularly ask Him to show us if any of our possessions or desires are getting in the way of our walk with Him. We must ask the Lord not only for wisdom regarding that, but also for strength to resist anything that tempts our heart to turn away from Him.

❧

> *God, I pray my treasure will always be in You and not in*
> *my possessions or the distractions of this world. Help me to*
> *never make an idol out of anything or anyone, or put them*
> *before You in any way. I give You honor and gratitude*
> *for all the good things You have given me. You are my*
> *greatest desire, and I put You above all else in my life.*

PRAYING *for* SOMEONE WHO DOESN'T DESERVE IT

❧ Read and Consider ❧

1 Kings 13:1-10

*"Then the king said to the man of God, 'Intercede
with the LORD your God and pray for me that my
hand may be restored.' So the man of God interceded
with the LORD, and the king's hand was restored
and became as it was before" (1 Kings 13:6).*

Have you ever felt God calling you to pray for someone who you thought didn't deserve it? Do you know of people who ignore or even mock God, but when disaster strikes they want God to make it better? Have you ever struggled with the temptation to say, "Why should I pray for you when you show such disrespect for God?" The prophet Ahijah had good reason to feel that way when God sent him to confront the king. But he prayed anyway.

Jeroboam led a rebellion against Solomon's son Rehoboam and became the king of the northern ten tribes of Israel. Ahijah the prophet had foretold Jeroboam's success (11:29-40). Because Jeroboam didn't control Jerusalem, he feared that people's loyalty would be undermined if they continued to travel to the temple there to worship. So he instituted his own religion, complete with golden calves and altars (12:25-33). When God's messenger, Ahijah, showed up with a prophecy against the pagan altar, the king was offended. But when he pointed toward Ahijah to have him arrested, the king's hand instantly shriveled up.

Immediately, Jeroboam asked Ahijah to "intercede with the LORD your God." Even though he needed help, Jeroboam couldn't bring himself to acknowledge God as the God he should worship; instead, this was the *prophet's* God, not his. The fact that God healed him can only be seen as God's grace extended toward a rebel. But Jeroboam missed that point because he continued to promote his own religion. But Jeroboam's persistent rejection of God led to the destruction of his entire family.

And Ahijah was willing to pray for Jeroboam immediately, in spite of the fact that Jeroboam had threatened his life. This kind of praying isn't easy. But we are commanded to do it. Ahijah was under orders to announce judgment on the false religion Jeroboam was leading, but given a chance to pray for the wayward king, he didn't hesitate. Jesus said, "Love your enemies and pray for those who persecute you" (Matthew 5:44). We must remember that God is willing to listen to prayers for *us* when we don't deserve it. And we must not hesitate to pray for *others* even when we think *they* don't deserve it.

❧

*Lord, help me to obey Your commandment to love my
enemies and to pray for those who persecute me. I know
You have heard and answered the prayers of others for
me when I didn't deserve it; help me to do the same
for them. Give me the heart of love You have so that
I can pray for people who hurt or disappoint me.*

LEARNING *to* PRAY BOLDLY

❧ Read and Consider ☙
─────────────────────
1 Kings 17:1-24

*"Now Elijah the Tishbite, from Tishbe in Gilead, said
to Ahab, 'As the LORD, the God of Israel, lives, whom
I serve, there will be neither dew nor rain in the next
few years except at my word'" (1 Kings 17:1).*

When Elijah prayed, things happened. Clouds dried up or gushed rain, ravens served as food waiters, oil and flour multiplied, fire fell from heaven, and a dead boy came back to life. Some of these miracles were examples of divine timing, and each one of them was an example of divine power. All of them remind us that nothing is impossible when God decides to act.

When people and churches make prayer a priority, they always see answers to their prayers. Those who pray boldly may have the thrill of seeing miracles. When people are unified in the spirit of praise and they pray in unity, God does amazing things. Some people may question that God would really change the weather because people prayed. But He did it in the Bible. "Elijah was a man just like us. He prayed earnestly that it would not rain, and it did not rain on the land for three and a half years. Again he prayed, and the heavens gave rain, and the earth produced its crops" (James 5:17-18). If Elijah was like us, then why can't we pray like he prayed? We don't have to understand everything about how prayer works; we just have to believe that it does. Most of us know little about car engines, but that doesn't keep us from driving. We just have to turn the key. Few of us understand electricity, but we still expect our appliances to work when we plug them in. Prayer is the key that gets things going. Prayer is the way we plug in to the power of God. We are instructed to "pray continually" (1 Thessalonians 5:17). And God has promised to hear and answer. Elijah saw some unique answers to prayer, but his ability to pray was not unique. When you pray, big things can happen too. That's because God hears and will answer according to His will.

❧

*Lord, I know You are the God of miracles and nothing is
impossible for those who pray in the power of Your Spirit.
Help me to pray boldly and believe for miracles in answer
to my prayers. Teach me how to not pray too small. I don't
want my prayers to stop short of what You want to see
happen in my life and in the lives of those for whom I pray.*

EXPECTANT PRAYER

*"'Answer me, O LORD, answer me, so these people will know
that you, O LORD, are God, and that you are turning their
hearts back again.' Then the fire of the LORD fell and burned
up the sacrifice, the wood, the stones and the soil, and also
licked up the water in the trench" (1 Kings 18:37-38).*

If there is anything like instant replay in heaven, countless believers
will want to watch the moment when Elijah gave the signal and
God's fire fell and consumed the soggy sacrifice. Elijah had made
it impossible to set the sacrifice on fire outside of a miracle from
God. And a miracle is what he expected God to do. This is in great
contrast to the hours of agonized pleading by the prophets of Baal,
urging their mute and impotent god to send a little spark and light
the fire under *their* sacrifice.

Years earlier, Moses had warned the people that "God is a consuming fire, a jealous God" (Deuteronomy 4:24). So the way God
answered Elijah's prayer was perfectly in character. God doesn't
reveal all of His glory because He knows we couldn't handle it.
That's why when God makes His presence known, even through
messengers, His first words often are "Don't be afraid." But when it
came to a showdown with Baal worshipers, God allowed His actions
to announce, "Be afraid! God and His consuming fire are here!"

When you pray, do you expect God to do something because
you know what He *is able* to do? Or do you half expect to be disappointed because you doubt that God could do something so great
for you? If you answered yes to the last question, ask God to give

you a heart filled with faith and expectancy of the great things He
will do in response to your prayers.

❧

*Dear Lord, I pray You would help me to have strong
faith to believe You will do great things in response to
my prayers. Your Word tells of the magnificent and
miraculous things You have done for people, and I
know You are the same today and in the future as You
were in the past. I believe You can do magnificent and
miraculous things in response to my prayers as well.*

GOD WILL POUR OUT *as* MUCH *as* YOU CAN RECEIVE

❧ Read and Consider ❧
2 Kings 4:1-7

"Elisha said, 'Go around and ask all your neighbors for empty jars. Don't ask for just a few. Then go inside and shut the door behind you and your sons. Pour oil into all the jars, and as each is filled, put it to one side'" (2 Kings 4:3-4).

The widow came to Elisha for help because her sons were about to be sold into slavery to cover her debts. When he asked her what she had in her house, she said all she had was one jar of oil. He instructed her to borrow empty jars, *but not just a few.*

The widow didn't know what God would do with these empty jars; she only knew He asked her to gather *many.* This woman's faith would be measured by how many jars she collected.

God took what the widow had in her one jar and multiplied it to fill all the containers she had borrowed and brought into her house. She was then able to sell the oil and pay her debts.

God will take what you have and multiply it to meet your needs as well. But how well are you able to contain all God has for you? Do you have faith enough to embrace the big things God wants to do in your life? If not, ask Him to give you big faith, and then determine to shut the door on doubt.

❧

Heavenly Father, give me a vision of all You want to do in my life. Help me to not think too small, even when I pray. I want to be available to whatever You have for me and not

*limit Your blessings by being unprepared to receive them.
Enlarge my heart and mind to understand how You can
take what I have and expand it beyond what I can imagine.*

OPEN MY EYES, LORD

❧ Read and Consider ❧
2 Kings 6:8-23

"And Elisha prayed, 'O LORD, open his eyes so he may see.' Then the LORD opened the servant's eyes, and he looked and saw the hills full of horses and chariots of fire all around Elisha. As the enemy came down toward him, Elisha prayed to the LORD, 'Strike these people with blindness.' So he struck them with blindness, as Elisha had asked" (2 Kings 6:17-18).

E lisha and his servant were surrounded by an enemy army, but Elisha knew something his servant didn't, so he prayed that God would open his servant's eyes—*really* open them. When God did just that, the servant saw an even greater army of God surrounding the whole scene.

Elisha's prayer is one we can all pray too. "Open my eyes, Lord. Help me to see the *real* picture, the big picture, the supernatural picture. Help me to see what You are doing. Lift the curtain off of my spiritual eyes so that I can see Your hand at work behind the scenes of the battles I face in life."

But there is another prayer in this story. After Elisha prayed that his servant would see the truth of God's supernatural protection, he then prayed that his enemies would be struck blind so they couldn't see what was around them. This would cause them to follow a different path. Both of Elisha's prayers were answered. There are times when we also need to pray Elisha's second prayer. We need to ask God to blind and confuse our enemy.

Ask God to give you the ability to see with spiritual eyes so you can better understand things from *His* perspective.

❧

Almighty God, I pray You would open my eyes to
see the truth about my situation. Give me clear
understanding—especially when I am facing the enemy—of
all You are doing in the midst of my situation. Help
me to trust Your hand of protection. Enable me to see
things from Your perspective so that I can stand strong.

Undeserved Answers *to* Prayer

*"Then Jehoahaz sought the LORD's favor, and the LORD
listened to him, for he saw how severely the king
of Aram was oppressing Israel. The LORD provided
a deliverer for Israel, and they escaped from the
power of Aram. So the Israelites lived in their own
homes as they had before" (2 Kings 13:4-5).*

Jehoahaz was not known for his wisdom and virtue. He was such
an evil king that God sent the oppressive team of King Hazael
and Prince Ben-Hadad of Aram as Jehoahaz's judgment. It seemed
he was finally getting what he deserved.

But then Jehoahaz did an unexpected thing. When the oppression became too great, he did what any of us would do when our
backs are against the wall and our best efforts are not enough—he
prayed. An evil man was desperate and turned to God. He asked
for God's help, and God gave it. That's what God does. He answers
the prayers of people *who don't deserve it.*

How easy it is to believe that our answered prayers have something to do with our being good enough. Or we think that if
God *hasn't* answered our prayer yet, it must be because we *aren't*
good enough. Or worse, we don't pray because we think we can't
impress God enough with our goodness to make Him want to
answer. We forget that our best goodness still would not *deserve*
God's favor.

Jehoahaz's prayer has a lot to teach us. He called out to God,
knowing full well that he had given God no good reason to answer.
He received God's favor, not because of who he was, but because

of who God is—a gracious and compassionate God who listens to honest, humble prayers. Don't forget that God always listens whenever you pray.

❧

Dear Lord, I thank You that You listen to my prayers and that You answer, not according to my own goodness, but according to Yours. Help me to not let anything discourage me from coming to You in prayer—especially not my own sense that I am undeserving of Your attention and blessing. I come entirely because You are full of grace and mercy.

AN UNDIVIDED HEART

❖ Read and Consider ❖

2 Kings 17:24-33

*"They worshiped the LORD, but they also appointed
all sorts of their own people to officiate for them as
priests in the shrines at the high places. They worshiped
the LORD, but they also served their own gods in
accordance with the customs of the nations from
which they had been brought" (2 Kings 17:32-33).*

I
f Samaria was anything, it was a house divided. Starting with King Jeroboam, this northern kingdom had allowed the worship of foreign gods—forgetting their spiritual roots. A succession of evil kings spiraled the nation deeper and deeper into sin, until God finally allowed it to be taken into exile by the Assyrians. The people of the northern kingdom were taken captive; then the king of Assyria brought other people from foreign lands and resettled them in Samaria. After some concerns about "what the god of that country requires" (17:26), the king sent a few exiled priests back to teach the resettled foreigners about the god of that land. The result was that people tried to combine the worship of Jehovah God with that of all the various false gods—including those whose worship practices were in direct violation of God's laws. That was a combination that was sure to bring serious consequences. When it comes to serving God, our loyalty to Him cannot be divided.

Centuries later, Jesus talked about a house divided. He had been accused of casting out demons by the power of Satan (a ludicrous accusation made by jealous people). Jesus pointed out to these accusers that He wouldn't be working against Satan by the power of Satan. A house divided is a house that will fall (see Matthew 12:24-29). And that's what happened to Samaria, not that the nation immediately disappeared, but that it never regained spiritual or political power.

Samaria is a good lesson for us. In the rush of our lives, it's easy to be divided—in our time, our energies, our focus. Without realizing it, we can be a lot like the Samaritans, serving God along with our other allegiances.

That's why prayer is so important. It unites your heart with God's. And it connects you to *who* matters more than anything else in your life. Prayer keeps your heart undivided.

❧

> *Dear God, I pray You would keep me from ever*
> *having a divided heart. I don't want to weaken my*
> *allegiance to You by showing any allegiance to the*
> *false gods of this world. Help me to stay in close touch*
> *with You through constant and fervent prayer. Unite*
> *my heart with Yours so that it never strays.*

REMEMBER ME, LORD

❖ Read and Consider ❖

2 Kings 20:1-11

*"Hezekiah turned his face to the wall and prayed
to the LORD, 'Remember, O LORD, how I have
walked before you faithfully and with wholehearted
devotion and have done what is good in your eyes.'
And Hezekiah wept bitterly" (2 Kings 20:2-3).*

The prophet Isaiah had informed Hezekiah that he was going to die. Perhaps you've faced a similar situation, whether from a potentially terminal illness, a near fatal accident, or an iffy report from a medical test. Whenever you face your own mortality, what do you do? Hezekiah prayed.

His prayer was a plea not to be forgotten by God. "Remember how I've served You, Lord. Remember the good things I have done."

When we find ourselves in desperate circumstances—especially in a life and death situation—we want to say, "Remember me, Lord. I love You and want to serve You longer." We know God doesn't owe us that. But we also know He is a God of mercy and grace. And we are asking for His grace to be extended to us now.

One of the things Hezekiah's prayer did was to clearly identify God as the source of his healing and deliverance. By turning to God with his whole heart, he was coming to the only One who could change his fate. God heard his prayer and the cry of his heart and not only healed him but gave him 15 more years to live and serve.

When you are in a difficult situation, cry out to God as the source of your healing and deliverance. Thank Him that He is a God of mercy and grace.

❖

*Lord, You are my Healer and Deliverer. In times
of sickness, injury, or affliction, I pray You would
remember me and heal me from anything that would
threaten to diminish or end my life. Help me to be
able to serve You longer and ever more effectively and
not succumb to the plans of the enemy for my demise.
Remember me with Your health and wholeness.*

BE BOLD *to* ASK

---

1 *Chronicles* 4:9-10

*"Jabez cried out to the God of Israel, 'Oh, that you would
bless me and enlarge my territory! Let your hand be with
me, and keep me from harm so that I will be free from
pain.' And God granted his request" (1 Chronicles 4:10).*

Apart from these two verses, Jabez doesn't show up anywhere else
in Scripture. Yet his brief mention here left a lasting impression.
He prayed boldly, and then "God granted his request."

Jabez, whose name sounded like the Hebrew word for "pain,"
made four requests: for God's blessing ("bless me"), for God's provision
("enlarge my territory"), for God's presence ("let your hand be
with me"), and for God's protection ("keep me from harm"). All of
these things are what God wants for us. It is God's pleasure to bless
us and provide for us, to be with us and protect us. But He wants us
to pray and ask. And so often we don't. Too often we think we don't
deserve His blessings or that it is being selfish to ask. Sometimes
we pursue things in our own strength and fail to recognize God's
goodness in wanting to be our provider. Often we don't want to
seem as if we are asking for too much, as if God is limited in what
He has to give.

If you have ever had thoughts like that, consider the words of
Jesus when He said, "Your Father has been pleased to give you the
kingdom" (Luke 12:32). That sounds like He wants to give us more
than we realize.

Have you ever prayed boldly like Jabez did? If not, start by
thanking God for all He has already given you and then ask for

the desires of your heart. Ask Him to bless you so you can serve His purposes and bless others.

Don't worry that in asking boldly you will ask for too much. God is not going to give you something that is not good for you or before you are ready to receive it. He will always answer your prayers according to His will and in His perfect timing.

❦

God, I thank You for all You have given me. I pray for Your continued blessings, provision, and protection. I pray Your presence will always be with me wherever I go and no matter what happens. Thank You that You are pleased to share Yourself and Your kingdom with me. Enable me to give back to You by helping and blessing others.

Pray Before You Act

"Now the Philistines had come and raided the Valley of Rephaim; so David inquired of God: 'Shall I go and attack the Philistines? Will you hand them over to me?' The LORD answered him, 'Go, I will hand them over to you'" (1 Chronicles 14:9-10).

David was finally made king of all Israel. Suddenly, he faced his first challenge as the ruler of the land. The Philistines decided to test his strength by invading territory under his control. The new king could have taken this threat as a personal challenge to prove his fitness to rule. Instead, he turned to God for wisdom in responding to the attack. He didn't do anything before asking God for direction. He prayed before proceeding.

Twice God instructed David to attack. His permission was specific. So was His promise of victory. Israel would defeat the Philistines because God would "hand them over." Interestingly, both armies took their "gods" into battle. The true God of Israel won; the gods of the Philistines were left lying on the battlefield like dry wood ready for burning. "The Philistines had abandoned their gods there, and David gave orders to burn them in the fire" (14:12).

Then the Philistines returned for round two. It's not clear exactly why. Perhaps they needed to rescue their gods or try out some new ones, or perhaps they thought David's first victory was just beginner's luck. David prayed again and received new marching orders. The Philistines were defeated again.

David's actions in this passage reveal several significant lessons about prayer. First, no matter how sudden or major a threat, we need to pray *before* we respond. Second, God brings the victory. Third, just because we have prayed and seen an "enemy" defeated doesn't mean we won't face that same threat again. Fourth, prayer allows us to receive direction from God that may include a different kind of action than we have taken previously.

Although we can't always see the problems we avoided because we prayed, all too often we see the bad things that happen when we act and don't pray. Ask God to help you always pray before you take any action or make any decision.

❧

Dear Lord, I pray I will always inquire of You first before I take action. I don't want to assume that because You instructed me in a certain way before, You will instruct me in the same way each time I am faced with a similar situation. I don't want to mistakenly think I have all the answers when only You have all the answers for my life.

GOD DOES MORE THAN
YOU CAN IMAGINE

❧ Read and Consider ❧
1 Chronicles 17:1-27

"And now, LORD, let the promise you have made
concerning your servant and his house be established
forever. Do as you promised, so that it will be established
and that your name will be great forever. Then men
will say, 'The LORD Almighty, the God over Israel, is
Israel's God!' And the house of your servant David will
be established before you" (1 Chronicles 17:23-24).

More than anything, David desired to build a magnificent temple to honor the Lord. He had big plans and all kinds of resources ready. Even Nathan the prophet thought a temple was a great idea. Then God spoke. Through a revelation to Nathan, God revealed that David would not be the one to achieve that goal. The message Nathan shared began with God's "no" but ended with amazing promises to David. One of David's offspring (Solomon) would indeed build the temple, and David's throne would be established forever.

Rather than complaining about being denied the temple project, David responded with deep humility, gratitude, and praise. God was giving more than he ever dreamed—a temple and an everlasting kingdom! David acknowledged that this great blessing had to do with God's character and grace, not David's own worthiness (17:16-19). He praised God saying, "There is no one like you, O LORD" (17:20). He described the parallel between God's gracious choice of his family and God's faithfulness to Israel, both examples of God's amazing willingness to work out His plans through frail and flawed people. Then David made a request: "Let the promise you have made…be established forever" (17:23). In today's language, David was praying, "Lord, these are the amazing promises You have made about my family. I know that because You have said it, it will be done!"

Whenever you sense that God is saying no to your prayer, don't focus on your disappointment over not having *your* will done. If you do that, you may miss the joy of something much better that can come about if *God's* will is done. God's will is always richer and better than anything you can imagine.

❧

Lord, I confess any disappointment I have had when my prayers were not answered the way I wanted them to be. I know my greatest blessing will come about because of Your will being done in my life. I also know that what You have for me is far greater than what I can imagine for myself. Forgive me for any time I did not trust that to be true.

REPENTING BEFORE GOD *in* PRAYER

❖ Read and Consider ❖
1 Chronicles 21:1-19

*"David said to God, 'Was it not I who ordered the
fighting men to be counted? I am the one who has
sinned and done wrong. These are but sheep. What
have they done? O LORD my God, let your hand fall
upon me and my family, but do not let this plague
remain on your people'" (1 Chronicles 21:17).*

King David had many highs of faith and obedience and some
real lows of sin and disobedience. How can someone with such
capacity for harmony with God be guilty of such sinful actions?
This episode begins with a reminder that David was a prime target
of Satan. Humiliating and defeating people whom God has called
seems to be a specialty of the enemy of our souls.

Satan tempted ("incited") David, and David took the bait (21:1-2).
Taking a census of fighting men appealed to the king's sense of
authority and power. It was a matter of sinful pride. Satan knew
just where David was weakest.

By the time Joab returned with the numbers, the king realized
he had sinned. To his great credit, David owned up to his sin. He
took responsibility and confessed it all to God in prayer. God used
this occasion to teach David an indelible lesson about responsibility:
When we sin, the consequences are real and often hurt others. When
a king sins, all the people suffer. God gave David a choice of consequences, each affecting both king and people. David chose to submit
to God's direct punishment rather than suffer under "the hands
of men" (21:13). But the effects of his choice overwhelmed David:
Seventy thousand men died from the plague. The king gained a
deeper, humbler, more painful perspective on the seriousness of sin

and the holiness of God. He begged God to punish him personally and spare the rest of the people. God called off the plague, and David offered sacrifices. Our last glimpse of David in this episode shows a king chastened and respectful before God, careful not to take Him for granted.

We all need to confess our sins in prayer to God. Especially the sin of pride, which we are each tempted to have. But if we include repentance and confession as part of our prayers and then ask God to help us not commit those sins again, it enables us to stay on target with God. Even though there may be hard consequences for sin we've committed, when we come before God with humble hearts, we can be forgiven and good can come out of it.

❧

*Lord, I see in Your Word the terrible consequences of
pride. I don't want to experience those consequences
in my life, and especially not to have my family suffer
because of my sin. Reveal any pride in me so that I
can confess and repent of it before You immediately.
Help me to always have a humble heart.*

The POWER of PRAISE-FILLED GIVING

❧ Read and Consider ❧
1 Chronicles 29:1-20

*"Wealth and honor come from you; you are the ruler of all
things. In your hands are strength and power to exalt and
give strength to all. Now, our God, we give you thanks,
and praise your glorious name" (1 Chronicles 29:12-13).*

D avid's life was winding down, and he wanted to pave the
way for his son's reign and for the construction of the great
temple. He arranged for vast sums of raw materials to be stockpiled
for the project. As one of his last official gestures as king, David
announced he would add his own personal gift from out of his
treasures as the king. He challenged others to give in the same spirit,
out of honor to God. "Now," he said, "who is willing to consecrate
himself today to the LORD?" (29:5). Other leaders stepped up and
gave. The resulting offering provided much of the funding for the
construction of the temple.

The people were amazed at their own generosity. King David
was deeply touched by their giving and lifted up one of the greatest
prayers of praise in the Bible. It wasn't a long prayer, but every word
exalted God and recognized Him as the ultimate supplier of all
things. What more appropriate way to acknowledge God as the head
over all and the owner of everything than by contributing generously
to the building of a grand temple that would honor Him? What
better way to show trust in God's future faithfulness than to give
from the abundance of His present faithfulness?

After King David gave his personal treasure and praised God, he
acknowledged the profound effect he had felt as the people gave their
offerings. And he fervently prayed that this spirit of generosity and

trust would always be a hallmark of God's people. David concluded by urging the people to "Praise the LORD your God" (29:20). They gave to God from their earthly treasures as well as giving praise to Him from their whole hearts.

Powerful prayer includes lavish praise to God for His generosity. It also includes giving to God out of a praise-filled heart. To do otherwise reveals that we revere our possessions more than our God, who has given us all that we have.

❧

Heavenly Father, I thank You and praise You for all
You have given me. Help me to give back to You with
the same heart of praise I have when I receive from
You. I want to be a cheerful giver. Help me to never
value my possessions more than I value You and Your
laws. Enable me to give the way You want me to.

INVITING GOD'S PRESENCE
and FORGIVENESS

✤ Read and Consider ✤
2 *Chronicles 6:12-42*

*"Now, my God, may your eyes be open and your ears
attentive to the prayers offered in this place. Now
arise, O LORD God, and come to your resting place,
you and the ark of your might. May your priests, O
LORD God, be clothed with salvation, may your saints
rejoice in your goodness" (2 Chronicles 6:40-41).*

Solomon's workers had completed the temple construction. David,
Solomon's father and predecessor, had gathered the materials,
but Solomon was charged with completing the actual structure.
Such attention to detail was given to this process that it took seven
years to complete the majestic temple. The walls and furniture were
covered with gold. The king of Tyre himself shipped the lumber in
from Lebanon.

Yet even with all its finery, it wasn't the temple building that
prompted Solomon's thoughtful prayer here. It was God's glorious
presence filling that temple. Finally there was a place for God to
dwell more permanently among His people. Since the nation's whole
identity was based on its relationship with God and His blessing,
this was a very significant moment.

In light of that, it's interesting to really listen to Solomon's prayer.
Rather than a formal prayer laced with high and holy phrases, it is
a very down-to-earth prayer filled with the tough stuff of real life.
Solomon covered the gamut of life situations that these people were
going to face as they worshiped for—what he hopes will be—many
centuries at this temple.

After describing all the possible tragedies that could happen, Solomon's prayer was, in essence, "Be with us." No matter how the people might stray, he wanted God to hear their prayers of repentance and forgive them. He wanted God's presence.

We should pray the same way—inviting God's presence to dwell in us and to forgive us whenever we stray from His ways.

❦

Holy Father, there is nothing more important than Your presence in my life. Help me to be a holy place for Your Spirit to dwell. Forgive me of all sin and cleanse my heart of all unrighteousness. Nothing is more comforting to me than to know You are with me, no matter what is happening in my life.

WHY WE MUST PRAY
for OUR NATION

"If my people, who are called by my name, will humble themselves and pray and seek my face and turn from their wicked ways, then will I hear from heaven and will forgive their sin and will heal their land" (2 Chronicles 7:14).

King Solomon dedicated the temple and saw God's awesome presence there. The people feasted for days and days. The king prayed a prayer that seemed to cover all possible contingencies, asking God for guidance, deliverance, and forgiveness. Once the festivities were over, God answered. Coming to Solomon in the night, God laid it out, plain and simple. *If* the people would follow God's ways, *then* He would hear their prayers and heal their land.

Looking back through Israel's history, it is obvious that every time the people did not follow God's plan, they did not receive what God had planned for them. When they worshiped other gods and did whatever they wanted, when they married into other tribes and made deals with wicked nations, they lost political strength and were ultimately defeated and taken away as exiles.

We can ask ourselves, how could they have missed it? God couldn't have been clearer in His instructions. And yet, we too often miss what God is saying. God is still saying that if we follow His ways our lives will be better, yet often we don't follow and then wonder why things go the way they do.

God is still saying, "Pray for your nation." Whether we like our leaders or greatly disagree with them, God calls us to humble ourselves and pray for them.

Our land needs healing. God's promise is that if we turn from our wicked ways, He will forgive and heal. That won't happen without prayer.

❧

Lord God, I come humbly before You and confess the sins of my nation. I pray we as a people would turn from our wicked ways and seek Your face so that You will hear our prayers, forgive our sins, and heal our land. We desperately need Your hand of blessing and protection upon our country. Pour out Your Spirit on us and work Your righteousness in the hearts of the people.

Praying *in the* Good Times

❧ Read and Consider ❧
2 Chronicles 15:1-19

*"Although he did not remove the high places
from Israel, Asa's heart was fully committed to
the LORD all his life" (2 Chronicles 15:17).*

When we live a lifestyle of praise and worship, we keep our
heart fresh and open to the working of the Holy Spirit in us.
Spending time in prayerful worship keeps us in the right attitude
to hear from God and be guided by Him. It positions Him as first
priority in our lives and helps us stay dependent upon Him, whether
things in our lives are going well or not.

When the Spirit of God came upon the prophet Azariah, he told
King Asa, "The LORD is with you when you are with him. If you
seek him, he will be found by you, but if you forsake him, he will
forsake you" (15:2). It can't get any clearer than that. If God is with
us as long as we're with *Him,* that should increase our motivation
to be with *Him.*

So what does it mean to be "with God"? We understand it pretty
clearly in the bad times. We come to God desperate for help. What
about when things are going well? The best advice when you are in
a season of peace and rest is to use that time to build and fortify
yourself in the Lord. Study His Word. Communicate with Him
in prayer. Spend time in His presence in worship and praise. Get
closer. Stay *with* Him. Use that time to fall in love with Jesus all
over again.

King Asa didn't always do everything right, but in the end he
was described as a king who had a heart fully committed to the
Lord. Even when you don't act perfectly, you can show God that

your heart is perfectly in love with Him by the praise you give Him every day.

❧

Father God, I worship You and thank You that You
are the God of love. Your love in my life has saved me
and is transforming me for Your high purpose. Help
me to remember to pray as fervently to You in the good
times as I do in the difficult times. Enable me to always
keep my heart open to what You are doing in my life.

DELIVERANCE MAY BE
ONLY *a* PRAYER AWAY

*"When the chariot commanders saw Jehoshaphat, they
thought, 'This is the king of Israel.' So they turned to attack
him, but Jehoshaphat cried out, and the LORD helped him.
God drew them away from him" (2 Chronicles 18:31).*

The kingdom of Israel had divided into two kingdoms, Israel and
Judah. While these kingdoms were often at odds, they did join
together to fight Aram. Judah's king, Jehoshaphat, was known for
being a righteous king, but this was not a trait that could be used
to describe Israel's wicked King Ahab. Even though the prophet
Micaiah had foreseen doom for Israel and the death of Ahab, the
two nations had a common enemy in Aram, so it seemed to make
political sense to go into battle together.

As a precaution against the prophecy of his own death, King
Ahab shrewdly suggested that he remain in disguise as a soldier,
while Jehoshaphat enter the battle in a king's full regalia. Even those
of us who've never entered a battlefield would know that the enemy
army is going to want to take out the leader. If the king is leading
his army, he is the primary target. But Jehoshaphat agreed. And sure
enough, when the enemy attacked, they went after the only king
they saw. But Jehosphaphat prayed, and God protected him. And in
keeping with the prophecy, a stray arrow found the chink in Ahab's
armor even though he was disguised as a mere soldier.

Jehoshaphat made several errors that day, not the least of which
was building an alliance with a competing and wicked king. He
asked for a prophet of God but didn't really listen when he came.

He let his faith slip in the face of political expediency, pride, or even fear. But one choice Jehoshaphat made was impeccable. Even in the heat of battle, he cried out to God.

Prayer is not something that only happens in the quietness of a moment. Acknowledging God's presence and power—talking to God—should be part of every aspect of life, the battles as well as the peace times. Always cry out to God in your desperate moments, remembering that deliverance is often only a prayer away.

❧

> *Lord, I pray You would strengthen my faith so that*
> *I will not give up praying in the heat of the battle*
> *of opposition from the enemy. I realize the very next*
> *prayer I pray may be the one to bring total deliverance*
> *from the strongholds the enemy is trying to erect in my*
> *life. Enable me to stand strong in prayer and worship,*
> *giving thanks for Your presence and delivering power.*

EVEN WHEN WE DON'T DO EVERYTHING RIGHT

"Although most of the many people who came from Ephraim, Manasseh, Issachar and Zebulun had not purified themselves, yet they ate the Passover, contrary to what was written. But Hezekiah prayed for them, saying, 'May the LORD, who is good, pardon everyone who sets his heart on seeking God—the LORD, the God of his fathers—even if he is not clean according to the rules of the sanctuary.' And the LORD heard Hezekiah and healed the people" (2 Chronicles 30:18-20).

Hezekiah had a heart like Jesus. Over and over again, Jesus broke the religious rules of His day. He understood that God's heart was bigger than any set of rules, even the ones meant to govern worship and holiness. Hezekiah's prayer revealed the same thing in him.

The people had come from far and wide to feast and worship. But some were not prepared. They were ceremonially unclean. Hezekiah realized, however, that what was happening—the reinstitution of the Passover, the most important national and spiritual ritual—was much larger than any rule regarding that ritual. If Hezekiah hadn't realized that, the festival would have caused division rather than unity. The work of God would have moved backward rather than forward. The whole point of the feast would have been missed—the point being that God saves His people based on His mercy, love, and the blood of a lamb.

Hezekiah's prayer showed how much he believed that God would be gracious and merciful to overlook imperfection and help His children worship Him. He healed them even though they had not done everything right.

Don't hesitate to come to God. Don't be afraid to ask God to help you honor and worship Him, even when you don't do everything perfectly. He will enable you to do that.

❧

God, I thank You that even when I don't do everything right, You see in my heart the desire to do so, and You bless me with answers to my prayers. I am grateful You look past my imperfections and see the perfect qualities of Your Son, Jesus, stamped on my heart instead. Help me to live Your way so that my ways are pleasing in Your sight.

GOD IS *on* YOUR SIDE

❧ Read and Consider ❧
2 Chronicles 32:1-23

" 'Be strong and courageous. Do not be afraid or discouraged
because of the king of Assyria and the vast army with
him, for there is a greater power with us than with
him. With him is only the arm of flesh, but with us is
the LORD our God to help us and to fight our battles.'
And the people gained confidence from what Hezekiah
the king of Judah said" (2 Chronicles 32:7-8).

King Hezekiah knew the king of Assyria was going to attack Jerusalem. It was only a matter of time. So he gathered his advisors and worked hard to build up his defenses and prepare the city. Then he gathered the people and reminded them that no matter the size of the army against them, God was bigger. "And the people gained confidence." By acknowledging and remembering who God was, they all found strength.

It's not wrong to be afraid of what you see *could* happen. That's realism. What *is* wrong is to not seek God's help immediately and humble yourself in worship before Him. Among other things, our praise reminds the enemy of who God is and how well we know Him. Always keep in mind that the enemy does not want you to worship God. So every time you attempt to build an altar to God in your life, the enemy will try to stop you.

Have you faced any frightening opposition in your life lately? Have you felt the enemy of your soul waging a full attack against you? Are you sometimes overwhelmed at how little strength and power you feel in the midst of it all? Don't worry; pray, and remember, "The one who is in you is greater than the one who is in the world" (1 John 4:4).

When King Hezekiah faced a strong enemy, he told his people the truth—God is greater. Keep in mind that when you acknowledge and praise God in the midst of enemy opposition, there is far more power with you than there is with the enemy.

❧

Thank You, Lord, that You are with me in everything that I face. No matter what comes against me, You are greater and more powerful. I ask You to be with me in the things I face today. I praise You and Your greatness in the midst of all that seems large and looming in my life.

The ANTIDOTE *for* FEAR

Ezra 3:7-13

"With praise and thanksgiving they sang to the LORD: 'He is good; his love to Israel endures forever.' And all the people gave a great shout of praise to the LORD, because the foundation of the house of the LORD was laid" (Ezra 3:11).

The people of Judah had been exiled. Jerusalem and its temple were in ruins. Outsiders had taken over the land—people who did not understand or revere the customs of the Jewish nation. So when the first Jews returned from their exile, they were fearful and a bit intimidated by the people around them. But they knew they must rebuild, and so they began. It was a slow and arduous process, but finally the foundation of the temple was laid.

And then the people pulled out all the stops, praising God, singing songs, shouting, and playing trumpets and cymbals. They were so *loud* that all the foreign neighbors heard them.

When you're struggling, or doubting, or fearful, or feel as if your foundation has crumbled, don't ever underestimate the power of praise! Don't just think about it. Do it. Pull out all the stops. Make praise your *first* response to fearful situations in your life. God wants us to praise Him at all times, but especially when we are afraid or discouraged. When we do, not only will He take away our fear, but He will also give us joy (Psalm 34:1-5).

Fear will tell you things that are not God's truth for your life. Fear denies that God's presence is powerful and fully active in your life. It cancels all hope and faith in God's desire to work in your behalf. But the truth is that faith, prayer, praise, and the Word of God will conquer your every fear.

❧

Lord, I praise Your name. You are almighty and far
above all things. Your presence in my life is greater
than anything I fear. I know faith in You and in Your
Word will conquer all opposition in my life. With Your
help, I will not dwell on my problems, but instead
I will praise You and Your name continually.

The POWER of FASTING with PRAYER

❧ Read and Consider ☙

Ezra 8:21-32

*"So we fasted and petitioned our God about this,
and he answered our prayer" (Ezra 8:23).*

E zra the priest, and those traveling with him, needed protection for what would be a long and difficult journey. They could have asked the king for horses and soldiers, but they didn't. They could have hired guards, but they didn't. In fact, Ezra says he was ashamed to do that. After all, they had told the king how powerful their God was. Surely He could protect them on their way.

So they fasted and prayed.

Prayer is always a strong weapon against the enemy. Fasting makes it even more so. When the Lord puts on your heart that a particular request needs to be accompanied by fasting, you would be wise to listen. Fasting takes prayer to a whole new level, keeping evil at bay and breaking down strongholds. Fasting is a way of saying, "I deny myself what I want most and put God first in my life." The enemy hates that because he knows it's a sure way of resisting and defeating him. Fasting cripples the power of evil spiritual forces in the realm of darkness so they cannot sustain their grip on your life, your mind, and your circumstances.

Fasting and prayer bring your body into submission by informing it that it is not in charge. Fasting says, "I'm a spiritual being before I'm a physical being. I'm physical, so I need to eat, but I'm spiritual too. I'm going to assert the supremacy of my spiritual allegiance beyond and before my allegiance to my body and its desire for food."

Ezra was facing a difficult but very important trip, so he fasted and prayed. Whenever you are facing a difficult circumstance or decision, you can be sure that when you fast and pray about it, much is being accomplished in the spiritual realm. In fact, far more is accomplished in the realm of the spirit during a fast than is ever manifested immediately in the physical realm.

The kind of fast God wants is that of an obedient heart willing to say, "Yes, God, I'll go without food for a period if that means a child may be healed, a friend in bondage may be set free, a lost family member may be found, someone in darkness may be moved into light, or that I might live in greater wisdom, peace, and power. Yes, God, a fast is a small price to pay for all that."

Be open to hear what the Lord says to you about fasting, for He *is* saying something. If you are able to fast, He wants you to do so because you trust Him, love Him, and acknowledge His power.

❧

Lord, help me to fast and pray regularly. Show me
how often and how long and give me the strength to
get through each fast successfully. With every fast, help
me to pray powerfully about the issues of my life and
the situations in my world. I want to deny my flesh so
that I can exalt You above everything else in my life.

BE WATCHFUL *in* PRAYER

❖ Read and Consider ❖
Nehemiah 4:1-9

*"But we prayed to our God and posted a guard day
and night to meet this threat" (Nehemiah 4:9).*

Working for good in this world will always meet opposition. The enemies of Jerusalem wanted the city to remain in ruins. They were angry when Nehemiah organized the people to rebuild the walls. First they ridiculed, then they threatened, then they planned to attack. The pressure to stop the work grew. Nehemiah prayed against the ridicule and the threats. He trusted God, and he "posted a guard day and night."

There are examples in Scripture when God instructed people to pray and stand back to see Him work (for example, in 2 Kings 19:35, where God wiped out an army laying siege to Jerusalem). But these occasions are rare. Prayer and faith are vital, but so is doing our part.

So how do we know when we should just pray, or when we should pray *and* do something else? The answer is to keep praying, and God will show you. Nehemiah was a man of constant prayer. His ongoing conversations with God gave him insight into what he was to do. At times, God said, "I'll take care of it." At times, God said, "I'll take care of it, but have the people post a guard. They'll all feel better about that." In any case, you can know what to do when you become sensitive to God's guidance as Nehemiah was. Nehemiah and the people never had to fight, but they had to be ready to do so. Their prayers renewed their trust in God; their actions showed that they were willing to have God work things out any way He decided. Whether they had to fight or not, they were not going to stop building the wall, for they were under God's orders. That was a greater motivator for Nehemiah and his people than anything the enemies could throw at them.

We have to be watchful in prayer and always available to do what God has instructed us to do. As we stay in close communication with Him, He will show us what action to take.

❧

Dear God, I pray You would help me to be watchful in prayer so that I am always aware of what I am supposed to be doing, as well as clearly understanding what I am not supposed to be doing. Help me to pray without ceasing so that I can stand guard against every plan of the enemy against me.

THANK GOD *for* HIS MERCY *to* YOU

✣ Read and Consider ✣

Nehemiah 9:1-37

*"But in your great mercy you did not put an end
to them or abandon them, for you are a gracious
and merciful God" (Nehemiah 9:31).*

Nehemiah and the people of Israel had just accomplished an impossible mission. They had rebuilt the massive walls of Jerusalem in record time. Against all odds and opposition they had succeeded. Now it was time for another kind of rebuilding—accepting and applying God's written instructions for His people. Nehemiah chapter 8 describes a national Bible study of sorts, as Ezra reintroduced God's law to the people. Chapter 9 records the effects of God's Word settling into the hearts and minds of God's people. They arrived at a clear understanding of how far they had drifted from God's ways, and so they gathered for a great service of national repentance and worship.

In God's presence, the people reviewed their history, highlighting the repeated sins of the nation as well as God's repeated mercy and faithfulness. This review wasn't to inform God, but to demonstrate to themselves that they understood how things had come to be. They were standing as a small remnant of a great nation that had been humbled under God's just judgment. In God's mercy they had returned to their land. Their very existence was an amazing tribute to God's faithfulness. Despite everything His people had done to violate the covenants He had made with them in the past, God had kept His word. They knew God was faithful, so they dared to start over.

Their prayer of confession offers us a good example. We need to review our spiritual history in prayer from time to time. Particularly when we have followed the Lord for a long time, we need to trace the journey we have traveled with Him. Perhaps we hesitate to do this because we realize our history with God is like the Israelites' was—full of our failures as well as God's faithfulness. God certainly takes no pleasure in our review of sins unless it leads us to repentance and a clearer understanding of all He has done to guard and guide us along the way. Thank God for all the times He has shown His mercy and grace to you.

❧

Lord, I am aware every day of Your great mercy toward me. Thank You that You have never judged me according to what I have deserved. Your grace toward me is beyond comprehension. Thank You that You will never forsake me. Help me to never forsake You in any way either. I pray that my attitude will always be right before You, and I will never take Your mercy for granted.

The POWER of ONE

Esther 4:1-17

"Go, gather together all the Jews who are in Susa, and fast for me. Do not eat or drink for three days, night or day. I and my maids will fast as you do. When this is done, I will go to the king, even though it is against the law. And if I perish, I perish" (Esther 4:16).

Have you ever thought, "I'm just one person. My prayers can't make a difference"? Many of us think that from time to time. But it's not true. Esther was the chosen wife of Xerxes, the powerful king of the Persian Empire. This king had made an example of his previous wife by banishing her for her disobedience to him. Now Esther was faced with an even more severe punishment if she dared approach the king on his throne without being summoned. She was literally risking her life. Yet her cousin, Mordecai, asked her to do just that. Her people, the Jews, were in great danger, and Esther was queen of the empire. "Who knows," her cousin had said, "but that you have come to royal position for such a time as this?"

Esther was just one person, but she was the one person in the right place at the right time—put there by God Himself to intercede for her people. So she called the people together and asked them to fast and pray for three days. She may have been the queen, but she still needed great courage, great faith, and God's guidance through the circumstances. More than her own life was at stake; the lives of millions of her countrymen were in jeopardy as well. But she courageously did what she had to do and saved her nation.

As believers, we each have to stand up for what is right, even if the result of our actions may bring ridicule or something worse.

It's easy to talk the talk when we're with our Christian friends, but those times when we are surrounded by scoffing unbelievers can be very challenging. Maybe you are the only Christian at work or at a family gathering—what do you do when confronted about your faith? Are you willing to risk banishment by your peers by standing up for what is right?

It would be easier to sit back and quietly wait for the moment to pass—that moment when you could have spoken up for the truth. It's far more challenging to take a risk and stand up for what's right. Esther fasted and prayed and followed God's leading. You can do the same. And you never know when it will result in the very thing for which you were created. You never know when your intercession and actions may save lives.

❧

> *Lord, I pray You would help me to be a person who
> has a heart for You and Your ways, and one who is
> in the right place at the right time. Enable me, as I
> fast and pray, to have a powerful effect on the world
> around me by standing up for what is right and
> following Your leading. Make my prayers powerful
> enough to save the lives of the people for whom I pray.*

PRAISING GOD *in* GOOD TIMES *and* BAD

"At this, Job got up and tore his robe and shaved his head. Then he fell to the ground in worship and said: 'Naked I came from my mother's womb, and naked I will depart. The LORD gave and the LORD has taken away; may the name of the LORD be praised'" (Job 1:20-21).

*I*f God is in control, then why is this happening to me? This may be your first reaction when calamity strikes. Everyone has times of suffering, some to a greater extent than others.

Suffering is unavoidable, inescapable, and often undeserved.

Job, the man who did nothing to deserve his fate, lost everything, including all of his children and his health. Life can't get worse than that. Through it all, however, and even in his greatest hour of grief, he never cursed God. He could have blamed God, but he didn't. He trusted Him instead. His reaction to the tremendous loss was to humble himself and worship God.

Job endured that terrible time without wavering in his worship of God, and his life was eventually restored. Job lost seven sons and three daughters, and in the end God gave him seven new sons and three new daughters. "The LORD blessed the latter part of Job's life more than the first" (42:12). You may be thinking, "Yes, that's nice, but Job still lost the first seven sons and three daughters. You can't just replace a child the way you can replace a house or a herd of sheep."

It's true that Job suffered greatly. But because of his attitude, God brought good out of it. Job did not blame the Lord and say, "Why did You let this happen, God?" Instead, he said that life contains good and bad situations, and we should accept each with the same amount of reverence for God. The Bible says to "consider blessed those who have persevered. You have heard of Job's perseverance and have seen what the Lord finally brought about. The Lord is full of compassion and mercy" (James 5:11). No matter what difficult time we go through, there will be a time when life is good again.

What a powerful illustration of what we should do in response to tragedy in our own lives. God gives us what we have, and He takes it away as He sees fit. We are to praise Him for all of it. We won't always know the reason for our suffering, but we can know that God allows things to happen to us for His purpose. This doesn't make our suffering any easier, but it does give us hope for the future.

Don't give up in the midst of great loss, disappointment, or failure, or you will miss the greatest miracle in your life. If instead you praise God through it, you will see the birth of something new and good.

❧

Dear God, I will praise You no matter what is happening in my life—in good times and in bad times. Even in the midst of loss, disappointment, sickness, or failure, I lift up praise to You because I know every time I do, You will work powerfully in my situation and be glorified in the process.

FACING YOUR FEARS

*"What I feared has come upon me; what I dreaded
has happened to me. I have no peace, no quietness; I
have no rest, but only turmoil" (Job 3:25-26).*

Job was considered by God to be a righteous man, and yet Job had
fear. He feared something happening to his children. He feared
failing health. He feared losing everything. When each one of these
fears came true, he said, "I have no rest, but only turmoil." Overwhelmed with grief, Job wished he had never been born. He had
lived according to God's laws, had worshiped God rather than his
possessions, and still he was afflicted. Who can criticize Job for his
reaction? How many of us have lost everything—including our
children, health, and possessions? How would we respond to such
a horrible situation?

When the thing we fear most comes upon us, the only way to
react is to praise God in the midst of it. That doesn't mean we have
to act as though nothing bad has happened. Besides, healthy grief is
important. But we must still recognize the things about God that are
always true no matter what is happening and how afraid we are.

Whatever your deepest fears are right now, bring every one of
them to God. Thank Him that He is greater than any of them.
Thank Him that in His presence all fear is gone. "Blessed is the man
who fears the LORD, who finds great delight in his commands...He
will have no fear of bad news; his heart is steadfast, trusting in the
LORD (Psalm 112:1,7).

God's love can take away your fear. His love gives the power
to stand against the enemy of your soul when he wants fear to

overwhelm you. And even if your worst fears do come upon you, God's love assures you that He will walk with you every step of the way toward restoration.

❧

Lord, I lift up to You my deepest fears and ask that You
would deliver me from them. Set me free from all dread
and anxiety about the things that frighten me. Thank
You that in Your presence all fear is gone. Thank You
that in the midst of Your perfect love, all fear in me
is dissolved. You are greater than anything I face.

Knowing God Is *with* You

"What is man that you make so much of him, that
you give him so much attention?" (Job 7:17).

Job was at the end of his rope. He was suffering greatly, with no understanding of why. His question came out of his frustration. In essence, he was saying, "We're worthless, God, so stop paying attention to us humans! Maybe then we'd be left in peace. Maybe then we wouldn't be tested and examined and constantly found wanting."

Job knew he wasn't a hypocrite. He knew he'd lived a life pleasing to God. In his pain he lashed out at God. But his friends concluded that he must have committed some horrible sin in order to deserve such unbearable punishment. Surely they understood that all people suffer—yet the extent of Job's suffering seemed to need an explanation.

When we are careful to obey God's rules and directions for our lives and repent when we sin, we may feel as if we should be exempt from suffering. After all, why would God allow faithful people to endure such hardships? But God uses difficulties, pain, suffering, and trials to make us stronger, wiser, and more able to comfort others.

God is the Lord, the Savior of our souls, the Lover of our hearts. He isn't sitting up in heaven watching us in our misery. He is with us every step of the way, working His perfect will in our lives.

God says, "As the heavens are higher than the earth, so are my ways higher than your ways and my thoughts than your thoughts" (Isaiah 55:9). You may not understand your suffering, just as you cannot understand the depth of God's love for you. But keep open the lines of communication between you and Him. If you feel angry because of your situation, tell Him. He understands. As you praise Him for who He is, He will heal your heart and bring good out of the situation.

❧

Heavenly Father, it is hard to comprehend the depth
of Your love for me and why You care about the details
of my life. I am grateful that in difficult times You are
with me, walking beside me all the way through to
the other side of pain and trouble. Where bad things
have happened and I have blamed You, I ask for Your
forgiveness. Thank You for working things out for my good.

Finding Peace *in the* Midst *of* Suffering

✤ Read and Consider ✤

Job 26:1-14

*"And these are but the outer fringe of his works; how
faint the whisper we hear of him! Who then can
understand the thunder of his power?" (Job 26:14).*

God's power and ways are immeasurable, far beyond our comprehension. We will never fully understand them this side of heaven. We don't understand His ways that allow us to suffer. And we don't understand His power to redeem and restore us. That's why we must praise God no matter what is happening in our lives. We should praise Him even in the midst of suffering because it strengthens us and refines our faith in Him. Trials, hardships, and pain all serve to strengthen not only the individual, but also a society or nation. How much more should we praise God when we know for certain that God loves us, has a purpose, and is working out His plan through our every experience.

Our suffering can be compared to the refining process of silver. The heat is turned up, and as the impurities rise to the surface they are skimmed away by the refiner. Because God is sovereign, nothing that happens to us surprises Him. And as difficult as it is to accept sometimes, God even allows us, His children, to suffer.

It is in those times of suffering that we may feel as if we're on a roller coaster, vacillating up and down as we wonder why God would allow us to endure such pain. Yet if we draw close to Him, we will have a sense of peace, knowing He is in control of the situation. In spite of all that Job went through, he never doubted God's unlimited power. Job said that God's power terrified him (23:15-16). He said, when referring to God's ability to calm a raging storm, "These are but the outer fringe of his works" (26:14).

So even in the midst of turmoil and grief, praise God for the path He has chosen for you and for His refining power and love. When the heat is on, allow the Refiner to purify your soul.

❧

Almighty God, Your power is beyond comprehension. I can't begin to understand the far-reaching greatness of Your restoration and redemption in my life. Help me to never doubt You and Your ability to restore and redeem me. Help me to have such unwavering faith in the midst of difficult times that I rest in peace, knowing You will take care of all I care about.

FINDING *a* SONG *in the* NIGHT

❖ Read and Consider ❖
Job 35:1-16

"But no one says, 'Where is God my Maker, who
gives songs in the night?'" (Job 35:10).

O f all Job's friends, only Elihu had a glimmer of wisdom. In fact, God rebukes the other three men for their inaccurate explanations of Job's pain (42:7-9). Elihu wasn't completely in tune with the sovereignty of God, but he understood that something good would come from Job's pain. He observed that people often cry out to God for deliverance, but rarely cry out for God Himself (35:10). King David experienced suffering, and God gave him a song:

> *I waited patiently for the LORD; he turned to me and*
> *   heard my cry.*
> *He lifted me out of the slimy pit, out of the mud and mire;*
> *   he set my feet on a rock and gave me a firm place to stand.*
> *He put a new song in my mouth, a hymn of praise to our*
> *   God.*
> *Many will see and fear and put their trust in the LORD*
> *   (Psalm 40:1-3).*

In your darkest time, when you seek God, He will give you a song in the night. It will be a song of worship and praise, and your heart will sing once more. It doesn't matter how terrible or difficult your situation is. Every time you praise God, He will move into the situation to redeem and transform it in some way. Praise God for how He will work through your pain, for the lives He will touch through your witness. You may never know how far-reaching your testimony will be, but rest assured that God will use you to glorify Him and to draw others closer to Jesus.

❦

Lord, Your Word says that when we seek You, You will give us a song in the night. When I am going through a dark night of the soul, I pray You would enlighten my darkness with Your presence. In the face of the darkest situation in my life, I lift up songs of praise to You, knowing Your presence will inhabit them.

GOD HEARS WHEN YOU CALL

❧ Read and Consider ❧
Psalm 4:1-8

"Know that the LORD has set apart the godly for himself;
the LORD will hear when I call to him" (Psalm 4:3).

Psalms is one of the most encouraging books in all of Scripture. There is no emotion we can experience, whether elation or depression, guilt or gladness, that we won't find first expressed in Psalms. This book is the ancient hymnal of the Israelites, and the 150 psalms contained in its pages are a combination of prayer, poetry, and praise. When you don't know what to say to God, pray the psalms back to Him!

Whenever you feel *desperate* to know that God is close and that He is hearing your prayers and will answer you, read this verse again. Remember that God hears the prayers of the godly. The Hebrew word for *godly* is often translated "saints." God sees you as a saint, and He has set you apart for Himself. If you've accepted Christ as your Savior, you are a saint, a child of God, set apart for His glory (Romans 8:16-17). Yet even though we know this is how God sees us, there are times when we don't feel close to God—times when He feels far away and our prayers seem to go no further than the ceiling.

Your prayers may appear to go unanswered for many reasons. God may simply be giving you the answer that you are to wait. It could be that some sin in your life is clouding your communication with Him. Isaiah wrote, "Your iniquities have separated you from your God; your sins have hidden his face from you, so that he will not hear" (Isaiah 59:2). Make sure that nothing in your life is acting as a barrier between you and God.

Be encouraged! As God's child, you have His ear. Stay close, and He promises to hear when you call.

❖

Thank You, Lord, that I am a child of Yours, set apart for Your glory, and that You hear my prayers. When I pray, help me to have the peace of knowing You have heard my prayer and will answer in Your way and in Your perfect timing. Show me if there is ever anything in my life that would become a barrier between me and You so that my prayers would go unanswered.

PRAISE IS YOUR GREATEST WEAPON

❧ Read and Consider ❧
Psalm 9:1-20

*"I will praise you, O LORD, with all my heart; I will tell of
all your wonders...For he who avenges blood remembers;
he does not ignore the cry of the afflicted" (Psalm 9:1,12).*

Have you noticed how many psalms either begin or end with
praise? Praise is *not* denial. The Bible never tells us to bury
our pain. Instead, we are to pour it out like water from a pitcher:
"I pour out my complaint before him; before him I tell my trouble"
(142:2). However, once we've expressed our distressing emotions to
God, He gives us a powerful weapon with which we can fight our
battles—the weapon of praise.

God wants us to *destroy* evil, not just try to outrun it. He doesn't
want us to only try to defend ourselves and stay alive; He wants us to
push the enemy back. He wants us to say as David did, "I pursued
my enemies and crushed them; I did not turn back till they were
destroyed. I crushed them completely, and they could not rise; they
fell beneath my feet. You armed me with strength for battle; you
made my adversaries bow at my feet" (2 Samuel 22:38-40).

Praise is one of our greatest weapons of warfare. "The weapons
we fight with are not the weapons of the world. On the contrary,
they have divine power to demolish strongholds" (2 Corinthians
10:4). When we praise God, our enemies have to turn back from
attacking because they cannot stand in His presence. Every time
you praise Jesus for His victory on the cross, it reminds the devil of
his greatest defeat. And he hates that.

You don't have to praise God *for* your troubles, but you can praise

171

Him in the *midst* of them. And rest secure that He "remembers; he does not ignore the cry of the afflicted" (9:12).

❧

Thank You, God, that You never forget me. You always remember me and my situation, and You never ignore my cries to You when I am in need. I praise You in the middle of the struggles I face, knowing that worshiping You is my greatest weapon against the enemy of my soul. Help me to not just survive the attacks of the enemy, but to push the enemy back and crush him.

Look *to* God *as* Your Protector

"'Because of the oppression of the weak and the groaning of the needy, I will now arise,' says the LORD. 'I will protect them from those who malign them'" (Psalm 12:5).

I know what it's like to have lived in the "bad part of town," where people are murdered, mugged, raped, and robbed. Where it wasn't safe to go out of the house. Fearing for my safety became a way of life there. In fact, many times I wondered if I would ever make it out of that place alive. No one stays in the bad part of town if they can possibly afford to live anywhere else.

After I came to know the Lord, I found the greatest comfort in being able to trust God as my Protector. God promises to rise up and protect the oppressed and needy from their oppressors. God did that for me. I intensely *yearned* for safety for years. He not only protected me in the dangerous place where I lived, but He led me to a place of safety.

We should never take for granted the protection of the Lord in our lives. We should not enter a plane, train, or automobile without praising Him as our Protector. We should not enter a day without *asking* Him for His protection and then thanking Him for it in advance. How many times have we been protected and spared from harm or disaster that we are not even aware of?

Remember, God also promises protection from those who malign you or who try to destroy your reputation without just cause. "It is mine to avenge; I will repay. In due time their foot will slip; their day of disaster is near and their doom rushes upon them" (Deuteronomy 32:35). He hears your prayerful groanings. He knows your needs.

When you are slandered or your life is threatened, rest assured that God promises divine protection. Your life is safe in His hands.

❧

Lord, I am grateful for all the times You have protected me from disaster. I'm sure there are countless ways You have kept me from harm that I am not even aware of. I pray You will always protect me and my reputation from anyone who would try to destroy me. Thank You that You hear my prayers for protection and You have promised to keep me safe.

PERSEVERING PRAYER

❧ Read and Consider ☙
Psalm 18:28-42

*"You armed me with strength for battle; you made
my adversaries bow at my feet" (Psalm 18:39).*

Perseverance has been described as the ability to see a problem or a situation through to its resolution despite the difficulties encountered on the way. It's not hard to persevere when everything's going your way, but when the road to resolution becomes a virtual obstacle course, we need the strength to persevere through the pressure.

God's Word tells us over and over again that perseverance, while it may not be fun, is actually good for us, "because we know that suffering produces perseverance; perseverance, character; and character, hope" (Romans 5:3-4). In fact, we are actually *commanded* to stay with the course God puts us on. "Run with perseverance the race marked out for us" (Hebrews 12:1).

Ask the Lord to help you do as David did and be aggressive against the enemy, who would try to wear you down with discouragement. Ask Him to help you stand strong against this enemy until he is completely destroyed. David didn't stop until the job was done, and neither should we. We should pray through until we see the answer.

Ask God to give you the strength you need in order to persevere in prayer. With His power flowing through you, you can not only withstand whatever pressures are coming your way, you can eliminate them. Remember, you don't run this obstacle course alone. God is with you and will arm you with strength for the battle. Because of that you will have the victory.

❧

*Lord, I am grateful that You have armed me with
the strength I need for the battle ahead. Help me to
subdue my enemies until they are completely destroyed.
Teach me to persevere in prayer and not let down.
Enable me to pray through each situation until I see
victory over all opposition. Thank You that You are
always with me, working things out in my favor.*

Your Heavenly Father
Waits *to* Hear *from* You

❧ Read and Consider ❧
Psalm 27:1-13

"Though my father and mother forsake me, the
Lord will receive me" (Psalm 27:10).

When Jesus' disciples asked Him to teach them to pray, He gave them a model beginning with the words "Our Father" (Matthew 6:9-13). Some of us have no problem thinking of God as a Father. We had good dads, or at least adequate ones, and the imagery of God in relationship to us as our Father is a positive one.

For others of us, however, thinking of God as a Father is troublesome, if not downright painful. Perhaps you're in that category. Your earthly father may have abandoned you or neglected you or even abused you. How do you wrap your mind around the concept of a heavenly Father when you have conflicted feelings about the earthly father who failed you in that category?

God says that in order to have a long, fruitful life and move into all He has for you, you must honor your father and mother (Exodus 20:12). It's a command! You may have had parents who were around and provided food and a place to live—and for that you certainly need to be grateful—but maybe they never put anything of themselves into your life. Maybe you could never expect Dad or Mom to support, encourage, or teach you anything.

But you still need to honor them, if for no other reason than that they gave you life. Without them, you wouldn't be here. But you can't fully honor your father and mother if you haven't forgiven them. No parent is perfect. No parent always does everything right. Ask God to show you if there is anything you need to forgive. Even if your parents are no longer living, forgiving them will clear the way for you to fully see God as your heavenly Father and to feel His love for you. He will heal and restore whatever you suffered or lost in your relationship with your parents.

Praise God that He is the perfect Father—loving, kind, accessible, helpful, encouraging, guiding, and comforting. Regardless of what your earthly father was like, your heavenly Father will be everything you need. Look to Him every day.

❦

> *Dear Heavenly Father, I thank You that You will never forsake or desert me. Thank You that You always accept me. I am grateful for Your love, guidance, and comfort. Show me any place in my heart where I have not forgiven my own father or mother for letting me down in any way. I want to honor You by honoring them with complete forgiveness.*

The BLESSING of CONFESSING

❧ Read and Consider ❧
Psalm 32:1-11

"Then I acknowledged my sin to you and did not cover up my iniquity. I said, 'I will confess my transgressions to the LORD'—and you forgave the guilt of my sin" (Psalm 32:5).

Sin always brings separation. When we behave badly toward our family members or use our tongues carelessly so that others are wounded, our sinful actions lead to barriers being built between ourselves and other people.

Sin separates us from God as well. When we break any of the commandments that He lovingly set forth for our own protection, we put up a wall between ourselves and the One who made us. It's a wall of our own construction. But God's Word provides a solution to this barrier. It's called confession.

Confession has been defined as "agreeing with God about our sin." The most common Old Testament words for sin are "transgressions" and "iniquity," and Psalm 32 contains frequent references to these actions that serve to separate us from God.

When we don't confess our sins, we end up trying to hide ourselves from God. Just like Adam and Eve in the garden, we feel we can't face Him. But the problem with attempting to hide from God is that it's impossible. The Bible says that everything we do will be made known—even the things we said and thought in secret. "Nothing in all creation is hidden from God's sight. Everything is uncovered and laid bare before the eyes of him to whom we must give account" (Hebrews 4:13).

What a frightening thought! If each of us will have to give an account, the quicker we get it straight with God—the better. In fact, the sooner we deal with the sins we *can* see, the sooner God can reveal to us the ones we *can't*. And only God knows how much of that is residing in each of us. Sin always has consequences. King David described it best when he wrote of his own unconfessed sin: "When I kept silent, my bones wasted away through my groaning all day long. For day and night your hand was heavy upon me; my strength was sapped as in the heat of summer" (32:3-4).

Confession has a "consequence" too—a good consequence! A free and happy heart! When we confess our sins to God, we are blessed. To be blessed means to enjoy the favor of God. There is no greater blessing than knowing that your sins have been forgiven by God.

❧

> *Dear Lord, I don't want anything to separate me from You and all You have for me—especially not my own unconfessed sin. I don't want to build a wall between You and me by failing to acknowledge anything I thought, said, or did that was not pleasing in Your sight. If I am too blind to see the truth about myself, reveal it to me so that I can confess it before You.*

PRAY *to* RESIST TEMPTATION

❧ Read and Consider ❧
Psalm 51:1-19

*"Create in me a pure heart, O God, and renew a
steadfast spirit within me. Do not cast me from your
presence or take your Holy Spirit from me. Restore
to me the joy of your salvation and grant me a
willing spirit, to sustain me" (Psalm 51:10-12).*

David wrote the words of this psalm after the prophet Nathan
confronted him following David's adultery with Bathsheba.
To his credit, David recognized his own sin, and this psalm is both
a passionate plea for purity and a prayer in which David is crying
out to God to be restored into the joy of right relationship. However,
David could have spared himself much grief and sorrow (as well
as for Bathsheba and her husband) if he had taken his feelings for
Bathsheba to God in the first place.

God wants us to live in stark contrast to the world. The world is
absorbed totally in the flesh. Sexual temptation of one sort or another
is everywhere. The attitude toward casual sex and immorality in
our society has gone far beyond what most people imagined it ever
could. Those who have any sense of their own purpose and who God
created them to be know that they cannot compromise in this area.
The price is way too high. The consequences are far too great.

God says we are to "abstain from sinful desires, which war against
your soul" (1 Peter 2:11). The things we lust after, whether they be
sex, material goods, prestige, money, or power, create havoc in our
souls. They cause peace to elude us. It's not that God doesn't want
us to ever have any of these things; it's that we are to submit to His
way and His timing and let *Him* bless us as He wills.

There is a way to resist all temptation of the flesh—especially sexual temptation—and that is to worship God. But it must be our *first* reaction, and not after the fact.

King David *should* have done this. Instead, when Bathsheba discovered she was pregnant, David tried to cover up the adultery by arranging to have her husband killed in battle.

This all began as one sinful thought. No one ends up in adultery without thinking about it first. It's at the *first thought* that prayer should arise. David was later confronted by the prophet Nathan about what he had done, and to his credit David confessed everything and was deeply repentant. Even so, there were stiff consequences for his actions, not the least of which was the death of David and Bathsheba's baby boy. And from that time on murder, death, and treachery became a part of his family and his reign.

Everyone makes mistakes. Don't let guilt over them separate you from God or make you feel distant from Him. That is the enemy's plan to keep you from all God has for you. The way to have victory over temptation is to go immediately before the Lord when temptation first crosses your mind. Don't wait the way David did. Don't entertain it for even a moment. Go to God right away and confess it. Then praise Him as the God who is more powerful than anything that tempts you.

❧

God, I pray You would create in me a clean and
right heart before You at all times. Help me to
come to You immediately at the very first sign of
temptation so that I can stop any wrong thoughts from
turning into sinful actions. I don't want to ever be
separated from the presence of Your Holy Spirit.

THIRSTING AFTER GOD

❧ Read and Consider ❧
Psalm 63:1-11

*"O God, you are my God, earnestly I seek you; my soul
thirsts for you, my body longs for you, in a dry and
weary land where there is no water" (Psalm 63:1).*

I f you were lost in the desert without anything to eat or drink,
you would seek food and water anywhere you could find it, even
if it wasn't good for you. You wouldn't care how many impurities
it had in it or how bad it tasted because you want to survive. But
God has so much more for you than just survival.

What do *you* hunger and thirst for right now? Is it more of the
Lord?

When King David hungered and thirsted for the Lord, he said,
"As the deer pants for streams of water, so my soul pants for you,
O God. My soul thirsts for God, for the living God. When can I
go and meet with God?" (42:1-2). He wanted the Lord more than
anything else. God's presence was food and water to him.

Have you ever been that thirsty for God? Sometimes we don't
experience that deep thirst until we know what it's like to wander
in the desert of our own desires. We grab for what the world has to
offer only to discover that it leaves us empty.

Jesus once said, "If anyone is thirsty, let him come to me and
drink. Whoever believes in me, as the Scripture has said, streams
of living water will flow from within him" (John 7:37-38). Jesus
was quoting from an invitation given in the Old Testament book
of Isaiah, in which the prophet recorded these words: "Come, all
you who are thirsty, come to the waters" (Isaiah 55:1). When we

quench our spiritual thirst in the Lord, His Spirit will flow *through* us, and streams of living water will flow *from* us.

Drink deeply of all that God has for you in His Word, in His presence, and in prayer and praise, and you will never be thirsty again!

❧

Lord God, more than anything else I want Your presence in my life. I long for more of You the way I long for water in the dry heat of summer. I come to You to quench my spiritual thirst as only You can do. Flow Your rivers of living water into me so they can revive my soul and then flow through me to a dry and thirsty world.

Praying *from a* Right Heart

"If I had cherished sin in my heart, the Lord would not have listened; but God has surely listened and heard my voice in prayer. Praise be to God, who has not rejected my prayer or withheld his love from me!" (Psalm 66:18-20).

The good thing about prayer—or the problem with prayer, depending on our perspective—is that we have to go to God to do it. This means we can't get away with anything. It means that any negative thoughts, bad attitudes, hardness of heart, or selfish motives are going to be revealed by the Lord. Fervent and honest prayer causes the depths of our hearts to be exposed. That can be uncomfortable. Even downright miserable. The verses above make it crystal clear that if we have any unforgiveness, bitterness, selfishness, pride, anger, irritation, or resentment in our hearts, our prayers will not be answered. Our hearts have to be right when we pray.

In the same way, God wants us to be right with others before we take our concerns or even our acts of service—our "gifts"—to Him. In what is called The Sermon on the Mount, Jesus explicitly instructed His followers on the importance of setting things right: "Therefore, if you are offering your gift at the altar and there remember that your brother has something against you, leave your gift there in front of the altar. First go and be reconciled to your brother; then come and offer your gift" (Matthew 5:23-24).

All of us jeopardize our own prayers when we don't pray them from a right heart. What is in our hearts when we pray has more effect on whether our prayers are answered than the actual prayer itself. That's why, when we come before God to pray, He asks us to first confess anything in our hearts that shouldn't be there. He does that so nothing will separate us from Him.

If you ever feel as if your prayers are not being heard, examine your heart and ask God to clearly reveal anything that you might need to confess before Him. Then that joy David felt will be your joy as well.

※

Lord, I don't want to entertain sin in my heart. I want my heart to be right before You so that You will always hear my prayers. I know I don't do everything perfectly, so I ask that by the power of Your Holy Spirit You will enable me to keep my heart pure and my hands clean. Thank You for loving me and helping me do what is right in Your sight.

COMMIT YOUR WORK *to* GOD

*"May the favor of the Lord our God rest upon
us; establish the work of our hands for us—yes,
establish the work of our hands" (Psalm 90:17).*

What's on your "To Do" list for today? Do you have a job to
get to, a home to clean, someone to care for? Do you feel
sometimes as if you're constantly busy, continually on the move, and
yet at the end of the day you wonder if you have accomplished all
that you should have? How about your work? Do you regularly ask
God to bless it?

The psalmist recognized that people "are like the new grass of the
morning—though in the morning it springs up new, by evening it is
dry and withered" (90:5-6). Our days, quite literally, are numbered.
"The length of our days is seventy years—or eighty, if we have the
strength" (90:10). This reminder of our own mortality reinforces
the need to commit every task we undertake to God and to ask for
His blessing upon it.

We can start by making it a habit to turn our day over to the Lord
when we first wake up. Then ask for His help in all that we have to
do and thank Him that He will enable us to do it. "The one who
calls you is faithful and he will do it" (1 Thessalonians 5:24).

When you thank God and give Him charge over every endeavor
you undertake, right down to the smallest detail of your day, He will
establish the work of your hands. When you ask God to bless the
work you do and to enable you to do it better and better, you will
see the quality of your work improve in the way you always dreamed
it would.

❧

Dear God, I pray You would bless my work and establish it. I commit all of the work I do to You so that it may be used for Your glory. Give me the strength to accomplish what I must do each day, and the wisdom and ability to do it well. Be in charge of every detail of my work so that it will find favor with others and be successful.

EXPERIENCING *the* POWER *of* PRAISE

❧ Read and Consider ❧
Psalm 100:1-5

"Enter his gates with thanksgiving and his
courts with praise" (Psalm 100:4).

Praising God is not just about singing praise songs in church once a week. Praise should be a part of every moment of your life. Praise should be what you do in the car while on the way to work, to school, or to the store. It's what you should have in your heart when you're in the mall, the airport, or the doctor's office. It's what you do when the kitchen sink stops up, the car has a flat tire, you become sick, or you've lost your keys for the fortieth time. It's what you speak fervently when you are in the emergency room, at a loved one's burial, or in the middle of a tornado. Praise should be an ongoing attitude of the heart—an attitude that doesn't change, no matter what else in your life does.

This is not about some kind of positive thinking. This is not a plunge into denial that says, "This isn't really happening" or "I'm going to pretend that I'm not actually feeling this way." Instead, it means, "Don't let yourself sink to the level of the problem; make yourself rise to the level of the solution."

One of the secrets of experiencing the power of praise is to make a decision that you will worship God no matter what your circumstances. When you get to the place where praise comes automatically, no matter what is going on, you will come to know God more intimately. And when you do, you won't be able to *stop* yourself from praising Him.

It's easy to praise God when great things happen or when you see answers to your prayers, but what about when everything is going wrong? What is your first reaction to difficult or bad things that happen? If you blame others, yourself, or God, this only compounds the problem, leading to more distress, misery, and difficulty. Instead, if you refuse to react to your problems in the flesh and move immediately into the realm of the spirit by praising God, you will find that everything turns out differently. When you make your first reaction to what happens in your life a reaffirming praise to God for who He is, you invite His presence to inhabit the situation and His power to come and change things. This is the hidden power of praising God.

God wants you to exalt Him and not your problems. This doesn't mean trying to convince yourself that your problems don't exist. It means you are saying, "Although I have these problems, I know that You, Lord, are greater than they are. You are my heavenly Father. You are a good God. In You is everything I need for my life, and I choose to exalt You above all."

When you become convinced of the power of praise in every situation and understand all that is accomplished when you truly praise God, your life will be changed forever.

❧

Lord, I come before You with praise and thanksgiving
for all You are and everything You have done for
me. No matter what happens in my life or in the
world around me, I will not sink to the level of the
problem. I will rise to the level of the solution and
praise You as the solution to all my problems.

PRAISE IS *the* PRAYER THAT CHANGES EVERYTHING

❖ Read and Consider ❖

Psalm 102:1-28

"Hear my prayer, O LORD; let my cry for help
come to you. Do not hide your face from me when
I am in distress. Turn your ear to me; when I
call, answer me quickly" (Psalm 102:1-2).

O nce when I was enduring tremendous physical suffering, I randomly opened my Bible for comfort. Instead of turning to where the ribbon marked my place of ongoing reading, I found myself at Psalm 102. What I read there was written thousands of years ago, yet it could have been written for me right then in terms of what I was experiencing. The writer was honest before God about the way he was feeling and all that he was suffering, and he cried out to God to hear his prayer and give him a future. After reading the psalm, I did the same thing. Like the writer, I recognized that God will exist forever and will never change, and I have an eternal future with Him. No matter how bad it is here, I have the hope that whether God chooses to heal me or not, I have a life forever with Him that is free of pain, and I praise Him for that.

I have found that no matter how bad I feel, when I praise God I always feel better. I have found great healing in worship services where many people are worshiping God together. I have also found healing when worshiping God by myself. Things happen when we worship Him because praising God is the prayer that changes everything.

If you need to see a change in your life, your health, your circumstances, your financial situation, your attitude, your spouse, your children, or your church, then praise God! Thank Him for all that He can and will do—and invite Him to do it in His way and in His time. The Lord "will respond to the prayers of the destitute; he will not despise their plea" (102:17). And His answers will be far better than anything you could have thought up for yourself!

❧

Dear God, I worship You and thank You that You are greater than anything I face. Thank You that You are a compassionate God of mercy and You hear my prayers and answer them. I thank You that You inhabit my praise, and that in Your presence my life and circumstances are changed. I am grateful that praising You changes me.

GOD HEARS YOU WHEN YOU PRAY

✤ Read and Consider ✤

Psalm 116:1-19

"I love the LORD, for he heard my voice; he heard my cry for mercy. Because he turned his ear to me, I will call on him as long as I live" (Psalm 116:1-2).

D o you have someone in your life who listens to you—I mean truly *listens?* Maybe it's a sister or a close friend, or even a coworker who is empathetic. If so, you are blessed. We've all experienced times when it seems as if everyone we know is either too busy or too distracted by their own problems to sit and listen to the cries of our heart. There are few times as lonely as when we are hurting and have no one to tell.

As a child of God, however, you always have someone who will listen to you: God Himself!

Over and over again we find these declarations in the psalms: "God has surely listened and heard my voice in prayer" (66:19). "I waited patiently for the LORD; he turned to me and heard my cry" (40:1). Waiting is never easy, but when the answer to one of your prayers comes, you know without a doubt that God has heard your cries.

God is never so far away that He cannot hear us. Scripture tells us that He turns His ear to us, and it is never a deaf ear. He loves us. He is ever present in our lives. And He hears us when we call to Him.

Never doubt that you have Someone in your life who is always willing to listen. And He alone has the power to change the situation you are facing. Take comfort in the reality that you are loved by God, and He has your best interests at heart. "Be at rest once more, O my soul, for the LORD has been good to you" (116:7).

❧

Lord, I take great comfort in knowing You hear my prayers.
Your Word tells me You listen and are never so far away
that You cannot hear when I call. Help me to be patient
to wait for Your answers, to not lose heart, and to never
fear that You have not heard. Help me to trust You enough
every day of my life to pray for all that concerns me.

THANK GOD THAT HE
KNOWS *and* LOVES YOU

*"O LORD, you have searched me and you know me. You
know when I sit and when I rise; you perceive my thoughts
from afar. You discern my going out and my lying down;
you are familiar with all my ways" (Psalm 139:1-3).*

God knows everything about you. He knows your thoughts even
before you think them. "Before a word is on my tongue you
know it completely, O LORD" (139:4). He knows your actions from
the time you rise in the morning until the moment you go to bed
at night. Even when sleep reduces you to unconsciousness, He is
watching over you still.

God is everywhere around you. There is nowhere you can go that
God is not there too. He is with you in the mountaintop experiences
of life, and He is with you in the valleys of despair. He is omnipresent.
Corrie ten Boom suffered in a Nazi prison camp during World War
II yet was able to write, "There is no pit so deep that God is not
deeper still."

God did a miracle in creating you! You may struggle with the way
you feel or how you look, and you may not feel much like a "miracle"
at all, but you are. You may feel more like a mistake, but you are
not. God formed you and loved you even when you were in your
mother's womb. You bear His image (Genesis 1:27).

Your life is no accident, and the purpose of your life was ordained
even before you were born. Your heavenly Father knows everything
about you, is present everywhere around you, and performed a

miracle when He made you. Praise God every day that He knows you and loves you!

❧

God, I thank You that You know everything about me and You still love me. You know my thoughts and my mistakes, and You still call me Yours. Thank You that You are always with me—teaching and guiding me, comforting and restoring me—and I am never alone. You, Lord, know me better than I know myself. Help me to know You better too.

The LORD IS NEAR WHEN WE PRAY

✤ Read and Consider ✤
Psalm 145:1-21

"The LORD is near to all who call on him, to all
who call on him in truth" (Psalm 145:18).

D o you experience times when God seems far away? Most of
us do. The psalmist speaks for us when he cries out, "Why, O
LORD, do you stand far off? Why do you hide yourself in times of
trouble?" (10:1). When He was hanging on the cross, Jesus cried out,
"My God, my God, why have you forsaken me?" (Matthew 27:46).

Our feelings may tell us that God is distant, but Scripture tells us
otherwise. When we call on Him in prayer, God is near to us whether
we *feel* it or not. At the same time, we might pray for something we
need and fail to see an answer after weeks, months, or even years
of passionate intercession. Why does God so often cause us to wait
for what we are so sure we need right away?

We may be denied certain things for a time because God wants us
to fervently pray and intercede for them. He wants to do something
great in response to our prayers, something that can only be birthed
in prayer. There may be things that won't happen in your life unless
you are praying long and fervently about them.

If you start becoming discouraged and feel as if your life won't
ever be any different than it is at this moment, know that the truth
is quite the opposite. It's at these very times, when you feel as though
you're not getting anywhere or you're missing the future God has for
you, that God is actually *preparing* you for your future. And when
the time is right, He has been known to do a very quick work. Draw
close to God in prayer, trusting that He is near. Thank Him that
He hears your prayers and will answer in His perfect way.

❧

*Lord, I draw close to You and thank You that You are
close to me. I confess the times when I have doubted
You were near to hear my prayers, because it seemed
my prayers went unanswered. Now I know that doubt
is contradictory to Your Word. Help me to pray even
more fervently during times of unanswered prayer
instead of being concerned that nothing will change.*

ACKNOWLEDGE GOD *in* EVERY AREA *of* YOUR LIFE

"Trust in the LORD with all your heart and lean not on your own understanding; in all your ways acknowledge him, and he will make your paths straight" (Proverbs 3:5-6).

We have to trust that God's ways are always right and not try to figure things out on our own or make up our own rules. And we have to acknowledge God in every area of our lives.

We have to acknowledge Him first of all as Jesus our Savior, as our heavenly Father, and as the Holy Spirit our Comforter. Then we have to acknowledge Him as the One who meets all of our needs and is Lord over every area of our lives. That means we acknowledge Him as Lord over our relationships, our work, our activities, our finances, our homes, our bodies, and our marriages.

Is there any place in your life that you have not turned completely over to God? If so, say, "Lord, I invite You to be Lord over this area of my life." If you are not sure, ask God to show you. He will. And when you see some area where you have not fully acknowledged God as Lord, pray, "Lord, I acknowledge You in this area of my life, and I ask You to reign there. I want to recognize You in everything I do so that I can honor and serve You. Thank You that You will direct my steps and make my paths straight."

❧

Heavenly Father, I ask that You would help me to trust
You and Your ways and not depend on my own limited
understanding of things. Help me to acknowledge You in

every area of my life. If I have shut You out of any part of my life, I ask that You would reveal this to me so I can invite You to reign there. Thank You for making my path straight.

The BENEFITS of WAITING on GOD

Proverbs 8:22-36

"Blessed is the man who listens to me, watching daily at my doors, waiting at my doorway" (Proverbs 8:34).

When you are sitting at a stoplight, standing in a long checkout line at the supermarket, or flipping idly through an old magazine in a physician's waiting room, do you ever think, "What a blessing it is to wait"?

If you're like most people, you probably hate to wait. We are busy people; we usually have more to do in any given day than we can possibly accomplish. And yet over and over again, Scripture speaks of the need for us to wait—and *commands* us to do so. "Be still before the LORD and wait patiently for him" (Psalm 37:7). The key is waiting for *Him*.

The Bible teaches that waiting for *Him* is actually a blessing in our lives.

This verse tells us that we are blessed when we listen to God and watch and wait daily at His doors. But how does God use times of waiting to bless us?

When God permits life's circumstances to delay us from our intended goal, we can be sure He has good reason. It might be to build our faith because the New Testament teaches that "faith is being sure of what we hope for and certain of what we do not see" (Hebrews 11:1). When we are forced to wait, our faith must become stronger.

Or God might use times of waiting to build our character as we wait for the character of Christ to be formed in us. "And we, who with unveiled faces all reflect the Lord's glory, are being transformed into his likeness with ever-increasing glory, which comes from the Lord, who is the Spirit" (2 Corinthians 3:18).

Or God may be wanting us to wait so that we can learn to be patient. As we wait with hopeful anticipation for Him to work in our situation, He has promised that we will be "strengthened with all power according to his glorious might so that you may have great endurance and patience, and joyfully giving thanks to the Father" (Colossians 1:11-12).

God loves us, so our times of waiting on Him must be ultimately beneficial to our emotional and spiritual growth. The next time you are tempted to become restless during a time of waiting on God, use that time instead to praise God for all the benefits and blessings that He has in store for you. And don't forget to thank Him that His timing is perfect.

❧

Lord, I wait on You and listen for Your voice. Speak to my heart about the things I need to hear. Teach me all I need to know. Thank You for the great blessings that await anyone who waits at Your door and listens for Your voice. In these times of waiting on You, may the character of Christ be formed in me and my faith be increased.

GOD HEARS *the* PRAYERS
of the RIGHTEOUS

❧ Read and Consider ❧
Proverbs 15:8-9,26,29

*"The LORD detests the sacrifice of the wicked, but the
prayer of the upright pleases him" (Proverbs 15:8).*

Certain principles in Scripture are repeated over and over again. Consider this chapter of Proverbs. Again and again we are reminded that "the LORD detests the way of the wicked but he loves those who pursue righteousness...The Lord detests the thoughts of the wicked, but those of the pure are pleasing to him" (15:9,26). Why the continual repetition of the importance of righteousness?

First, we need to remember what righteousness is *not:* It is not simply doing "good works." Scripture does not teach that we will obtain righteousness through our own efforts. Rather, we *become* righteous through our relationship with Jesus Christ. This is spelled out for us in the New Testament: "But now a righteousness from God, apart from law, has been made known...This righteousness from God comes through faith in Jesus Christ to all who believe" (Romans 3:21-22).

Any righteousness imparted to us, then, is due to our faith in Christ. Yet once we receive Christ as our Savior, God expects us to live as redeemed people—individuals who are characterized by spirits of humility, repentance, and submission to God's will in our lives. "What does the LORD require of you? To act justly and to love mercy and to walk humbly with your God" (Micah 6:8). Living according to His commandments and all the teaching found in His Word is righteous living. And we are promised that God will hear our prayers when we live His way.

❦

*Dear God, how grateful I am that You see me as righteous
because of my relationship with Jesus. But I know You
also want me to choose to live righteously as well. I
pray my thoughts, words, and actions will always be
pleasing in Your sight so that my prayers will be pleasing
to Your ears. Enable me every day to do what's right.*

TEN GOOD REASONS *to* ASK GOD *for* WISDOM

❧ Read and Consider ❧

Proverbs 23:12,19,23

"Buy the truth and do not sell it; get wisdom,
discipline and understanding" (Proverbs 23:23).

If you were given a choice between wealth and wisdom, which would you choose? The Bible never promises that financial gain will bring us increased happiness, but Scripture consistently teaches that we *should* ask for wisdom. Think of wisdom as the ability to exercise good judgment and discern correctly at all times. Wouldn't it be wonderful to have that ability? All we have to do is ask God for it! "Wisdom is supreme; therefore get wisdom. Though it cost all you have, get understanding" (4:7).

Here are ten good reasons to ask God for wisdom:

1. *To have longevity, blessings, and honor.* "Long life is in her right hand; in her left hand are riches and honor" (3:16).

2. *To live a good, peaceful life.* "Her ways are pleasant ways, and all her paths are peace" (3:17).

3. *To enjoy vitality and happiness.* "She is a tree of life to those who embrace her; those who lay hold of her will be blessed" (3:18).

4. *To be protected.* "Then you will go on your way in safety, and your foot will not stumble" (3:23).

5. *To experience refreshing rest.* "When you lie down, you will not be afraid; when you lie down, your sleep will be sweet" (3:24).

6. *To gain confidence.* "The LORD will be your confidence and will keep your foot from being snared" (3:26).

7. *To live in security.* "Do not forsake wisdom, and she will protect you; love her, and she will watch over you...When you walk, your steps will not be hampered; when you run, you will not stumble" (4:6,12).

8. *To be promoted.* "Esteem her, and she will exalt you; embrace her, and she will honor you" (4:8).

9. *To be saved from evil.* "For wisdom will enter your heart, and knowledge will be pleasant to your soul. Discretion will protect you, and understanding will guard you. Wisdom will save you from the ways of wicked men, from men whose words are perverse" (2:10-12).

10. *To be guided in the way you should go.* "Let the wise listen and add to their learning, and let the discerning get guidance" (1:5).

Ask God today to give you wisdom in all things.

❧

Lord, I pray You would give me wisdom so that I will
have a long life of peace, blessing, and happiness. Give
me wisdom that brings confidence, protection, security,
promotion, and guidance. I pray to have the kind
of wisdom that saves me from evil and enables me
to make right decisions. Along with all that, help me
to live with understanding, discipline, and truth.

WHEN OUR PRAYERS DISPLEASE GOD

✣ Read and Consider ✣

Proverbs 28:9

*"If anyone turns a deaf ear to the law, even his
prayers are detestable" (Proverbs 28:9).*

C an it be that there is a time when our prayers actually *displease*
God?

Scripture tells us that a consequence of disobedience is that our
prayers will not be heard. In fact, the word "detestable" means
something that is revolting, abominable, or loathsome. None of us
wants God to see our prayers that way!

In order to grow in the Lord, it's important to keep asking God
to show us what He wants us to do. If we don't ask, we won't know.
Even when we think we are doing everything right, it's always good
to pray, "Lord, show me any place in my life where I am not obeying
You. I want to live by Your rules."

One of the consequences for disobedience is not getting your
prayers answered. You cannot receive all God has for you if you
are not living in obedience. Jesus said, "If you want to enter life,
obey the commandments" (Matthew 19:17). He knew that nothing
would give people more peace and confidence than knowing they
are doing what God wants them to do. God's Word promises that
by being obedient to His ways you will find mercy (Psalm 28:6),
peace (Psalm 37:37), and blessing (Proverbs 29:18). *Not* living in
obedience brings harsh consequences (15:10), unanswered prayers
(28:9), and the inability to enter into the great things God has for
us (1 Corinthians 6:9).

Walking in obedience has to do not only with keeping God's

commandments but also with heeding God's *specific* instructions. For example, if God has instructed you to rest and you don't do it, that's disobedience. If He has told you to stop doing a certain type of work and you keep doing it, that's disobedience. If He has told you to move to another place and you don't move, that's disobedience too. Or God may ask you to take a different job, stop a certain activity, join a certain church, or change the way you've always done something. Whatever He asks you to do, remember He does this for your greatest good.

God's ways are always better than ours, and obedience to His Word clears the path for our prayers to be heard.

❦

Almighty God, help me to know Your laws. Teach me Your Word so that I understand it better every time I read it. Give me insight into Your ways so that they become part of me. Speak to my heart if my thoughts, words, or actions start getting off the mark. Keep me on the right path so that my prayers are never detestable to You.

TIMING IS EVERYTHING

❖ Read and Consider ❖

Ecclesiastes 3:1-11

"He has made everything beautiful in its time. He has also set eternity in the hearts of men; yet they cannot fathom what God has done from beginning to end" (Ecclesiastes 3:11).

When it comes to prayer, most of us think about timing—that is, we think about what the timing of God's answers should be. *When the answer doesn't come immediately,* we anxiously wonder why. But Ecclesiastes tells us, "There is a time for everything, and a season for every activity under heaven." God's timing is not the same as ours. His ways are not our ways. We live our lives with a sense of earthly time. God sees things from an eternal perspective. Living in our time-bound world and waiting for God's timing is often hard, especially when we ask for things we want or need now.

We have to remember that even though we pray and have faith, the final outcome and timing are in *God's* hands. He says there is "a time to heal" (3:3). So if you pray for healing and nothing happens, don't beat yourself up or be mad at God. God sometimes uses physical ailments to get our attention so He can speak to us. He wants us to fervently turn to Him. So keep praying and don't give up hope.

The same is true when praying that God will save someone's life. We don't have the final say over anyone's hour of death. The Bible says there is "a time to die" (3:2), but we are not the ones who decide that. God does. And we must accept His decision. We can pray, but *He* determines the outcome. We have to allow Him to do that without resenting or getting angry at Him.

God's timing is perfect. And it is liberating when we surrender to it. There is great freedom in simply laying our concerns and desires before Him and then trusting Him for the outcome. What joy there is in looking for God's goodness to us in the midst of our times of waiting. While you may not be able to understand exactly what God is doing, you can trust that He is doing something. He has your best interests at heart. And He will make everything in your life beautiful in *His* perfect time.

❦

Lord, I know Your timing is not the same as mine. I want all the answers to my prayers right now. But You want me to be patient and wait on You. I lay my concerns before You and leave the outcome in Your hands. Help me to rest in the knowledge that Your timing is perfect, just as everything You do is perfect.

A STREAM *of* REFRESHING

❧ Read and Consider ❧
Song of Songs 4

"You are a garden fountain, a well of flowing water streaming down from Lebanon" (Song of Songs 4:15).

Wouldn't it be wonderful to be thought of as a well of living water, flowing like a refreshing stream? Especially by the people around us and those closest to us in our lives. Wouldn't it be great to be loved, adored, and appreciated in the way that adoration is described in chapter 4? But that is the way God thinks about His people. He loves us with a beautiful and unfailing love.

We all want to have a committed, deep, pure, unconditional, sacrificing, heart-uniting relationship in our lives with someone who will not leave or forsake us for someone better. We all want to be thought of as spotless and flawless. We all want to be remembered as pleasing and beautiful. And that is the way God already thinks of us. He sees us through His Son, Jesus, who is all those things. And because we have received Jesus into our lives, His beauty, purity, and perfection is what God sees in us. And the more we spend time with the Lord and surrender our lives completely to His will, the more others will see *Him* in us.

The Holy Spirit flowing in us is what enables us to be a stream of refreshing for other people. All we have to do is open up to His flow in our lives by inviting His presence to fill us afresh each day. When we do, He will pour out on us His river of living water and His everlasting flow of love. That, along with the beauty of His presence in us, will be more than enough to attract others with a refreshing that will wash over their souls.

❧

*Lord, fill me afresh with Your Spirit today and overflow me
with Your healing stream so that when I am with anyone
else, they will sense Your presence. Make me to be like a well
of refreshing water flowing out to others. I know You see me
through Your Son, Jesus. I pray others will see Jesus in me,
even if they don't fully understand what it is they are seeing.*

Standing Before Our Holy God

❧ Read and Consider ❧

Isaiah 6:1-8

*" 'Woe to me!' I cried. 'I am ruined! For I am a
man of unclean lips, and I live among a people
of unclean lips, and my eyes have seen the
King, the LORD Almighty' " (Isaiah 6:5).*

When Isaiah, one of God's greatest prophets, had a vision of
God with the angels worshiping Him around His throne,
he realized his own unworthiness and sin. He said, "I am ruined!"
When he confessed his sin, God touched him and purified him.
God's holiness made him aware of his own lack of it. It also made
him whole.

Sin chips away pieces of our soul. With enough sin, we become
a pile of broken pieces. But God's holiness is what purifies us and
helps us to separate ourselves from all that is *unholy.* There is a
correlation between God's holiness and our wholeness. That's why
when we are in His presence, we become more whole. *God's holiness
makes us whole.* Whenever the great men of faith in the Bible, such
as Job, Abraham, and Moses, had a close encounter with God, they
saw their own failings. That's what happens to us too.

You may be thinking, *Why do I need to become more aware of my
own failings? I am already well aware of them. Thinking about them
is just going to make me feel worse about myself than I already do.*

But understanding God's holiness doesn't make you feel bad
about yourself in a way that leads to depression. It makes you feel
drawn toward His holiness in a way that leads to restoration. It
convicts you rather than condemns you. It's actually liberating.

The Bible tells us to "approach the throne of grace with confidence, so that we may receive mercy and find grace to help us in our time of need" (Hebrews 4:16). We certainly should be humble as we bring our unworthiness to His throne. Yet we can be confident because we know we are called and loved. We can come to God anytime, knowing that He wants us there and that He will cleanse our hearts and make us more like Him.

Ask the Lord to help you comprehend His holiness. Then acknowledge your own lack of it and pray that who He is will rub off on you.

❧

Dear Jesus, whenever I sense Your holy presence, I am greatly aware of my own unworthiness. And that makes me even more grateful for how much You sacrificed for me so that I can come before Your throne with confidence and find Your mercy and grace in my time of need. Touch me and purify me and help me to separate myself from all that is unholy.

I WILL PRAISE YOU

❧ Read and Consider ❧
Isaiah 12

*"I will praise you, O LORD. Although you were angry with
me, your anger has turned away and you have comforted
me. Surely God is my salvation; I will trust and not
be afraid. The LORD, the LORD is my strength and my
song; he has become my salvation" (Isaiah 12:1-2).*

The Lord gets angry about sin. We must not fool ourselves by
thinking that God overlooks our sin just because He loves us, or
that we can somehow get away with sin because we're one of God's
kids. Sin is ugly. Sin caused the death of His beloved Son. Sin will
not be tolerated by our holy God.

But sin is a part of our nature. Paul wrote, "I know that nothing
good lives in me, that is, in my sinful nature. For I have the desire
to do what is good, but I cannot carry it out. For what I do is not
the good I want to do; no, the evil I do not want to do—this I keep
on doing" (Romans 7:18-19). Although we are saved from sin, we
continue to struggle with it. We've been set free from sin, but our
sin nature still rears its ugly head. Satan constantly tries to wear
us down and tempt us to sin so we can be rendered ineffective for
God's kingdom.

While sin is a reality, and God's anger at sin is a reality, so is our
good standing with God. The battle is real, but He has armed us
for the battle (Ephesians 6:10-17). We have the ultimate weapons,
which are God's Word and our praise.

The Bible says, "The angel of the LORD encamps around those
who fear him, and he delivers them" (Psalm 34:7). Whenever the
enemy tries to drag you into sin, use your sword, which is the Word

of God, and drown the enemy out with praise. Thank God that He is the Deliverer and you are being delivered even as you praise Him.

If you ever seem to be sliding back into the very sin you've already been set free of, don't even waste time getting discouraged. Often what seems like the same old sin coming back again may be another layer surfacing that needs to come off. You're not going backward—you are going deeper. Those deep layers of bondage can hurt far worse than the earlier ones. But the deeper you go, the stronger you get, the more mature you become, the readier you are to move into all God has for you.

If you fall (and everybody does at times), remember that you have the weapon of repentance. Go to God immediately. Confess your sin and clear the air. Show Him your repentant heart. His anger will turn away, and He will comfort you (Isaiah 12:1).

Then praise God for all the glorious things He has done and is doing in your life.

❧

Lord, even though I don't always do, say, or think the
right thing—and I know sin displeases You—I thank
You that You always love me and will hear my confession.
Give me the discernment to hide myself in You when
I see temptation coming. You are my Savior and my
Deliverer, and I lift up praise to You whenever I sense
the enemy trying to draw me away from Your path.

Having Peace About Your Future

✢ Read and Consider ✤

Isaiah 26:1-9

"You will keep in perfect peace him whose mind is steadfast, because he trusts in you" (Isaiah 26:3).

W e all would like to experience "perfect peace," but as we look around at our world, at our lives, at our futures, it's hard to imagine that the peace we experience can ever be perfect. Although God promises us a future full of hope and blessing, it doesn't just happen automatically. There are some things *we* have to do. One of them is to pray (Jeremiah 29:11-13). Another is to obey God.

Every time you pray and obey, you are investing in your future. Although you live in a world where everything in your life can change in an instant, and you can't be certain what tomorrow will bring, God is unchanging. Although you may not know the specific details about what is ahead, you can trust that God knows. And He will get you safely where you need to go. In fact, the way to get to the future God has for you is to walk closely with Him today.

Walking with God doesn't mean there won't be obstacles. Satan will see to it that there are. While God has a plan for your future that is good, the devil has one too, and it's not good. But the devil's plan for your life cannot succeed as long as you are walking with God, living in obedience to His ways, worshiping only Him, standing strong in His Word, and praying without ceasing.

Your future is in *God's* hands. The only thing that is important is what *He* says about it. He doesn't want you to be concerned about your future anyway. He wants you to be concerned with *Him,* because *He* is your future. Remember that you are God's child, and He loves you. As you *walk* with Him, you will become more like Him every day (1 John 3:1-3). As you *look* to Him, you will be "transformed into his likeness with ever-increasing glory, which comes from the Lord, who is the Spirit" (2 Corinthians 3:18). As you *live* with Him, He will take you from strength to strength.

God is looking for people who will be committed to living His way and stepping into the purposes He has for their lives. You are one of those people. I pray that you will be equipped and ready when God says, "Now is the time," and the doors of opportunity open. Just keep doing what's right, and when you least expect it, you will get a call from God giving you your assignment.

Perfect peace can be a reality. Remember, God "is able to do immeasurably more than all we ask or imagine, according to his power that is at work within us" (Ephesians 3:20). He has more for you than you can imagine. And now may "the God of hope fill you with all joy and peace as you trust in him, so that you may overflow with hope by the power of the Holy Spirit" (Romans 15:13). Stay focused on God. As Isaiah wrote, God will keep you in "perfect peace" because you trust in Him.

❧

Dear God, the only reason I have peace about the
future is because my future is found in You. Even
though I don't know the details about what is to
come, I know You know everything, and my future is
in Your hands. Help me to walk faithfully with You
every day—in prayer and in Your Word—so that I
can move into the purposes You have for my life.

KNOWING WHICH WAY *to* GO

❧ Read and Consider ☙
Isaiah 30:19-26

"Whether you turn to the right or to the left, your
ears will hear a voice behind you, saying, 'This
is the way; walk in it'" (Isaiah 30:21).

We pray about a lot of things—things we need, things we want, safety for our families, traveling mercies, strength in times of grief. Very often, we pray for guidance. We need to know God's will about a big decision, how to solve a problem, how to deal with people, how to face adversity. We want to know God's will because it is a place of safety. When we live outside of God's will, we forfeit His protection.

We all want to be in the center of God's will. That's why we shouldn't pursue a career, move to another place, or make any major life change without knowing that it is the will of God. The way we find out is to regularly ask God to show us what His will is and then ask Him to lead us in it. When you ask Him to speak to your heart, He will do that. He will give you peace about a certain thing and *lack* of peace about others. What joy to have peace that as we confidently set foot in a certain direction, God is leading us on that particular path. We can be confident that whatever happens along the way, we don't have to worry because we are right where God wants us to be.

But all too often we don't hear that voice behind us. We hear the voices clamoring around us instead; we hear our own internal concerns and issues; we're in a hurry, and so we just forge ahead on the path and hope that everything will work out in the end.

When Isaiah gave this promise of God's guidance, it was in the midst of a description of people turning their hearts back to God. He had just prophesied to them about God's compassion in waiting for them to get their priorities in line. When they established right priorities, when their hearts were drawn in the right direction, God's voice would guide them.

As you seek guidance, listen for God's voice. It will be there. Take a few quiet moments to wait on Him and give Him time to respond.

❧

Lord, speak to me about Your will for my life so that I can always walk in it. Your will is a place of safety and protection for me, and I need to know I am headed in the right direction. Help me to hear Your voice speaking to my heart telling me what to do, especially with regard to the decisions I need to make each day of my life.

PRAISE IS *the* PUREST FORM *of* PRAYER

❧ Read and Consider ❧
Isaiah 43:6-21

"I provide water in the desert and streams in the wasteland, to give drink to my people, my chosen, the people I formed for myself that they may proclaim my praise" (Isaiah 43:20-21).

My definition of prayer is simply *communicating with God*. It's a love relationship first and foremost. Prayer is baring your soul to the One who loved you before you even knew of Him and letting Him speak to your heart.

Far too often prayer becomes a complicated issue for people. In fact, there can seem to be so many aspects to it that people can become intimidated. They fear that they can't pray well enough, right enough, long enough, or eloquently enough. They are afraid that their prayers won't be heard because they themselves are not good enough, holy enough, or knowledgeable enough. In all the books I have written, I have sought to dispel that kind of fear and intimidation and make prayer accessible to everyone.

One of the most important forms of prayer—or *communicating with God*—is praise and worship. Worship is the *purest* form of prayer because it causes our minds and souls to focus entirely on God and away from ourselves. It communicates our love, devotion, reverence, appreciation, and thankfulness to God, exalting Him for who He is, communicating our longing for Him, and drawing close to Him for the sake of being close. When we worship God, we are the closest to Him we will ever be. That's because praise welcomes His presence in our midst.

We were created to praise God. And God wants to make praise and worship of Him a way of life. Not necessarily with a hymn and a harp, but with a song in our heart that breaks forth through our lips as praise to the One who created us, formed us, gave us life. When we walk with Him, stay in fellowship with Him, use the gifts He has given us, serve Him wherever we find ourselves, and live for Him at all times, we can't help but praise Him for who He is and all He has done. When we do that for which we were created, we connect with our purpose. It fills our souls. It sets our path right.

Make praise and worship of God the way you live your life every day, and you'll sleep in peace every night.

❦

God, I want to show my love, reverence, devotion, and appreciation for You as I lift You up in worship. I praise You for who You are and for all You have done in this world and in my life. Help me to live every day with praise and thanksgiving in my heart so that I will fulfill my greatest purpose and calling on this earth—which is to worship and glorify You.

How *to* Respond *to* Unanswered Prayer

Isaiah 54:1-8

" 'Sing, O barren woman, you who never bore a child;
burst into song, shout for joy, you who were never in labor;
because more are the children of the desolate woman than
of her who has a husband,' says the LORD" (Isaiah 54:1).

When the prophet Isaiah foretold of Jerusalem's coming restoration, he likened its condition to a barren woman. He told the Israelites to sing in the face of it. This is exactly how we should respond to unanswered prayer or to the barren or unfruitful situations in our own lives. We are to sing praise to the One who can bring to life the places in us and our situations that appear to be dead. The One who can birth something new in us and our circumstances. The One who hears our prayers and answers in His way and His time. Whenever you have a dream in your life that seems to go unfulfilled year after year and there is no way possible to make it happen, determine to worship God in the face of it. When hope that this thing can ever be brought to life completely dies, then praise God for His resurrection power. The Bible tells us that not only can God bring to life things that are dead, but we are actually to prepare for that possibility because of who He is and what He does.

Have you ever experienced times when you are praying fervently from your whole heart and yet it seems that heaven and earth are silent? Do you ever wonder if God has even heard your prayers? If so, you are not alone. We've all felt that at times. But be assured that God hears and will answer. He may fall silent for a time, but His silence does not mean that He has not heard or that He has forgotten your request. What God has promised, He will perform. And when He does, you will be amazed that the answer is far beyond what you could have imagined. Until that time, sing praise to the Lord and see things come to life that you thought never would.

❧

Lord, Your Word says to sing praise in the face of unfruitful situations in our lives. So even when my prayers seem to be unanswered I will still praise You, because I know that You can breathe life into any situation—even one that appears dead. Help me to always trust that You have heard my prayers and have not forgotten my request.

Praying God's Word

*"As the rain and the snow come down from heaven,
and do not return to it without watering the earth
and making it bud and flourish...so is my word that
goes out from my mouth: It will not return to me
empty, but will accomplish what I desire and achieve
the purpose for which I sent it" (Isaiah 55:10-11).*

Sometimes we get discouraged when we pray fervently about a situation and get no response. We may even wonder if God hears us. But Isaiah 55 promises that God's Word, like the rain and snow, does what it needs to do wherever it goes. It accomplishes what God desires and achieves the purpose for which He sends it.

That means there is a power in praying God's Word. And we need to remember that, especially when we are in the midst of a battle. We can't see it in the quiet of our prayer time, but the words we raise to heaven are weapons of warfare. Because of our prayers, angels fight with demons to bring about God's will.

God's Word is "living and active. Sharper than any double-edged sword, it penetrates even to dividing soul and spirit, joints and marrow; it judges the thoughts and attitudes of the heart" (Hebrews 4:12). Paul placed the Word of God as part of every Christian's armor, saying that we must carry "the sword of the Spirit, which is the word of God" (Ephesians 6:17). In short, God's Word pierces everything it touches. It is *never* ineffectual.

That's why it is so important for you to not only pray, but to also read your Bible daily. Underline it, claim its promises, pray the words back to God. When you don't know what to pray, look up a psalm and read it aloud as your prayer. You can never be at a loss for words when it comes to prayer because God has given you everything you need. When you pray His words, you tap into His power and wield His sword. God promises that great things will happen when you do.

The battle for our lives, and the lives and souls of our children, our husbands, our friends, our families, our neighbors, and our nation is waged on our knees. When we don't pray, it's like sitting on the sidelines watching those we love and care about scrambling through a war zone, getting shot at from every angle. When we *do* pray, however, we're in the battle alongside them, appropriating God's power on their behalf. If we also declare the Word of God in our prayers, then we wield a powerful weapon against which no enemy can prevail.

❧

*Heavenly Father, I thank You that Your Word
always accomplishes the purpose for which You sent
it. Enable me to secure the power and life that is in
Your Word by having it planted so firmly in my heart
that it guides everything I do. Help me to weave Your
Word into my prayers so that it becomes a powerful
weapon against which the enemy cannot prevail.*

God's Chosen Fast

Isaiah 58:6-14

"Is not this the kind of fasting I have chosen: to loose the chains of injustice and untie the cords of the yoke, to set the oppressed free and break every yoke?" (Isaiah 58:6).

God gives us many wonderful keys for spiritual growth—keys such as speaking and reading His Word, praise, prayer, faith, and also fasting. Don't let your life be locked up because you are not using all of your keys. Fasting is a key to total health in every part of your being.

Fasting is not the easiest of disciplines, but it's not the hardest either. If you have a disease or health problems, check with your physician to see if it is safe for you. If it is, fasting can provide an especially close time with your heavenly Father. If you can begin the discipline of fasting for even one day each month, you will feel fresh, renewed, and cleansed in body, mind, and soul. And you will experience a special fellowship with God as you deny your physical desire for food and turn your focus on God.

Fasting is a spiritual discipline that is a denial of self. When you deny yourself, you position the Lord as *everything* in your life. This breaks the bonds of oppression. It causes things to change. Deliberately denying yourself food for a set period of time in order to give yourself more completely to prayer and closer communication with God has great rewards.

There are many religions in which fasting is a regular spiritual practice. There are also many people who fast who have no religious beliefs related to fasting but want a natural cure or cleansing for the body. We, as believers in Jesus who take seriously the written Word of God, must do our fasting unto the Lord to honor, worship, and glorify Him. It is not just a religious exercise; it is a step of obedience to God for the purpose of ministering unto Him. This is a personal matter between you and God—an offering to Him—and should be approached prayerfully and by the leading of the Holy Spirit.

Fasting goes hand in hand with prayer, so always fast with the intent of praying too. Fasting is not intended to twist God's arm into getting what you want out of Him, or something you do to win His approval, but it is a time of offering your concerns to Him.

If you desire to delve into the discipline of fasting, or if you already do it, take the time to read Isaiah 58 every time you fast. It's rich with purposes, promises, and truth. This passage describes the kind of fasting God desires—the kind of fast He has chosen, what fasting is intended to accomplish, and what the promise is for those who fast. God will speak to you through it. You will be reminded of why you are fasting: "to loose the chains of injustice," "to set the oppressed free," and to "break every yoke." It also serves as a reminder of what you should do: "Share your food with the hungry," "provide the poor wanderer with shelter," and do not "turn away from your own flesh and blood." And He tells you of your rewards: "Your light will break forth like the dawn, and your healing will quickly appear," and "the glory of the LORD will be your rear guard. Then you will call, and the LORD will answer." Ultimately, you are assured that "you will find your joy in the LORD." Now, that's worth skipping a meal for and praying instead.

❧

*Dear God, help me to be disciplined enough to fast and
pray as You would have me to. I want to deny the desires
of my flesh in order to focus entirely on my desire for more
of You. I want to break every yoke of oppression in my life
and in the lives of others so that we see great breakthrough.*

TEARING DOWN *the* WALL *of* SEPARATION

❧ Read and Consider ❧
Isaiah 59:1-8

"But your iniquities have separated you from
your God; your sins have hidden his face from
you, so that he will not hear" (Isaiah 59:2).

Nothing works in our lives when we don't live God's way, not the least of which is that our prayers are not answered. This verse says that our sins separate us from God so that He will not hear us when we pray. Don't let unconfessed sin separate you from God and hinder your prayers.

If you can't think of any sin in your life, ask God to show you whatever you need to see in that regard. All of us get things in our hearts, souls, minds, attitudes, and emotions that shouldn't be there and are not God's best for our lives. Often we have sin in our hearts and lives and don't even realize it until we start paying the consequences for it. Don't let any separation happen between you and God. Talk to Him daily about the condition of your heart. Ask God often to keep you undeceived. And when He reveals any sin, confess it immediately so that you can be cleansed of it.

We all fail at times, so don't let any failure on your part hinder your prayers in any way. If you take care of this issue by yourself with God in the daytime, by confessing and repenting of all sin as soon as you are aware of it, then you won't have to be dealing with the effects of it when you are trying to sleep at night.

❧

Lord, I know my life does not work when I am not living Your way. Help me to stay undeceived about my own sin so that I can confess it immediately and be cleansed of it. I don't want anything to separate me from You and hinder my prayers by causing You to not hear them. Show me how to tear down any wall of separation that may arise because of sin in my heart.

RECEIVE BEAUTY *for* ASHES

❧ Read and Consider ❧
Isaiah 61

"He has sent me...to bestow on them a crown
of beauty instead of ashes, the oil of gladness
instead of mourning, and a garment of praise
instead of a spirit of despair" (Isaiah 61:1,3).

The Jews had plenty to grieve about. The nation had struggled for many generations with taking God at His word and following Him faithfully. The prophet Isaiah was a strong voice for God, calling His people to renewed faithfulness. And he didn't leave anyone out. Isaiah confronted the wealthy and even the royalty with their lack of commitment to God's ways. The real problem in Jerusalem was that not enough people were grieving. In fact, they were not concerned at all that they were, in essence, snubbing their noses at God.

But for those who willingly turned their faces to God and repented of their sins, Isaiah had some good news. God promised comfort for those who grieved, beauty instead of ashes, oil instead of mourning, praise instead of despair. There was hope for those who understood that the Lord's favor would come upon all who sincerely sought to love and obey Him.

Do you ever grieve over the sins of your life or your own community or nation? If so, bring your grief to God and let Him trade it for gladness. Do you ever look at the ashes of your life or the lives of others and feel that great sense of loss? If so, God wants to give you beauty in exchange.

God knows what to do with despair. So seek Him. Sit with Him. Grieve with Him. Repent before Him. Let Him renew your life.

Ask Him for beauty, gladness, and a garment of praise. Then you can say with the ancient prophet, "I delight greatly in the LORD; my soul rejoices in my God. For he has clothed me with garments of salvation and arrayed me in a robe of righteousness" (61:10).

❧

*Dear God, I grieve over my own sins and over any time
I have not lived Your way. I don't know how much I
must have lost, or the blessings I have forfeited, because
I have lived my way. But I confess my sins of thought,
word, and action to You now and ask that You would
give me beauty instead of ashes, gladness instead of
mourning, and a garment of praise instead of despair.*

FINDING DELIVERANCE

❧ Read and Consider ❧
Isaiah 62

"For Zion's sake I will not keep silent, for Jerusalem's sake I will not remain quiet, till her righteousness shines out like the dawn, her salvation like a blazing torch" (Isaiah 62:1).

Isaiah interceded for the deliverance and restoration of his nation with fervency and desperation. Yet he also prayed with the hope of a man who had a vision for the future of his people.

We need to pray with that same combination of desperation and vision. Once we recognize that our only hope for deliverance and restoration in our lives is found in God, it causes us to pray with passion. Yet we are hopeful because we know that nothing is impossible with God. We know that in His hands, anything is possible. In His hands the situation will be resolved, the question answered, the wound mended, the oppression dissipated.

Isaiah's prayer reminds us of several things. First, it reminds us of the passion we must have in prayer not only for our own lives, but also for the lives of others in our family, our city, and our nation. Next, it reminds us that our only hope is in God, even if we fool ourselves into believing for a time that we can take care of things ourselves. Finally, Isaiah's prayer reminds us that no matter how hopeless the situation seems, God is our hope. We are never in a dark situation with no light. He is our light, and we just have to open our eyes and see Him.

All lasting deliverance comes from the Lord, and it is an ongoing process. It is God who has "delivered us from such a deadly peril, and he will deliver us. On him we have set our hope that he will continue to deliver us" (2 Corinthians 1:10). God does a complete work, and He will see it through to the end. So don't give up because it's taking longer than you hoped. Be confident that "he who began a good work in you will carry it on to completion until the day of Christ Jesus" (Philippians 1:6).

No matter how difficult your situation seems, don't give up because God will not rest until your righteousness shines out like the dawn and your salvation like a blazing torch (Isaiah 62:1).

❧

Lord, I know my only hope for deliverance and restoration in my life is found in You. You have saved me for eternity and for Your glory, and nothing is impossible with You. I pray You will not give up on me until I am completely set free and restored to total wholeness, and my righteousness shines forth like the morning sun.

Praying Without Excuses

Jeremiah 1:1-10

"But the LORD *said to me, 'Do not say, "I am only a child." You must go to everyone I send you to and say whatever I command you.'...Then the* LORD *reached out his hand and touched my mouth and said to me, 'Now, I have put my words in your mouth'"(Jeremiah 1:7,9).*

There was Jeremiah, simply minding his own business, when "the word of the LORD came" (1:2). And not just any word, but a word of divine appointment. God was giving him a whole new job description: to speak for Him to the nations. Feeling completely inadequate, Jeremiah humbly declined. After all, he couldn't speak well, and besides, he was just a kid. But God completely rejected Jeremiah's excuses.

The Lord immediately dismissed Jeremiah's concern about his youthfulness, but He did respond to Jeremiah's fear about speaking in a very specific way. The prophet described it like this: "The LORD reached out his hand and touched my mouth" (1:9). How wonderful and comforting that touch must have been. Jeremiah knew he did not need to worry any longer.

When we think up excuses for not doing God's will, what we are really saying is that we understand things better than God does. We are also saying that we think it's up to us and our abilities, rather than up to God's power and enablement. Feeling inadequate is good when it drives us to depend on God. But it's not good when that insecurity and fear cause us to say no to what God wants.

When it comes to prayer, we often have excuses for why we can't. We may see someone who needs prayer and yet we don't step out and do it. We may think, "My prayers aren't powerful enough." "God can't use me, I'm not eloquent." "I haven't walked with God long enough."

But we must remember how God told Jeremiah that He had put words in his mouth. The Lord will do that for us when we ask Him to help us pray.

God has given us the most powerful tool in the universe: *prayer.* The power of prayer is unlimited because it's God's power, not ours. If our words release God's power to change people's hearts, bring down spiritual strongholds, or build up nations, then we are participating in the most potent force in the universe.

When you pray, start by saying, "Lord, please touch my mind and mouth and give me Your words to pray." And then pray as the Lord leads. Of course, it's only in heaven that you will be able to see all the miracles that have been brought about by your prayers. But even on earth you will one day say, "I prayed about that situation, and look what God did!"

❦

Father God, I don't want to make excuses for not doing
Your will, but I feel inadequate to do the things You are
calling me to do—especially in prayer. Yet I don't want fear
to keep me from doing it. I want to depend on You to do it
through me. I pray You would put Your words in my mouth
so that I can intercede for others by the power of Your Spirit.

PRAYING *for* YOUR NATION

❖ Read and Consider ❖
Jeremiah 6:16-19

"This is what the LORD says: 'Stand at the crossroads and look; ask for the ancient paths, ask where the good way is, and walk in it, and you will find rest for your souls. But you said, "We will not walk in it."...I am bringing disaster on this people, the fruit of their schemes, because they have not listened to my words'" (Jeremiah 6:16,19).

Notice what God said to the sinful nations: "Stand...look... ask...walk." In other words, "Look for the right way to go and then follow it." And the reward for doing that meets everyone's deepest longing—"and you will find rest for your souls." Unfortunately, the response of far too many nations to God is, "We will not walk in it."

The consequence for any nation that forsakes God and His ways is serious. Even though you and I and millions of other believers have not forsaken God and His ways, many others in our nation have. But God gives us a way to respond to His warnings of judgment by confessing the sins of our nation before Him and asking Him to heal our land: "If my people, who are called by my name, will humble themselves and pray and seek my face and turn from their wicked ways, then will I hear from heaven and will forgive their sin and will heal their land" (2 Chronicles 7:14).

He didn't say that all people in a nation must be perfect in their heart and actions in order to receive His blessings. If that were the case, there would never be a nation that was blessed. We can, however, "stand in the gap" and be the one person willing to pray. Ezekiel described the sad situation when not one person could be found to pray: "I looked for a man among them who would build up the wall and stand before me in the gap on behalf of the land so I would not have to destroy it, but I found none" (Ezekiel 22:30).

God allows those of us who are called by His name to humble ourselves and repent for the sins of our nation so that we can continue to receive the blessings He has for us. We can stand in the gap on behalf of our unrepentant nation. Let's pray that we will be the ones who stand at the crossroads, look for the ancient paths, ask where the good way is, and walk in it. And may many others follow our example.

❧

*Lord, I come humbly before You and confess the sins of my
nation. Even though there are many people who believe
in You, far too many have refused to walk Your way. I
stand in the gap at the crossroads and look for the good way
and pray for many more to join me in walking according
to Your law so that disaster will be averted in our land.*

BOASTING *in* GOD ALONE

✤ Read and Consider ✤
Jeremiah 9:13-26

"This is what the LORD says: 'Let not the wise man boast of
his wisdom or the strong man boast of his strength or the
rich man boast of his riches, but let him who boasts boast
about this: that he understands and knows me, that I am
the LORD, who exercises kindness, justice and righteousness
on earth, for in these I delight'" (Jeremiah 9:23-24).

Everyone wants to accomplish something significant with his life.
We all desire to do things well. Who doesn't want to accomplish
something worth boasting about, even if we are not the ones doing
the boasting? But God says we are to boast about one thing only,
and this is that we know *Him*.

Men and women of the world boast about their accomplish-
ments. These verses mention three things people commonly boast
about, and those are wisdom, strength, and riches. But even if we
have *all* of these characteristics, we can't get prideful about them as
though *we* did something great. That's because everything we have
comes from God.

The one thing we can brag about is that we have a relationship
with the Lord. The only reason we have the potential to do something great is that we are His and His Spirit dwells in us. Because
of His greatness *in* us, He will accomplish great things *through* us.
Perhaps the greatest things we will do in life are acts that no one
will ever know about—such as interceding in prayer or caring for
the needy—the impact of which we will not comprehend this side
of eternity.

✤

> *God, I confess any pride I have over anything in my*
> *life, for I know all the good things have come from*
> *You. Help me to never even appear to boast about*
> *anything other than the fact that I know You. And*
> *the only reason I have the potential to do something*
> *good is because Your Holy Spirit dwells in me.*

Being Honest Before God

❦ Read and Consider ❦
Jeremiah 12:1-13

*"You are always righteous, O LORD, when I bring a
case before you. Yet I would speak with you about your
justice: Why does the way of the wicked prosper? Why
do all the faithless live at ease?" (Jeremiah 12:1).*

One remarkable thing about Jeremiah was he never hesitated
to tell God what was on his mind. He didn't edit his prayers.
He trusted God enough to be completely honest. God listened and
responded with mercy. In this particular case, Jeremiah came to
God with a compliment and two complaints. He recognized God's
faithfulness—"You are always righteous" (12:1). Then Jeremiah
began to pour out a list of issues he felt God needed to resolve.
Among these were the prosperity and peaceful living of wicked
people, which greatly irritated the prophet. Why did God allow
such people to succeed?

God's response presents a beautiful picture of His patience. He
gently told Jeremiah that he was out of his league in attempting to
give God direction. He didn't rebuke Jeremiah; He simply told him
that what he observed was a small part of a much larger picture.

God wants us to be honest with Him. He lets us bare our souls
and share our hearts. Like a loving parent, He listens and is not
angry or impatient. So if you have concerns and questions, bring
them before your heavenly Father and lay them all at His feet. Often
He will help you to see things from His perspective. God already
knows what is in your heart. He wants you to be completely honest
with Him about it.

❦

*God, I know You are always good and just, and I
don't question Your ways, but I confess that sometimes
I wonder why certain people seem to get away with
murder while others, who are Your servants—and seem
to have done nothing wrong—have so much suffering
in their lives. Help me to see these things from Your
perspective so that I might help others do the same.*

Praying *for* Healing

"Heal me, O LORD, and I will be healed" (Jeremiah 17:14).

Healing and body care are two different things. When you ask God to heal you, this is something *He* does. Taking care of your body is something *you* do. Both are vitally important.

God knows we are a fallen race and can't do everything perfectly. That's why He sent Jesus to be our Healer. But He also calls us to be good stewards over everything He gives us, including our body. He wants us to live in balance and temperance and to take care not to abuse our body in any way. He wants us to glorify Him in the care of our bodies because we are the temple of His Holy Spirit.

Many of us tend to think, "Everything I have is the Lord's—except for my eating habits. Those are mine." Or we think, "My life is the Lord's, but my body belongs to me, and I can do with it whatever feels good." But when we are the Lord's, our body has to be surrendered to Him just like everything else. Caring for our body is not something we can do successfully independent of God.

I've actually heard people say, "I don't worry about taking care of my body because the Lord can just heal me when I get sick." This kind of presumptuous thinking is dangerous and can get us into trouble. Satan's plan for our lives is to do the very thing that will hurt us the most. We help him along by that kind of attitude. We sabotage our lives by not doing what's best for our bodies and our health. Ask God to help you resist what is bad for you and to be disciplined enough to do what's right. God loves and values you. He created you. You are where His Holy Spirit dwells. He wants you to love and value yourself enough to take good care of your body.

However, even after all of our efforts toward taking proper care of ourselves, we can still get sick. And we need Jesus, our Healer, to heal us. Don't hesitate to ask Him for His healing touch upon your body.

❧

Dear Lord, how grateful I am that You came as our Healer. Thank You for mercifully understanding how much we need Your healing hand. I ask for Your healing touch upon my body today and whenever I need it. I know when You heal me, I will be healed completely. At the same time I ask for Your guidance and wisdom in knowing how to take care of my body.

ASK GOD *for* DISCERNMENT

Jeremiah 23:16-32

*"This is what the LORD Almighty says: 'Do not listen to
what the prophets are prophesying to you; they fill you
with false hopes. They speak visions from their own minds,
not from the mouth of the LORD'" (Jeremiah 23:16).*

Just as the Israelites centuries ago, we all long to hear directly from
God. We want to hear prophetic words of truth. We need words
of hope. Sometimes we're so desperate for it that we're willing to
listen to just about anyone who says, "God told me…" But Jeremiah
spoke about the dangers of listening to the wrong voices.

Someone claiming to speak for God must meet a very high
standard—perfection! God declared that His prophets would always
be correct in their pronouncements. What they said would come true.
Any mistake would make their message null and void (Deuteronomy
18:20-22). We make a serious mistake if we describe predictions as
truly "prophetic" when they come from someone with a track record
of wild guesses and incorrect declarations.

But then, how do we know for sure whether what we are hearing
from someone is the truth?

Our first tool of evaluation is God's Word. Those who contradict
or twist what God has already declared cannot be trusted. God says
not to listen to voices that speak lies, for "they speak visions from
their own minds, not from the mouth of the LORD" (Jeremiah 23:16).
Any vision for the future that is full of failure and empty of hope is
not from God (Jeremiah 29:11). And "positive" visions that discount
God's power often express someone's wishful thinking. So always
check out what you hear against the teachings of Scripture.

Our second tool of evaluation is the Holy Spirit. When we are born again, the Holy Spirit comes to dwell in us. Jesus called the Holy Spirit our "Counselor" and the "Spirit of truth," promising that He would "guide you into all truth" (John 16:7,13). When in doubt about what someone is saying or teaching, always pray for the Spirit to show you the truth.

Whenever you pray, ask the Holy Spirit to give you discernment and the ability to identify what is from Him and what is not. If people are giving you advice you're not sure about, ask Him to give you revelation regarding that.

Each time you read God's Word, ask Him to speak to you through it. If you have confusion about things people have spoken to you, ask Him to show you whether their words line up with *His* Word. Don't listen to people with visions from their own minds and not from the mouth of God.

❧

God, help me to hear Your voice speaking to my heart. Give me discernment so I can always distinguish between those who speak Your truth and those who give false prophesies filled either with fear or false hope. Help me to examine what I hear against the teaching of Your Word. Holy Spirit, guide me in all truth just as You have promised. Help me to identify what is from You and what is not.

GOD'S PLANS STILL REQUIRE PRAYER *on* OUR PART

❖ Read and Consider ❖

Jeremiah 29:4-14

> *"'For I know the plans I have for you,' declares the*
> *LORD, 'plans to prosper you and not to harm you, plans*
> *to give you hope and a future'" (Jeremiah 29:11).*

Jeremiah had some good news and some bad news from God for the people. The bad news was extremely bad. They would spend 70 years in captivity in Babylon (29:10). The good news was that God would bring His people home in the end. He had plans for them—plans to prosper and not harm them, plans to give them hope and a future. But that still meant that an entire generation would come and go before the hopeful promise in Jeremiah 29:11 would come true.

Sometimes God's plans can take a long time to come to pass. (You probably know that already.) And in those long waiting times, we can lose heart or get discouraged. That's why it's important to remember that a future filled with hope and blessing doesn't just happen automatically. There are things we need to do.

The first thing you need to do is to seek God and pray about your future. "Then you will call upon me and come and pray to me, and I will listen to you. You will seek me and find me when you seek me with all your heart" (29:12-13).

The second thing you need to do is to be diligent to obey God. Every step of obedience you take today will take you into the future God has planned for you. "Whether you turn to the right or to the left, your ears will hear a voice behind you, saying, 'This is the way;

walk in it'" (Isaiah 30:21). You have to listen for God's voice leading you every step of the way.

The Holy Spirit is God's guarantee to you that He will help you do what you need to do and bring to pass everything He promised. "Having believed, you were marked in him with a seal, the promised Holy Spirit, who is a deposit guaranteeing our inheritance until the redemption of those who are God's possession—to the praise of his glory" (Ephesians 1:13-14).

Every time you seek God and obey Him, every time you pray and listen for His voice, you are investing in your future. God promises that you have a good future and a reason to have hope. Trust Him for both. It may not happen as quickly as you would like, but God promises, and He will deliver.

❦

*Lord, I thank You that Your plans for me are for good—to
prosper me and give me a future and a hope. Help me
to obey You in every area of my life so that I don't do
anything that would thwart Your plans for my future. I
seek You about my future now and ask You to help me
to hear Your voice leading me every step of the way.*

LEARNING *to* LISTEN

*"Therefore, this is what the LORD God Almighty, the
God of Israel, says: 'Listen!'"* (Jeremiah 35:17).

This is not a complicated direction God is giving His people. It can't get any simpler than, "Listen!" He said it then, and He's still saying it today. God wants us to listen to Him only. That's why we have to be discerning about what we allow into our minds.

We have a choice about what we will accept into our minds and what we won't. We can choose to "take captive every thought to make it obedient to Christ" (2 Corinthians 10:5), or we can allow the devil to feed us lies and manipulate our lives. Every sin begins as a thought in the mind. "For from within, out of men's hearts, come evil thoughts, sexual immorality, theft, murder, adultery, greed, malice, deceit, lewdness, envy, slander, arrogance and folly" (Mark 7:21-22). If we don't take control of our minds, the devil will.

That's why you must be diligent to monitor what you allow into your mind. What TV shows, magazines, and books do you look at? What music, radio programs, or CDs do you listen to? Do they fill your mind with godly thoughts and feed your spirit so you feel enriched, clear-minded, peaceful, and blessed, or do they deplete you and leave you feeling empty, confused, anxious, and fearful? "God is not a God of disorder but of peace" (1 Corinthians 14:33). When we fill our minds with God's Word and godly books and magazines written by people in whom God's Spirit resides, and we listen to music that praises and glorifies Him, we leave no room for the enemy's propaganda.

Refusing to entertain unrighteousness in your thought life is part of resisting the devil. If you want to determine whether your thoughts are from the enemy or the Lord, ask yourself, "Are these thoughts I would *choose* to have?" If you answer no, then they are probably from your enemy.

Don't live with confusion or mental oppression. You never have to "live as the Gentiles do, in the futility of their thinking. They are darkened in their understanding and separated from the life of God because of the ignorance that is in them due to the hardening of their hearts" (Ephesians 4:17-18). Instead, ask God to give you clarity and knowledge. Ask Him to give you ears to hear His voice. Ask Him to make you a good listener.

❧

Almighty God, help me to be a good listener to Your voice speaking to my heart. I don't want to drown it out with the noise and busyness of life. Help me to take every thought captive in obedience to Your Word. Keep me from entertaining unrighteousness in my thought life. Enable me to be diligent in not allowing anything into my mind that does not glorify You.

Paying Attention *to* God's Direction

*"Zedekiah son of Josiah was made king of Judah
by Nebuchadnezzar king of Babylon; he reigned
in place of Jehoiachin son of Jehoiakim. Neither he
nor his attendants nor the people of the land paid
any attention to the words the LORD had spoken
through Jeremiah the prophet" (Jeremiah 37:1-2).*

This passage in Jeremiah reads like a script for a movie. Danger, courage, betrayal, drama, war, and political intrigue abound. Tensions stay at a fever pitch in a large city under siege. Our hero Jeremiah may not live to see another day. Special forces led by Ebed-Melech the Cushite have to pull off a daring rescue. Outside the walls, the mighty Chaldeans are waiting for the city to collapse. When and how will Jerusalem fall? Will God actually let that happen? When the end comes, who will be left standing? And why isn't anyone listening to the one prophet who is speaking for God? He's the good guy.

We can see it so clearly, why can't they?

We can see things in that Old Testament scene because we have perspective and access to other information. But when you're in the middle of a situation, things aren't always so clear. As our life stories unfold, sometimes it's obvious who to listen to and who *not* to listen to; sometimes it's not. Sometimes we pay attention; sometimes we don't. The Director of our life movie is giving just enough information to bring us along on the right path. There may be surprises in the plot along the way—but He is not surprised. It's all part of the story. He gives directions and guidance, telling us where to go and what to do so that the story falls into place as it should. We just have to pay attention.

King Zedekiah kept asking Jeremiah for God's counsel, but then when he received God's directions, he didn't act on them. The king *wanted* to know, but he was unwilling to do anything with that knowledge. How often do we plead for God's direction and, not liking what we hear, decide to go our own way? We hear from God but then, for one reason or another, we don't immediately act on it.

When you are asking God for direction, ask Him to give you ears to hear it and the will and strength to follow it. Say, "God, show me what to do and enable me to do it."

❧

Father God, I ask You for clear direction in my life. Help me to hear and understand what it is. I don't want to miss Your instructions to my heart because I wouldn't listen. Help me to act immediately on the guidance You give me and not ignore it. Show me what to do and enable me to do it.

GOD WILL GET YOU THROUGH

❖ Read and Consider ❖
Jeremiah 45

"Should you then seek great things for yourself? Seek them not. For I will bring disaster on all people, declares the LORD, but wherever you go I will let you escape with your life" (Jeremiah 45:5).

Jeremiah's scribe, Baruch, surely suffered as much as Jeremiah. After he recorded everything Jeremiah heard from the Lord, he read the prophecies publicly. Then he had to read them again before a group of leaders, after which he was instructed to go into hiding with Jeremiah. A little later he heard his scroll had been sliced to pieces and burned. To his surprise (and probably terror), Jeremiah gave Baruch another scroll and said, "God has told me to do it over. Let's start." Baruch became discouraged and afraid, but he also prayed. And God answered.

God gave Jeremiah a special message for Baruch. He told Baruch he would preserve his life in all circumstances. God warned him to not seek great things for himself because *everyone* would experience adversity. But God promised to rescue *him*.

The assurance of God's presence must have been a powerful comfort to Baruch. That same assurance is available to us. God has said, "Never will I leave you; never will I forsake you" (Hebrews 13:5). Jesus promised, "I am with you always, to the very end of the age" (Matthew 28:20).

These promises do not mean that nothing bad will ever happen to us. They mean that we can count on God's presence as we face all that life brings our way. Even in the midst of terrible circumstances, God is with us, saving us in ways we may not even be able to comprehend at the time. Jesus said, "I have told you these things, so that in me you may have peace. In this world you will have trouble. But take heart! I have overcome the world" (John 16:33).

It doesn't matter what your circumstances are at this moment, God has a future for you that is filled with good things. Even though you may have to go through tough times, take God's hand and walk with Him. He promises He won't let you fall.

❧

Lord, I pray You will be with me in the most difficult and trying areas of my life, helping me in ways I may not even be able to comprehend. I know that even though there may be troubles ahead, when I walk with You, You won't let me fall. When I go through difficult situations, I won't complain, for I know You will make a way through or a means of escape.

FINDING HOPE *in the*
MIDST *of* SORROW

❧ Read and Consider ❧

Lamentations 2

*"Arise, cry out in the night, as the watches of the night
begin; pour out your heart like water in the presence of the
Lord. Lift up your hands to him" (Lamentations 2:19).*

When Jeremiah wrote Lamentations, the echo of Jerusalem's crumbling walls were possibly still ringing in his ears. The cries of despair and weeping over those who had died could yet be heard. All that was left for the Israelites was the grim prospect of a bleak future.

Jeremiah, known as the "weeping prophet," responded with a grief-filled lament over the city and over the people. Like much of Jeremiah's prayer life, these verses are filled with raw emotion. They include deep reverence, anger, worship, confidence, despair, questions, and answers. All aspects of grief find expression in this brief book. Here we see how deeply the human heart can break. There's no joyful worship here, only agony.

If you ever feel such sorrow, do as Jeremiah says and "pour out your heart like water in the presence of the Lord." In your toughest hour, God invites you to hold nothing back, not even your raw emotions. In God's loving presence you will find hope.

Jeremiah finds hope in the midst of his affliction, but the promises God made to Jeremiah are for you as well. As you pour out your pain to God, as you are surrounded with bitterness and hardship (3:5), as you call out for help and it feels as if He has shut out your prayers (3:8), as your heart is pierced (3:13), as you are deprived of peace and prosperity (3:17), remember these words of Jeremiah: "Yet this I call to mind and therefore I have hope: Because of the LORD's great love we are not consumed, for his compassions never fail. They are new every morning; great is your faithfulness. I say to myself, 'The LORD is my portion; therefore I will wait for him.' The LORD is good to those whose hope is in him, to the one who seeks him; it is good to wait quietly for the salvation of the LORD" (3:21-26).

There is hope to be found in the midst of your pain. The darkness, the heartbreak, the sorrow, and the grief are not permanent. The Lord's compassion never fails. He is good to those who hope in Him, who seek Him, who wait quietly for Him.

❦

Lord, I pour out my heart before You regarding the things in my life that cause me grief. I lift my hands to You because I know You are my hope and Your compassion for me never fails. Heal me of all emotional pain, and use the sorrow I have suffered for good. I pray that in Your presence I will find total restoration.

FINDING *a* NEW HEART

❧ Read and Consider ❧
Ezekiel 11:16-25

"I will give them an undivided heart and put a new
spirit in them; I will remove from them their heart of
stone and give them a heart of flesh" (Ezekiel 11:19).

There's an old hymn that contains these poignant words: "Prone to wander, Lord, I feel it; prone to leave the God I love." Many of us experience the temptation to wander spiritually—to drift away from the God we love. Our hearts and emotions can be desperately deceptive, convincing us all too easily that we want what someone else has and not what God has planned for us. "The heart is deceitful above all things and beyond cure. Who can understand it?" (Jeremiah 17:9).

There is One, however, who *does* understand how emotionally fragmented our hearts can become, and He has promised to give us an undivided heart. What does this mean? Simply this: God promises that when we relinquish control of our hearts to Him, He will transform us from the inside out. If you think you can't give up that destructive habit, those inappropriate thoughts, that illicit relationship, then seek God. Cry out for His help. Ask Him to give you an undivided heart. God specializes in spiritual surgery on hearts that are open to Him.

God also promises to remove our hearts of stone. Have you experienced such pain and trauma in your life that you have determined never to allow yourself to be that hurt again? Has your warm heart for the things of the Lord ever become cold and distant? When we invite God's Spirit to truly take up residence within us, He lights a fire in the hearth of our hearts that cannot be put out. Ask God today to ignite a fire within your heart so that it can burn away all hardness. Ask Him to give you a new heart filled with His love.

❧

> *Dear God, I pray You will fill me with Your love, and*
> *help me to keep my heart from wandering away from You.*
> *Make my heart to be undivided and take away any hard-*
> *heartedness in me. I invite You to take charge of my mind*
> *and emotions and help me to give complete control to You.*
> *Light a flame of desire in me for You that never goes out.*

The PROMISE *of a* FRESH START

❧ Read and Consider *❧*

Ezekiel 18

*"Rid yourselves of all the offenses you have committed,
and get a new heart and a new spirit. Why will
you die, O house of Israel?" (Ezekiel 18:31).*

How do we get rid of each and every transgression from our lives? How can we divest ourselves of those sins of which we're not even aware? How do we get free of attitudes and actions we don't yet even recognize as being wrong? The answer is to ask God for it.

Scripture teaches that none of us is perfect. "All have sinned and fall short of the glory of God" (Romans 3:23). Because of our fallen nature, we need to ask God to bring to light any hidden sins that have taken root in our hearts so they can be dealt with now rather than later, when the consequences may be far more serious. God will do that, for "He knows the secrets of the heart" (Psalm 44:21). We've all heard stories of the "nice, likeable man" who beats his wife, abuses his children, or goes on a killing spree. You can be sure that he was a man who had hidden sin in his heart. We can be just as sure that any hidden sin in us will eventually display itself in an undesirable way. The time to catch it is now. "Turn away from all your offenses; then sin will not be your downfall" (Ezekiel 18:30). Ask God to bring any hidden sin to light so there won't be a physical or emotional price to pay for it.

Sin leads to death, but repentance leads to life. "For the wages of sin is death, but the gift of God is eternal life" (Romans 6:23). We don't confess our sins in order for God to know about them. He already knows. Confession is a chance for us to clear the slate.

Repentance is an opportunity for us to start over. We need to do
both! We need a new heart and a new spirit. We need a fresh start—
today and every day.

❦

*Lord, I pray You would take away everything in my
heart that is not right before You. Help me to be
rid of bad attitudes and wrong thinking. Show me
anything that has taken root in my heart that should
not be there so that I can free myself of it before there
is a serious price to pay. Help me clear the slate and
begin again with a new heart and a right spirit.*

GETTING FREE *of the* BURDEN *of* SIN

❧ Read and Consider ❧
Ezekiel 20:30-44

"There you will remember your conduct and all the actions by which you have defiled yourselves, and you will loathe yourselves for all the evil you have done" (Ezekiel 20:43).

I f you have children of your own or you work with children in any capacity, you know the importance of insisting that they admit when they've done wrong. If a child lies or steals or cheats and is never held accountable for his actions, he will be tempted to see what more he can get away with the next time.

The same principle holds true for us as adults. Just as confession and repentance are two life principles we insist upon for our children, they are equally important for us as children of God. Unconfessed sin puts a wall between us and God. Repentance, which literally means "turning away and deciding not to do it again," is manifested when we say, in effect, "I did this, I'm sorry about it, and I'm not going to do it again." If sin is not confessed and repented of in that way, we can't be free of the bondage that goes along with it.

King David knew all about unconfessed sin when he wrote, "When I kept silent, my bones wasted away through my groaning all day long…Then I acknowledged my sin to you and did not cover up my iniquity. I said, 'I will confess my transgressions to the Lord'—and you forgave the guilt of my sin" (Psalm 32:3,5).

What God said to the Israelites who disobeyed Him and didn't repent was that they would remember their evil and hate themselves for it. We all have experienced that sense of shame when we remember some words we've said or actions we've done that we now deeply regret. But even though we may never forget those things, we can still be set free from the bondage and the burden of guilt by confessing and repenting of those sins. This allows God to take away the burden and make us new.

❧

Lord, I don't want to look back over my life—even as recently as yesterday—and feel bad about myself because of the things I have done wrong. Help me to quickly recognize and confess sin. Enable me to live in such a way that I don't have regret over my words, thoughts, or actions. Help me to fully repent so that You will fully lift the burden of sin from me.

STANDING *in the* GAP
for OUR NATION

*"I looked for a man among them who would build
up the wall and stand before me in the gap on
behalf of the land so I would not have to destroy
it, but I found none" (Ezekiel 22:30).*

I t's difficult to read this verse without feeling tremendously sad. The Lord is speaking through the prophet Ezekiel to the people of Israel and explaining why judgment could not be averted on their land. God said He was looking for just one person who would pray and intercede for the nation so it wouldn't be destroyed, but He could not find even one person. What a tragedy.

How can we read this passage and not think of our own country with all its sin and rebellion? Our day of judgment will come as well. As surely as there is a physical law of gravity, there is also a spiritual law of reaping what we sow. There may be a time lapse between what we have sown and what we reap, but the harvest will come.

Bad things don't come from God. They happen because we have sown bad seeds or as a result of the enemy's work. Either way, God gives us the opportunity to avert both of those things by standing in the gap through prayer. In spite of everything that is wrong in our country, we still enjoy the blessings we have because countless people have stood in the gap on behalf of our nation.

When God looked for a person to pray and couldn't find *one*, the land of Israel was taken over by enemies. Do you see how significant a role each of us can play as we learn to pray together for the protection of our nation today? As we pray according to God's Word and invoke God's power as intercessors, we can affect the outcome of events and avert judgment on our land.

Let's stand in the gap together and see what great things God will do.

❧

Almighty God, I lift up my nation to You, with all
its sin and rebellion, and ask that You will have
mercy upon us and help us not to reap the full
consequences of what we have sown. I stand in the
gap to invoke Your power on our behalf. Do not judge
us as we deserve, but rather pour out Your Spirit
over this land and bring millions of people to You.

MOVING *in the* SPIRIT

❧ Read and Consider ❧
Ezekiel 36:24-32

"And I will put my Spirit in you and move you to follow my decrees and be careful to keep my laws" (Ezekiel 36:27).

We all have to do things we don't want to do. Even in the best of jobs, there are still aspects we don't enjoy. When we do things we don't like simply because we know we need to do them, it builds character in us, makes us disciplined, and forms us into leaders God can trust. Besides, there's always a price to pay when we forsake the things we *need* to do in order to do only the things we *feel* like doing. We must be willing to make sacrifices for the blessings we want.

When we ask God for it, He will give us the discipline we need in order to do all the tasks that are distasteful to us. When God asks us to do something, He also promises to equip us to carry it out. "The one who calls you is faithful and he will do it" (1 Thessalonians 5:24). Look at the men and women in Scripture whom God singled out for extraordinary assignments. Moses was in his senior years, David was only a shepherd boy, and Jesus' mother, Mary, was most likely just a teenager. None of them felt qualified for the work to which God called them, and yet they responded in obedience and faith, and God enabled them to do what they needed to do.

God has promised to put His Spirit within you. Wherever you go and whatever tasks are before you, you have the pledge of His powerful guidance. But you have to be continually tapped into Him. You have to be in constant communication with Him in order to be plugged into His power. You have to be moving in the Spirit in order to do all He has for you to do.

❧

Lord, lead me by the power of Your Holy Spirit so that I will always obey Your Word and follow Your laws. Give me the discipline I need to do what I must do. Thank You that You have put Your Holy Spirit within me to guide me in all things. Help me to follow Your leading and not run ahead or behind chasing after my own ways.

Bringing Dead Things *to* Life

✤ Read and Consider ✤
Ezekiel 37:1-14

*"This is what the Sovereign LORD says to these
bones: I will make breath enter you, and
you will come to life" (Ezekiel 37:5).*

One of the most amazing things that God has placed within
nature is its ability to recreate itself. Who doesn't rejoice
at seeing flowers pop up from the ground, or leaves and blossoms
budding on trees after a long winter when everything appeared
lifeless and dead?

On the spiritual level as well, God specializes in bringing life
where things might have seemed dead. This powerful story in Ezekiel
is actually a metaphor—a word picture—of God's ability to restore
life in seemingly hopeless situations. With God's hand upon him
and led by His Spirit, the prophet Ezekiel sees a vision of an entire
valley full of dry bones. God asks Ezekiel whether he thinks these
bones can live. The prophet answers wisely: "You alone know" (37:3),
and God proceeds to cover the bones with tendons, flesh, and skin.
Then God gives Ezekiel the order to use His holy name to command
the breath of life to enter the bones. To Ezekiel's amazement, a great
army rises to its feet.

Just as this vision was a symbolic representation of God's intention to restore the nation of Israel after its years of captivity, it has
also come to signify His ability to breathe new life into any seemingly
hopeless situation. Have you ever used the word "dead" in connection with your life? Has the life gone out of your marriage? Does
the church you attend seem lifeless and dull? Is your own heart for
God without vibrancy? Does your work feel like it's sucking the life

out of you? Just as God commanded Ezekiel to take action in His power, He has given us the power of prayer.

If your marriage lacks love, pray! If your church is without vitality, pray! If your walk with God is dry, pray! If your work is killing you slowly, pray! God is waiting to work through you to bring His life into places and situations you thought were dead. If dry bones can become a vast army, your situation is not beyond hope. You can see dead things brought to life through prayer.

❧

Dear God, there are areas of my life that seem dead
to me; they need a new infusion of Your life. There
are dreams I have had that seem as if they have died
because it's been a long time and still they have not
been realized. I know if You can make dry bones into
a vast army, You can bring life to anything worth
praying about, no matter how dead it seems.

SEEING GOD *in the* DARK

❧ Read and Consider ❧

Daniel 2:17-23

"During the night the mystery was revealed to Daniel in a vision. Then Daniel praised the God of heaven and said: 'Praise be to the name of God for ever and ever; wisdom and power are his'" (Daniel 2:19-20).

Why is it that during the daylight hours when we're active and busy, our problems don't seem as serious? But when darkness falls and the lights go out, our fears and worries loom larger. Perhaps it's because we forget that we serve a God who never sleeps and is sovereign over our affairs both day and night. The sovereignty of God is a major theme of the book of Daniel. Throughout this book we see multiple reasons that Daniel and his friends had to praise God for His power and ultimate authority over the situations that literally kept them up at night.

Are you facing situations that cause you to lose sleep at night? If so, you're not alone. For centuries God's people have experienced what are sometimes called "dark nights of the soul." Take comfort in the fact that God uses these times of darkness to teach us invaluable lessons we might never learn in the light. He desires to teach us things about Himself that we will only learn in the dark—when we are holding tightly to Him and He has our undivided attention. During those times, we will be the losers if we resist Him and what He is trying to teach us. He wants to share His secrets with us. "He reveals deep and hidden things; he knows what lies in darkness, and light dwells with him" (2:22).

One of the biggest mistakes we can make is to be angry with God because of things that happen. Or don't happen. "Woe to him who quarrels with his Maker" (Isaiah 45:9). Instead, allow God to use these dark times to give you "the treasures of darkness, riches stored in secret places, so that you may know that I am the Lord, the God of Israel, who summons you by name" (Isaiah 45:3).

❧

Lord, it seems that in the middle of the night all problems appear larger. At those times I am reminded that You never sleep, and I can come to You and cling to Your presence. I pray that at those times You will give me the treasures of darkness, stored in secret places, as You have spoken of in Your Word. I pray You will fill my darkness with Your light and give me peace.

CRYING OUT *for* GOD'S MERCY

Daniel 9:4-19

"Now, our God, hear the prayers and petitions of your servant...We do not make requests of you because we are righteous, but because of your great mercy" (Daniel 9:17-18).

Daniel had many reasons to be deeply alarmed. His own people were in exile, and he was pleading with God for the end of their captivity and their return to Jerusalem. But Daniel wasn't asking God for His help because the people deserved it. He was making his request because he knew God was a merciful God. Daniel cried out, "but because of your great mercy." Daniel was begging God to extend compassion and mercy to the people because of who *the Lord* was, not because of who the people were. His passionate prayer was a petition to a holy and righteous God—a God who grants grace in difficult situations because of His nature. Grace is not something that we can ever earn or deserve. Even our very salvation is a work of God's grace. "For it is by grace you have been saved, through faith—and this not from yourselves, it is the gift of God—not by works, so that no one can boast" (Ephesians 2:8-9).

When we are going through difficult circumstances, we can ask God's help even though we don't deserve it. Just like the tax collector Jesus described in one of His parables, we can say, "God, have mercy on me, a sinner" (Luke 18:13). Then praise Him that His help isn't dependent on what we do or on our "works," but on who *He* is.

❧

Dear God, I come to You, not because I am worthy, but because You are. You are full of mercy, and I need Your

*mercy extended to me today. I need help with all things,
but especially with certain situations in my life right
now. I thank You that Your help isn't dependant upon
my good works, but upon Your goodness, love, and grace.*

FINDING FAITH *to* WAIT
for the ANSWER

✤ Read and Consider ✤
Daniel 10:1-14

"Then he continued, 'Do not be afraid, Daniel.
Since the first day that you set your mind to gain
understanding and to humble yourself before your
God, your words were heard, and I have come in
response to them. But the prince of the Persian kingdom
resisted me twenty-one days'" (Daniel 10:12-13).

Have you ever waited anxiously for a promised letter or package to arrive, only to have days, weeks, or maybe even months pass by with no sign of it? How do you know for certain that it was placed in the mail in the first place or that it wasn't delivered to the wrong address?

When it comes to prayer, most of us will have times when we wonder whether the answer to our request has been "lost." Did God hear us at all, and is He planning to respond?

The book of Daniel contains one of the most encouraging yet sobering conversations recorded in the Bible when it comes to receiving an answer to prayer. Daniel had been faithfully fasting and praying for weeks without seeing any response. After 21 days, he had a vision of an angelic being who appeared to him and told him the reason for the delay: A spiritual battle was being waged in the heavens. Daniel was told that the messenger had been sent in response to his prayers from the first day, but he had been detained by opposition from "the prince of the Persian kingdom," a reference to an evil supernatural force. When Daniel persisted in prayer, help was sent to the first messenger in the form of the archangel Michael, and the messenger finally reached Daniel with a word from God for the future.

What an encouragement this is for us! God has promised to hear our prayers when we come to Him in faith, but we need to remember that Satan may throw obstacles in the way of our receiving the answers God has sent. What are we to do? Continue to pray! The prayers of a righteous man or woman are powerful and effective (James 5:16). Don't give up when the answer doesn't come right away. God hears and will answer. You have His Word on it!

❦

Heavenly Father, help me to wait patiently for the answers to my prayers. Increase my faith to know that when I pray, You hear the cries of my heart and will answer in Your perfect timing and Your perfect way. Help me to continue to pray and not give up, no matter how long it takes or how many obstacles the enemy throws in my path.

FINDING GOD'S
FORGIVENESS *and* LOVE

❧ Read and Consider ❧

Hosea 14

*"Take words with you and return to the LORD. Say to
him: 'Forgive all our sins and receive us graciously, that
we may offer the fruit of our lips'" (Hosea 14:2).*

The book of Hosea is an unusual love story of a husband, an
unfaithful wife, and a love that forgives and redeems even when
the relationship seems irreparably broken. Put yourself in Hosea's
place. God tells you to take an adulterous wife, give your kids odd
names that represent divine messages, and pay to get your wife back
after she has disgraced herself with other men. Then God instructs
you to forgive her and love her more than before.

Your reaction might be, "Are You joking, God? You want me to
what?" But Hosea didn't question God. Instead, he did exactly as
God said. As a result his life became a beautiful metaphor of God's
love for the unfaithful nation of Israel and for each of us individu-
ally. It parallels God's love for His "bride" (His people) and the
reconciliation that God's true love brings about.

Hosea calls the people of Israel to repentance, to turn back to
God. He even gives them the words to say: "Forgive all our sins and
receive us graciously…for in you the fatherless [we] find compassion"
(14:2-3). These simple but amazing words, when prayed with honesty
and a contrite heart, are as relevant today as they were 2500 years
ago. No matter how faithless we have been, God will be faithful
and just to forgive us (1 John 1:9).

Forgiveness begins when we recognize how sinful and needy
we are. We can't save ourselves, and no amount of money, fame, or

power can save us either. Our only hope is to throw ourselves upon the mercy of our Creator, knowing we don't deserve it. God loves us so much that He paid in blood to redeem us. Jesus Christ, His only Son, gave His life that we might forever have God's compassionate forgiveness.

When you are tired of trying to be good on your own, weary of a life of sin, when your friends and family desert you, when you feel yourself sinking in the quicksand of guilt, lift your voice to God. Ask Him to forgive you for your sins and for trying to do it all on your own. He will wash away your past, start you on a new path, and walk with you. Together, you and He will write your own love story, a story that will last forever.

❧

Dear God, I recognize how sinful and needy I am. I know I cannot save myself in any way, but You have saved me in every way. That's why I humble myself before You, first of all in confession of my sins. Secondly, I praise You for all You have done for me by extending Your forgiveness, love, and mercy my way. I love You above all else.

IT'S NEVER TOO LATE
to TURN *to* GOD

*"I will repay you for the years the locusts have
eaten—the great locust and the young locust, the
other locusts and the locust swarm—my great
army that I sent among you" (Joel 2:25).*

Up to this point, Joel's prophecy was gloom and doom for
those who had turned their backs on God. He warned of a
day of judgment coming—a day so dreadful that he asked, "Who
can endure it?" Even so, Joel kept reminding the people to repent
and seek God's forgiveness.

The people had sinned greatly. They had bowed to other gods
and succumbed to the idolatry in the world around them. They had
been far from God for a long time.

Joel says it's not too late. God would forgive and bless them if
they would return to Him in prayer and repentance.

When we pray, repenting of our sinfulness, our hearts become
soft toward God, and we gain a renewed vision. We see there is
hope. We have faith that He will restore all that has been devoured,
destroyed, and eaten away. Even years of life that have been wasted
in godless living can be restored. Trust God to take away all pain,
hopelessness, hardness, and unforgiveness. Have faith in His ability
to resurrect love and life from the deadest of places. Understand that
He wants to restore what has been lost so that you will know He is
God and glorify His name.

What is broken in your life? What have the "locusts" eaten? What has been lost, destroyed, or ruined? God says He will restore it when you turn to Him. It's never too late.

❦

Dear God, I thank You that it is never too late to turn to You and see restoration happen in my life. Even though I feel there has been time wasted when I didn't live fully for You, I pray that You would redeem the time and help me to make up for it. Restore anything that has been lost, wasted, or ruined so I can give You the glory.

Pray *for* Godly Friends

Amos 3

*"Do two walk together unless they have
agreed to do so?" (Amos 3:3).*

So much is made of the importance of the right kind of friends in the Bible that we can't treat this part of our lives lightly.

The main quality to look for in a close friend is how much that person loves and fears God. What Amos wrote is a picture of being in agreement on many levels. You will have all different kinds of friends, but your closest friends—those with whom you walk closely—should be the kind of friends who impart something of the goodness of the Lord to you every time you are with them.

Following are signs of a desirable friend:

A desirable friend tells you the truth in love. "Wounds from a friend can be trusted, but an enemy multiplies kisses" (Proverbs 27:6).

A desirable friend gives you sound advice. "Perfume and incense bring joy to the heart, and the pleasantness of one's friend springs from his earnest counsel" (Proverbs 27:9).

A desirable friend refines you. "As iron sharpens iron, so one man sharpens another" (Proverbs 27:17).

A desirable friend helps you grow in wisdom. "He who walks with the wise grows wise, but a companion of fools suffers harm" (Proverbs 13:20).

A desirable friend stays close to you. "A man of many companions may come to ruin, but there is a friend who sticks closer than a brother" (Proverbs 18:24).

A desirable friend loves you and stands by you. "A friend loves at all times, and a brother is born for adversity" (Proverbs 17:17).

A desirable friend helps in time of trouble. "Two are better than one, because they have a good return for their work: If one falls down, his friend can help him up!" (Ecclesiastes 4:9-10).

A desirable friend is not rebellious. "Do not join with the rebellious, for those two [the LORD and the king] will send sudden destruction upon them, and who knows what calamities they can bring?" (Proverbs 24:21-22).

A desirable friend is not often angry. "Do not make friends with a hot-tempered man, do not associate with one easily angered, or you may learn his ways and get yourself ensnared" (Proverbs 22:24-25).

Pray that God will give you good, godly friends who will influence and encourage you to grow deeper in Him.

❧

Lord, I pray I would always have good, godly friends, and
that we would influence, encourage, and inspire each
other to walk closer to You. I pray for friends who will
tell me the truth in love, give me sound counsel, and be
a help in times of trouble. Enable me to be that kind
of friend too. Send desirable friends into my life.

DELIVERING GOD'S MESSAGE

❧ Read and Consider ❧
Jonah 4

"Should I not be concerned about that
great city?" (Jonah 4:11).

God had given Jonah a second chance. "Go to the great city of Nineveh" had been the directive (1:2), and Jonah had gone the other direction. But God caught up with him, sent a fish to provide personal transportation back to shore, and said again to Jonah, "Go to the great city of Nineveh" (3:2). And this time, Jonah went.

What a compassionate God! He could have let His reluctant prophet drown in the ocean, but He didn't. He had a message for Nineveh, and He wanted Jonah to deliver it.

God always offers His grace and compassion to everyone—even those who might seem to be least deserving. Somewhere in Nineveh surely someone was seeking divine intervention, someone believed there had to be more to life, and they were looking to God for help. And God heard their prayer and sent Jonah to bring a message—with powerful results. The people's hearts were ripe to hear from God.

God hears the cries of those who seek Him. When people call out to Him on behalf of a city, He will send someone with a message. When people don't seek God, and when their hearts become hard and filled with evil desires, God will allow destruction to come upon them.

You have surely received God's compassion and seen His loving touch on your life. All around you are people who need to know God's love and compassion for them, too. Many of them may look carefree, but who knows the deep longings in their hearts and the questions they may be asking. They may be praying, "Lord, send someone to speak the truth and show me the right way to live."

Ask God to show you if perhaps He is sending you or asking you to intercede on someone's behalf.

❦

*Lord, I know there are people all around me who need
to hear Your message of hope and truth—people whom I
might not even notice, but whom You love deeply. Reveal
them to me so I can pray for them and perhaps speak
an encouraging word from You to them. Prepare their
hearts to receive from me and most of all from You.*

Rising Up *out of the* Darkness

"Do not gloat over me, my enemy! Though I have
fallen, I will rise. Though I sit in darkness, the
Lord will be my light" (Micah 7:8).

No one is perfect. The people of Judah knew this very well—
they had failed God miserably. And to make matters worse,
their enemies were laughing at them.

Being good can be a daily struggle for many people. Our human
nature is instinctively selfish, causing us to strive to satisfy our own
desires. Yet God has given us His Word and His Spirit to help us
combat our sinful nature. Still, we all fall into sin, some deeper
than others. In those times we have a choice to make: wallow in
the darkness of self-pity or repent and look to Jesus. "The Lord
will be my light," wrote Micah. Sin is a dark path that first draws
us in with promises of the gratification of our human desires. But
when the light of the Word shines upon it, all the snares, traps, and
quagmires are revealed.

Always remember that no matter how much we've failed, God
is ready to forgive us when we ask Him to. He doesn't want any of
His children to sink without hope of rescue. That's why He gave us
His Son, Jesus, to offer us His lifeline. Reaching out in repentance
is our decision. Picture a person drowning and crying out for help,
when suddenly a strong arm reaches into the water. That the person
would obviously reach for the strong hand immediately and be saved.
Confession of sin and repentance are a strong hand that reaches to us
when we are drowning in our own failures, yet many people choose
to reject that means of restoration. Perhaps they don't realize the

danger they are in, or maybe they reject the hope offered, thinking they can save themselves. But Jesus is always there ready to pull us up and out of the darkness, no matter how deep or how many times we slip and fall. Whenever you feel yourself sinking into the darkness, say this prayer:

> Lord, help me to trust Your light in my life. I look to You to be my treasure in darkness. I worship You as the Light of my life and thank You that You will enlighten the dark for me. Though I have fallen, I will rise.

❦

> *Thank You, Lord, that even if I were to fall off the path You have for me to walk, You will always be there to lift me up and back on it again when I repent of my sins. I thank You that even if I sink into darkness, You will be my light. I praise You as the light of my life and keeper of the flame that burns in my heart for eternity.*

KEEP PRAYING NO MATTER WHAT

❧ Read and Consider ☙
Habakkuk 1:1-11

"How long, O LORD, must I call for help, but
you do not listen? Or cry out to you, 'Violence!'
but you do not save?" (Habakkuk 1:2).

Isn't it interesting to note that Habakkuk felt the same way about society as Christians feel today? There seems to be no justice upon the wicked.

You might see a situation and wonder, *Where is God in the midst of this? Why do bad things happen to good people? How are the evil-doers getting away with cheating, violence, oppression, and perversion?* Habakkuk saw the evil around him, and he cried out to God for answers. He didn't doubt God's omnipotence; rather, he didn't understand why God would allow sin to run rampant in the world. God answered the prophet, telling him exactly what He planned to do.

Today injustice, evil, and sin continue to appear to prosper, but not because God is indifferent. God has a plan. He wants us to partner with Him in this plan by praying. Whenever you feel sad over what you see happening in the world today, pour out your concerns to God in prayer. Pray that you and your fellow believers might be a light in a darkened world, bringing the hope and peace of Jesus to those with whom you interact every day. God will answer those prayers.

Habakkuk knew that he would need to persevere no matter what. We must do the same. "Though the fig tree does not bud and there are no grapes on the vines, though the olive crop fails and the fields produce no food, though there are no sheep in the pen and no cattle in the stalls, yet I will rejoice in the LORD, I will be joyful in God my Savior" (3:17-18). We must learn to say, "No matter how bad it gets, Lord, I will be joyful and not stop praying until Your will is done on earth."

❧

Lord, help me to have the understanding and faith I need to keep praying and not give up if my prayers are not answered right away. I know Your ways are perfect. Help me to not become discouraged in the time of waiting for Your help, but rather to continue praying until I see Your will done in all the things You put on my heart to pray about.

Thank God *for* His Love

Zephaniah 3:8-20

"The LORD your God is with you, he is mighty to save. He will take great delight in you, he will quiet you with his love, he will rejoice over you with singing" (Zephaniah 3:17).

The Lord is with you. What joy there is in knowing that God is with you! You always have a line of open communication with Him because He is omnipresent. Whether your prayers are long or short, the Lord hears them all. Thank Him that He is a God who is close to you.

The Lord is mighty to save. Rejoice that you have been snatched from the jaws of hell because of God's great love. He has provided salvation through His Son, Jesus Christ, and He accepts your repentance for sin no matter how many times you come to Him with a repentant heart. Thank Him for His salvation and continuing forgiveness.

The Lord takes great delight in you…He will rejoice over you with singing. Just as you rejoice in the victories of others, God will rejoice over you with gladness. Like the Father that He is, He is proud of His children. He is glad when you follow His will and live a life that will cause others to want to know Him. Thank Him for His joyful delight in you.

The Lord will quiet you with His love. In times of turmoil, if you turn to the Lord, He will quiet you with His love. There is peace in knowing that whatever circumstances come your way, God will be there to guide you through. In good times and bad, His love will comfort your pain and soothe your weariness. Thank Him for His peace in you.

Rejoice daily in this profound relationship you have with the Almighty God. Thank Him again and again for His presence and love in your life, even when you know you don't deserve it.

❧

*Lord, I have great joy in knowing You are always with
me and have the power to save me from the plans of
the enemy. Help me to remember at all times—even
when I go through difficult situations that shake the very
foundation of my soul—that my foundation is in You
and my security is sustained by Your great love for me.*

Don't Neglect Your Walk With God

❧ Read and Consider ☙
Haggai 1:1-11

" 'You expected much, but see, it turned out to be little. What you brought home, I blew away. Why?' declares the LORD Almighty. 'Because of my house, which remains a ruin, while each of you is busy with his own house' " (Haggai 1:9).

In Haggai's time, the people had been returned to their land after exile in Babylon. But instead of getting down to work rebuilding their spiritual lives by rebuilding God's temple, they were more concerned with the condition of their own homes, more concerned with how they looked to others than with the time they spent in communion with God.

It is a warning to us to not be concerned with outward appearances and selfish pursuits, but rather to be concerned with the condition of our hearts and the things that touch the heart of God.

Haggai had stern words for his people. He admonished them to get their priorities straight! We too have to always place God first in our lives and remember that any work we attempt for Him without His blessing and guidance will be unproductive. Our material possessions will not satisfy us like He will.

Don't allow anything to keep you from your daily prayer time. Do whatever it takes to be with God. Ask Him to help you not neglect your relationship with Him. What you do in the Spirit—your praise, worship, and prayer—lasts for eternity.

❧

*God, help me to not be concerned with outward
appearances, selfish pursuits, and the condition of my
own house, but rather to be concerned with spiritual
growth, unselfish service, and the condition of Your house.
I want to always have my priorities in order so that my
walk with You continues to grow closer and deeper.*

By His Spirit

❖ Read and Consider ❖

Zechariah 4

"So he said to me, 'This is the word of the LORD to Zerubbabel: "Not by might nor by power, but by my Spirit," says the LORD Almighty'" (Zechariah 4:6).

Zerubbabel was given a huge responsibility: to rebuild the temple in Jerusalem. While the prophets encouraged him in this task, it was Zerubbabel's sole responsibility to see it through to completion. How inadequate he must have felt!

Every time you feel you are unable to do what God has called you to do, when you feel as though you don't have what it takes to move into the life God has for you, worship is the way to respond. First of all, be grateful that you feel the way you do because that means you are humble and dependent on God. Rejoice if you feel inadequate to the task because that means you are going to have to depend on God to enable you to do it. And He will, because "the one who calls you is faithful and he will do it" (1 Thessalonians 5:24).

You don't have to make your life happen; you just have to worship God and let *Him* make it happen. You don't have to strive to figure out your purpose; you have to strive to know God, for *He* knows your purpose. Your praise will illuminate the path by which God will guide you into your future and the purpose He has for you. You won't accomplish it; He will. Not by might or power, but by His Spirit.

❖

Almighty God, I acknowledge I cannot do all You have called me to do, except that Your Spirit enables me to do it. I depend on You to help me get where I need to go. I worship You as the light of my life who illuminates my path and guides my every step. I praise You as the all-powerful God of the universe for whom nothing is too hard.

DEVELOPING *a* HEART *for* WORSHIP

❧ Read and Consider ❧
Zechariah 7

"Ask all the people of the land and the priests, 'When you fasted and mourned in the fifth and seventh months for the past seventy years, was it really for me that you fasted?'" (Zechariah 7:5).

Zechariah had a message for his people—and it wasn't a pleasant one. He wanted them to understand that just worshiping, fasting, and keeping all the rituals of the faith was of no value. It meant nothing to God because it meant nothing to the people. They were not doing these acts out of love and devotion for God.

It's not enough that you should read about worship, hear worship songs, or listen to other people worship; you must actually worship God with a heart full of love for Him. It's in your own personal worship times that you will develop an intimate relationship with Him. If you are ever worshiping God by yourself and you don't sense His intimate presence, continue to praise and worship Him until you do. It's not that you have to try hard to get God to be close to you. He has chosen to dwell in your praise. But you do have to give Him time to break down the barriers in your soul and penetrate the walls of your heart so that He can pour Himself into you.

God must always be the complete focus of your worship. But when you worship Him, there will be gifts and blessings that He will pour out on you.

In worship you will sense why you were created. You will hear God speak to your heart because He has softened it and made it less resistant. In worship you will experience God's love. He will change your emotions, attitudes, and patterns of thought. He will pour out His Spirit upon you and make your heart open to receive all He has for you. He will give you clarity of mind so you can better understand His Word. He will refresh, renew, enrich, enlighten, heal, free, and fulfill you. He will breathe life into the dead areas of your existence. He will infuse you with His power and His joy. He will redeem and transform you and your situation. He will fill your empty places, liberate you from bondage, take away your fear and doubt, grow your faith, and give you peace. He will break the chains that imprison you and restore you to wholeness. He will lift you above your circumstances and limitations, and motivate you to help others find life in Him.

❧

Dear Lord, help me to never get to the point where I take Your presence in my life lightly. Help me not take for granted the things I do for You so that they lose their life and meaning in my heart. I know my fasting, praying, and worshiping mean nothing to You if they mean nothing to me. Help me to do all things in a way that pleases You.

Jesus Teaches Us How *to* Pray

❧ Read and Consider ❧

Matthew 6:9-13

"This, then, is how you should pray: 'Our Father in heaven, hallowed be your name, your kingdom come, your will be done on earth as it is in heaven. Give us today our daily bread. Forgive us our debts, as we also have forgiven our debtors. And lead us not into temptation, but deliver us from the evil one'" (Matthew 6:9-13).

Few people can enter a church without hearing this prayer either spoken or sung. It's known around the world. In Jerusalem there is a building that has over one hundred beautiful ceramic tiles inscribed with the words of this prayer in many languages of the world. Some people call it the "Our Father" or the "Lord's Prayer." Whatever title you use, it's accurate to say that this is probably the best known and most repeated prayer in the Christian world.

It is called the Lord's Prayer because Jesus, our Lord, taught His disciples to pray in this manner. He did not intend for them to mindlessly repeat this prayer over and over. Rather, He was laying out a pattern of prayer for them, and for us today as His disciples, to follow. There is rich meaning in each phrase.

Our Father in heaven, hallowed be your name is a declaration of praise acknowledging that God is holy and to be revered. His name is never to be taken lightly. Not only is He Lord of heaven and earth, but He is also our heavenly Father.

Your kingdom come, your will be done on earth as it is in heaven reminds us that God wants us to pray for His will to rule and reign in our world. As we pray and invite God to manifest His power in the midst of earth's suffering and pain, He will move in response to our prayers. His power and presence will enter our lives and will work out on earth what He has willed in heaven.

Give us today our daily bread declares our dependence upon God as our provider. All that we have now has been provided by His gracious hand. Everything we need in the future will come from Him day by day as we seek Him for it.

Forgive us our debts, as we also have forgiven our debtors is a statement in which we not only ask God for forgiveness, but we are also reminded that we must forgive others. Just as we are indebted to God because He forgave our sins, so we must willingly forgive those who have sinned against us.

Lead us not into temptation, but deliver us from the evil one. Jesus was not saying that God tempts people but that we have an enemy of our souls who would like nothing better than to defeat us. We all go through times of temptation from which we need divine deliverance. But Jesus paid an enormous price so we could be free and have power over the evil one.

Some manuscripts include: *For yours is the kingdom and the power and the glory forever. Amen.* All that God is and all that God does lives forever. There has never been and never will be anything greater than God in all the universe. This declaration reminds us of that.

❧

Heavenly Father, I praise Your holy name. I pray You will reign in my life and rule in this world. Pour out Your Spirit on this land so that we may do Your will. I depend on Your provision, forgiveness, and protection from the enemy. I praise You for all You are and all You do.

ASK, SEEK, *and* KNOCK

❦ Read and Consider ❦
Matthew 7:7-12

"Ask and it will be given to you; seek and you will find;
knock and the door will be opened to you. For everyone
who asks receives; he who seeks finds; and to him who
knocks, the door will be opened" (Matthew 7:7-8).

I f Jesus instructs us to ask, seek, and knock, why do we sometimes struggle to pray as much as we should? One reason could be that we doubt God will really hear and answer. Or we fear being disappointed if we ask for too much or for the wrong thing. Or our own self-sufficiency may keep us from total dependency upon God. Or perhaps we feel that if God knows what we need before we ask, why do we need to ask?

Yet Jesus Himself, who knew the heart of Father God better than anyone, teaches us that we must be diligent to tell God our needs and pursue Him by faith. "Without faith it is impossible to please God, because anyone who comes to him must believe that he exists and that he rewards those who earnestly seek him" (Hebrews 11:6).

Often we feel reluctant to bring our needs to God because we think our problems are too big, or too small, or our own fault—therefore, we can't bother God about them. But the good news is that we are God's beloved children, and He is our loving Father. We can feel free to ask Him for the desires of our heart and that they be in alignment with His will. "Seek his kingdom, and these things will be given to you as well" (Luke 12:31).

Jesus' promise is that if we imperfect parents desire to give good gifts to our children, "how much more will your Father in heaven give good gifts to those who ask him!" (Matthew 7:11). So don't hesitate to ask, seek, and knock, knowing that your heavenly Father hears and will answer.

❦

Lord, I come to You in faith, believing You are
God, and that You reward those who diligently seek
You. Your Word says You desire to give good gifts to
those who ask for them. I ask that the desires of my
heart be aligned with Your will so that they will
come to pass. I knock on the door of opportunity for
my life, and anticipate it being opened by You.

The VALUE of TIME
ALONE with GOD

✤ Read and Consider ✤

Matthew 14:22-23

"After he had dismissed them, he went up on a
mountainside by himself to pray. When evening
came, he was there alone" (Matthew 14:23).

Solitude—time alone—means different things to different people. Some have too little of it and treasure times of quiet with no one else around. Others who live alone may feel they have too much of it. "Alone" to them means "lonely."

There are examples throughout the Gospels of the value Jesus placed on solitude. He was surrounded each day by His disciples who He was teaching and training, and also by crowds of people who were hungry for His touch. Although He was fully God, He was also fully human. In order for Jesus to have the strength to minister continually, He had to make prayer a priority. When painful things happened, Jesus handled them by spending time alone with His Father. "When Jesus heard what had happened [the death of John the Baptist], he withdrew by boat privately to a solitary place" (14:13). Jesus was often alone, but never lonely. He was always spending time with God.

We don't have to ever be lonely either. When we are alone, we can be with God. On the other hand, if Jesus depended on regular times away to communicate with God in solitude, how much more do *we* need to make such times of quiet a priority in our lives!

We often speak of "finding" time to be alone with God, but that valuable time has a way of getting lost in the midst of our overcrowded schedules. We must change our focus from trying to

299

find time to *making* time. I heard of one mother who paused each day and threw her apron over her head. When the children saw that, they knew it was Mama's time alone with God! It doesn't matter *how* we do it, we just have to do it.

If you find it hard to make time for solitude, remember that your heavenly Father is wanting and waiting to spend time with you. "The LORD your God is with you, he is mighty to save. He will take great delight in you, he will quiet you with his love, he will rejoice over you with singing" (Zephaniah 3:17). Don't keep God waiting.

Whether you are surrounded by a noisy family or you live entirely isolated, take great joy in making time to be alone with God. "Alone" never has to mean "lonely" when you have the Lord in your life!

❧

> *Dear Lord, help me to find the time I need every day to be alone with You. Escaping all the diversions and busyness seems to be a constant struggle, and I need a greater ability to shut out everything and find solitude with You in prayer. Help me to secure a place of peace and quiet so that I can hear Your voice speaking to my heart.*

CREATING *a* SYMPHONY *of* PRAYER

Matthew 18:18-20

"Again, I tell you that if two of you on earth agree
about anything you ask for, it will be done for you
by my Father in heaven" (Matthew 18:19).

O ne of the first things we need to learn about praying with others is the need for unity. Jesus said "If you agree...it will be done." That word *agree* is very important. The Greek word for "unity" is *sumphoneo*. It's where we get the word "symphony." In order to have harmony, there are a number of things we need to agree on.

First of all, we need to agree on the basics, which are the very foundation of our faith. Foremost among these is that Jesus is "the way and the truth and the life" and "no one comes to the Father except through" Him (John 14:6). We must also agree that the Bible is inerrant—without fault in its original translation—and inspired by God. We agree that Jesus was born of a virgin and lived a sinless life, that He died for our sins and rose from the dead, and that whoever believes in Him will have everlasting life.

Second, we need to be in agreement about what we are requesting from God. For example, if your marriage is in trouble, you can pray with your spouse or with a trusted friend and agree together that marriage is a covenant ordained by God. Then ask God to be at the center of your marriage and a reflection of Christ's love for His people (Ephesians 5:31-32). Or another example is if you are in need or struggling in an area, you can join one or more people and agree that Satan will not have victory in this situation.

The Bible says that one can put a thousand to flight and two can put ten thousand to flight (Deuteronomy 32:30). If you do the math, you will see how powerful two or more people can be when they join together and agree in prayer about whatever concerns them.

Unity within the body of Christ is extremely important to God, and unity in prayer is a critical part of that. The very night He was betrayed, Jesus prayed for all believers everywhere that we might experience true unity. "May they be brought to complete unity to let the world know that you sent me and have loved them even as you have loved me" (John 17:23).

When we agree together in prayer, our words create a rich symphony of intercession that is carried to the very throne of God. Nothing is more beautiful to the ear of the Lord than the sound of the unified prayers of His people. Let the music begin.

❧

Lord, help me to find believers with whom I can
agree in prayer on a regular basis. I pray we will be
in agreement about the truth of Your Word and the
power of Your Holy Spirit. You have said that one can
put a thousand to flight and two can put ten thousand
to flight. I pray for enough prayer partners to put all
of the enemy's forces attacking our lives to flight.

LEARNING *to* BELIEVE

*"If you believe, you will receive whatever you
ask for in prayer" (Matthew 21:22).*

What a great promise from our Lord! All we have to do is believe. But that's not so easy, is it? It's easier to doubt than it is to have faith to believe for the answers to our prayers. But faith is not about trusting in faith itself, it's about trusting God and what He says in His Word. It's about confidently claiming the promises of God, believing that God means what He says.

Jesus promised His disciples, "You'll receive whatever you ask for in prayer," on one condition: "If you believe." Believe in what? In our own request? Does this mean we can get whatever we ask for, anything at all, no matter how grandiose our desires? The answer is no. Are we to believe in our own great faith? We would be foolish to do that. We are to believe God and trust in His perfect will.

It's important to remember that God's will never contradicts His Word. Yes, we are to pray for whatever we need, but if those needs and desires run contrary to the will of God, He is not going to give them to us. Our loving Father will not go against His own nature or give us that which is detrimental to the best that He has for us. At times, something may seem to us to be perfectly within God's will—and we should pray with all our heart—but we should still remember that only God sees the big picture. In the long run, what we are praying for may not be what's best at all.

Praying is not telling God what to do. Praying is communicating the desires of your heart. It's trusting that *God* knows what to do and He will answer in His way and in His time. Faith is believing God hears and will do the right thing. When you also pray that God's will be done in your life, you can release your requests into God's hands, believing He has heard you and will do what's best.

Faith has to do with believing that God is who He says He is and will do what He says He will. In order to increase your faith, read God's Word and ask Him to help you learn to believe Him. Ask Him to give you a greater measure of faith and the ability to walk confidently in the faith He has given you.

❦

Dear God, increase my faith to believe for great things. Help me to have faith enough to not pray too small. I know it is not about trusting in faith itself, but trusting in You. It's not about believing in my own ability to believe, but rather it is believing in Your ability and promise to hear and answer. Take away all unbelief in me.

WANTING GOD'S WILL

*"Going a little farther, he fell with his face to the
ground and prayed, 'My Father, if it is possible,
may this cup be taken from me. Yet not as I
will, but as you will'" (Matthew 26:39).*

It's important to pray for God's will to be done in our lives, but how do we align our own desires and will with what God wants? How do we learn to *want* God's plan for us more than we want our own?

Jesus' passionate prayer in the garden of Gethsemane is the greatest model for us of praying with absolute honesty and total submission. He knew He would be arrested, tortured, and put to death as part of God's plan of redemption for the world. The "cup" that He was about to drink was the cup of divine wrath for the sins of humanity, and He was about to take upon Himself the penalty for that sin. He anticipated the physical pain and suffering as well as the emotional agony of being separated from His Father, and He asked that this cup of suffering be taken away. The intensity of this prayer gives us a glimpse of Jesus' humanity. If it wasn't going to be painful, He would not have agonized to this extent.

You and I face times that aren't easy. We look ahead and sense God saying, "Stay in this difficult marriage," "Love that rebellious child," "Return kindness to that belligerent boss." Just like Jesus did, we can ask God to remove the cup of pain from our lives, to give us an easier way out. But like Jesus, we have to also say: "Yet not as I will, but as You will." The easy way may not be the best way. The easy way is often not the way God has for you.

God wants us to pray about all things, but He wants us to pray according to His will. That's why it's important to ask God to reveal His will to us and help us pray accordingly. When we don't know what God's will is, we should always include in our prayer, "Lord, let Your perfect will be done in this situation."

❧

Heavenly Father, more than anything I want Your will to be done in my life. Even though I want You to take away all my pain and suffering, and I want all of Your blessings, and I want things to turn out the way I want them to, above all I want Your will to be done and not my own. Reveal Your will and help me to pray accordingly.

The POWER to FIGHT TEMPTATION

❧ Read and Consider ❧

Mark 1:9-13

*"He was in the desert forty days, being tempted
by Satan. He was with the wild animals, and
angels attended him" (Mark 1:13).*

How often is the word *temptation* used lightly? We might comment on some food that looks particularly "tempting," or we laughingly say we're "yielding to temptation" when we buy something we want but don't absolutely need.

Most often, however, temptation is not a laughing matter. When we crave, desire, or are enticed by something that is wrong for us, we are experiencing temptation in its most dangerous form. The Bible says we have an enemy, Satan, who would like nothing more than to tempt us to sin and destroy our lives.

Jesus knew what it was to experience temptation. Immediately following His baptism, Jesus was led into the desert by the Holy Spirit where He was tempted by Satan for 40 days. God allowed this time of testing in Jesus' life, but it was Satan who did the tempting (Matthew 4:1-11).

Even though Jesus was God incarnate, He was also fully human. How could any human being withstand a full 40 days of intensive satanic attack? Based on what Scripture relates of the life of Christ and His regular habit of spending time alone with God, we know that Jesus did not enter this grueling time of temptation unprepared. Prayer and His knowledge of the Scriptures girded Him for battle. We should strive to be like Him in our preparation for enemy attacks.

The best time to pray about temptation is *before* you fall into it.

After the lure presents itself, resisting temptation becomes much more difficult. The model prayer Jesus taught us to pray as a matter of course is a good place to start. "Lead us not into temptation, but deliver us from the evil one" (Matthew 6:13). We can also prepare to do as Jesus did and rebuke the enemy with God's Word. That means we must read it enough to know what it says. In addition to that, we can call on the Lord. "Because he himself suffered when he was tempted, he is able to help those who are being tempted" (Hebrews 2:18).

None of us is immune to temptation. We might think that as we mature in the Lord, temptation will be less intense. But the truth is, we must continue to watch out for subtle temptations and ask God to give us discernment. Never hesitate to cry out to God when you are tempted. The temptation is not the sin. Whether we sin or not has to do with whether we *entertain* the temptation or turn to God immediately. God is not only able to help us stand strong against temptation, but He can also deliver us out of it.

❧

Lord, equip me to resist all temptation from the enemy.
Enable me to be so prepared before temptation happens
that I recognize the enemy's tactics from the moment
they manifest. Teach me to rebuke the enemy by having
a great knowledge of Your Word. Enable me to resist
entertaining temptation for even a moment, but rather
to turn to You immediately so that I can stand strong.

FINDING FREEDOM FROM WHAT KEEPS YOU BOUND

❧ Read and Consider ❦

Mark 9:14-32

*"He replied, 'This kind can come out
only by prayer'" (Mark 9:29).*

Jesus' disciples attempted to exorcise a demon from an afflicted boy, but they failed. After Jesus responded to the frantic father's plea for help, the demon left the child and the disciples were left bewildered. Why had Jesus succeeded where their sincere efforts had not?

Jesus said that prayer was the key to releasing this person from bondage to satanic forces. Some manuscripts include fasting along with prayer. Fasting always increases the power of our prayers. The disciples had apparently not prepared themselves well enough by praying and fasting first.

In Matthew 18:18, Christ taught, "Whatever you bind on earth will be bound in heaven, and whatever you loose on earth will be loosed in heaven." God gives us His authority on earth. When we call on that authority, God releases power to us from heaven. Because it's God's power and not ours, we become the vessel through which His power flows. When we pray, we bring that power to bear upon the situation, allowing the power of God to work through our powerlessness. When we pray, we are humbling ourselves before God and saying, "I need Your presence and Your power, Lord. I can't do this without You." When we don't pray, we are in effect saying that we have no need of anything outside of ourselves.

If you are facing a difficult situation within your own life, you have authority in the name of Jesus to stop evil and permit good. You can submit to God in prayer whatever bondage controls you—such as alcoholism, addiction, laziness, depression, infirmity, abusiveness, confusion, anxiety, fear, or failure—and fast and pray to be released from it. God will set you free.

❧

Lord, I see in Your Word that prayer is the key to being set free, and prayer with fasting together is even more powerful. I pray You will help me to understand the authority You have given me in prayer to release Your power from heaven in order to see freedom happen in my life and in the lives of those for whom I pray.

Nothing Is Impossible *with* God

❦ Read and Consider ❦

Mark 10:17-31

*"Jesus looked at them and said, 'With man this
is impossible, but not with God; all things
are possible with God'" (Mark 10:27).*

The most exciting thing about God being all-powerful is that it
means *with God, all things are possible.* There is nothing too hard
for Him. Gabriel told Mary that "nothing is impossible with God,"
and look what happened to her (Luke 1:37). Jesus said, "All things
are possible with God," and look what He accomplished! There is
nothing that God cannot do. God's power is not limited.

If you have ever lived through an earthquake, tornado, or hur-
ricane, you know that their power is overwhelming and frightening.
Yet God has absolute power over all those things. May I suggest
that we don't really *want* to experience the *full* magnitude of God's
power?

Suffice it to say that God has far more power than is necessary
to meet your needs and lift you above your situation. He has more
than enough power to rescue you from your circumstances and help
you do things you could not do without Him. If God is so powerful
that He can create something from nothing or give life to the dead,
then think what He can do in your life. He has the power to do
whatever is necessary, and He doesn't want you to doubt it.

❦

*God, You are all-powerful and nothing is too hard for You,
not even changing the most difficult circumstances of my
life. What is impossible for me is not impossible for You,*

so I ask that You would do the impossible and transform
me into a holy person full of Your love, peace, and joy.
Enable me to do great things by the power of Your Spirit.

The POWER *of* FORGIVENESS

❧ Read and Consider ☙

Mark 11:20-25

"And when you stand praying, if you hold anything against anyone, forgive him, so that your Father in heaven may forgive you your sins" (Mark 11:25).

O f all the commands in Scripture, the instruction to forgive those who have hurt us is one of the most difficult to keep. Our natural human tendency is to hold on to the hurt inflicted upon us, to nurse our wounds and hold grudges. Or, at the very least, we separate ourselves forever from the individual who is the source of our pain so that we cannot be hurt by that person again.

There are times, such as in cases of abuse, when physical separation is necessary. When a crime has been committed, justice and forgiveness go hand in hand. The courts of law must hold a perpetrator accountable, and God will hold that person accountable in the final judgment, but we must still forgive that person. In these verses, Jesus was talking about the spiritual obligation that we have to forgive each other because we have been so graciously forgiven by our heavenly Father. To refuse to forgive others reveals that our hearts do not understand the level of forgiveness we have received.

To forgive does not mean we necessarily forget; we may remember, but we choose not to allow the memory to keep us bitter. We don't replay the offense over and over in our mind. To forgive does not mean to say that what happened to hurt us doesn't matter; it *does* matter or it wouldn't need forgiveness. But we must remember that forgiving someone doesn't make that person right; it makes *you* free. When you forgive, you are set free from the bondage of carrying around the hurt, the pain, the grudge. You can let it go and move on with your life.

When we choose not to forgive, we end up stuck in the past and walking in the dark (1 John 2:9-11). Because we can't see clearly, we stumble around in confusion. This throws our judgment off and we make mistakes. We become weak, sick, and bitter. Other people notice all this because unforgiveness shows in the face, words, and actions of those who have it. People see it, even if they can't specifically identify what it is, and they don't feel comfortable around it.

The good news is that when we choose to forgive, not only do we benefit, but so do the people around us.

❧

> *Lord, I pray You would reveal any place in my heart*
> *where I have not forgiven someone. I know I have*
> *asked this before, but I also know how easy it is to let*
> *resentment build up, even though I try not to allow that*
> *to happen. I don't want to inhibit the forgiveness You*
> *have for me because I have not forgiven someone else.*

OUR GOD-GIVEN AUTHORITY

❖ Read and Consider ❖
Luke 10:17-22

*"I have given you authority to trample on snakes
and scorpions and to overcome all the power of the
enemy; nothing will harm you" (Luke 10:19).*

What does it mean that we have authority to overcome all the power of the enemy? Why did Jesus think it was so important to tell us this? Because our enemy is powerful, and he is working every day to hurt us, destroy us, and make us ineffective for God.

If we don't take our enemy seriously, it is much easier for Satan to manipulate and deceive us. We are all involved in a spiritual battle with an enemy who won't let up. Even though it is people who do evil things to us, we have to keep in mind that it is our ultimate enemy, the devil, who is behind it. "For our struggle is not against flesh and blood, but against the rulers, against the authorities, against the powers of this dark world and against the spiritual forces of evil in the heavenly realms" (Ephesians 6:12). Even when we are being attacked by a person, recognizing who our real enemy is will be the first step in standing strong.

The second step has to do with acknowledging the authority that has been given to us by Christ Himself. Our enemy is not as powerful as he wants us to believe. Satan is not even close to being as powerful as God is, but he wants us to think he is. And he will overpower anyone who doesn't understand that. Because of what Jesus accomplished on the cross, the devil is a defeated foe. He can't take our life and do what he wants with it unless we allow him to. He can't have our soul unless we give it to him. He can only accomplish what he does through lies and deception. It's our responsibility to recognize his lies and expose them for what they are. We do that by standing on the ultimate truth, which is the Word of God. The Word of God says that we have been given authority "to overcome all the power of the enemy." But so often we let the enemy get away with too much because we don't exercise our God-given authority to control his access to our lives.

When we face difficulty or oppression, we never need to live under the assumption that it's "just our bad luck." Instead, we can go before God in prayer, asking Him for discernment, wisdom, and strength to exercise the authority He has given us. Then we can get up and walk through our day as children of the King with all the honors, privileges, and authority of rightful heirs.

❧

Dear God, help me to fully understand the authority You have given me over the enemy of my soul. Thank You, Jesus, that because of what You accomplished on the cross, the enemy is defeated. Enable me to always recognize his lies and deception and be able to stand strong on the truth of Your Word so that I can control his access to my life.

WHY PRAYER WORKS

❧ Read and Consider ☙
Luke 11:5-13

*"I tell you, though he will not get up and give him the bread
because he is his friend, yet because of the man's boldness he
will get up and give him as much as he needs" (Luke 11:8).*

This parable about prayer gives us some insight into how Jesus
expects us to pray—Boldly! Understanding why prayer works
can help us to pray boldly. Here are a few reasons we can pray with
confidence:

Prayer works because of what Jesus did. When we pray we are
applying Jesus' victory through the cross, taking the rule away
from Satan and establishing the rule of God. In that way we stop
the devil's work and establish the Lord's will. We take things that
are wrong and make them right. When we become believers, God
doesn't take us to heaven right away—and for a good reason. There
are things He has for us to do on earth. He wants us to expose
the enemy's lies and proclaim God's truth. He wants us to bring
down the enemy's strongholds and set the captives free. He wants
us to bring health where there is sickness, love where there is fear,
forgiveness where there is condemnation, revelation where there is
spiritual blindness, and wholeness where there is a fracture in our
lives. God's Word reveals that this can be accomplished when we
pray. When we understand this, it's easier to pray boldly.

Prayer works because we live God's way. In order to get our prayers
answered, we need to walk in obedience to God's laws. "We have
confidence before God and receive from him anything we ask,
because we obey his commands and do what pleases him" (1 John
3:21-22). You may be thinking that this is enough to disqualify you

The Power of Praying Through the Bible

right there. How can you always do what pleases God? But God is merciful in this too, because we can pray about these issues as well. He will even help us to obey if we ask Him. Remember, the answers to our prayers are not earned by our obedience. But our privilege to pray boldly is rooted in our relationship with Father God. And He has called us to walk as obedient children.

Prayer works because we don't hesitate to ask. God wants us to be bold in our asking. Being bold isn't stomping into the throne room of God and demanding what we think we deserve, but it is recognizing that God wants to do above and beyond what we think possible (Ephesians 3:20). This knowledge makes us courageous to ask God to do great things in us, through us, and around us. Jesus' story about the man who persisted in asking for bread from his neighbor suggests that we not only ask persistently but boldly as well.

I once had someone tell me they prayed only about the "big stuff" because they didn't want to waste any of their prayers on small things, as if God only allows us a certain number of prayer requests per lifetime, so we had better make our prayers count. God says we are to ask continually—to pray without ceasing. He wants us to pray *all* the time about *everything*. God is always ready to hear from us. He wants us to ask because He wants to answer.

❧

Lord, help me to be bold and persistent in prayer. I don't want to be arrogant or presumptuous, as if You owe me anything, but rather to be confident in what Jesus accomplished on the cross that took away Satan's rule and established Your own. Help me to have great faith that prayer works so that I am confident enough to ask for great things, knowing that You will answer in a great way.

LET TIME *with* GOD TAKE *the* PLACE *of* WORRYING

❧ Read and Consider ❧
Luke 12:22-34

*"Who of you by worrying can add a single
hour to his life?" (Luke 12:25).*

None of us can add a single moment to our lives by worrying. In fact, the opposite is probably more true; we actually *lose* life when we worry. We are wasting the time we spend worrying, and we may be causing health problems that could ultimately shorten our lives.

Jesus tells us to refuse to worry because no matter what problems we have, He has already overcome them. "In this world you will have trouble. But take heart! I have overcome the world" (John 16:33). We can find freedom from anxiety just by spending time with Him. "When anxiety was great within me, your consolation brought joy to my soul" (Psalm 94:19).

When you are anxious, it means you aren't trusting God to take care of you. But He will prove His faithfulness if you run to Him. "Do not set your heart on what you will eat or drink; do not worry about it. For the pagan world runs after all such things, and your Father knows that you need them. But seek his kingdom, and these things will be given to you as well" (Luke 12:29-31).

God says we don't need to be anxious about *anything;* we just need to pray about *everything.* So instead of worrying, actively bring your cares to Him. Prayer is not empty, powerless, wishful thinking. It is a powerful connection with the One who is the source of our comfort, strength, and hope. So take your worries about the future to the One who holds your future in His hands.

❧

Dear God, I pray You would help me to stop worrying about things and start spending more time in Your presence. I know the time I waste by worrying is better used to pray and to hear Your voice speaking to my heart. You are my source of strength, hope, love, peace, and rest, and I want to be connected with You and not the things that worry me.

The HIDDEN POWER of PRAISE

❧ Read and Consider ❧
Luke 17:11-19

*"One of them, when he saw he was healed, came
back, praising God in a loud voice" (Luke 17:15).*

Ten lepers cried out to Jesus to heal them, and He did. But only
one of the ten returned and glorified God. How often are we like
the other nine? God does something great for us, and we just take it
in stride and don't fall down on our face at His feet and thank Him
for it. We often do that with healing, even when it is an answer to
a specific prayer we prayed. Many people think, *Well, this would
have happened anyway*. We often take the blessings of our health
for granted, instead of praising Him every day and giving thanks
that He is our Healer.

We need to praise Jesus that He is our healer whether we are
healed at that moment or not. We have to remember that God
heals in His way and in His time. Though Jesus came to earth as
our Healer, not all sickness or injury gets healed in this lifetime—at
least not the way *we* always want it to be. If He doesn't heal us the
way we ask Him to, it's because He has a greater plan and His glory
will be seen in it.

Some sickness comes from the enemy. God allowed Job to be
made sick by Satan. God allowed it for a reason. And even though
we don't understand the reason that God doesn't always heal us, we
can trust that He will bring good out of our suffering. If nothing
else, suffering forces us to draw closer to Him. And the closer we
are to Him, the more we will praise Him.

Praying passionately and fervently for our own healing is not a
problem because we are never apathetic about that, in fact we feel

quite strongly about it. And the sicker, the more miserable, pained, and incapacitated we are, the more fervently we pray. The Bible says that if we are suffering, we are to pray, and we are to pray with passion. That means burning, devout, sincere, wholehearted, and enthusiastic prayer. That means with our whole heart. When we pray for healing, we pray passionately, knowing that the answer is all up to God. He is our Healer, but not all of us find the healing we want when we want it. Sometimes the healing is delayed and we can grow weary in the waiting. Time passes very slowly when we are in pain or are suffering.

In God's presence there is healing. When we praise God, it invites His presence into our lives in a powerful way. Praising God for His presence and healing power in the midst of our sickness, pain, weakness, or misery, opens up a channel through which His healing presence can penetrate our lives to heal us or to sustain us as He sees fit. That is the hidden power of praising God.

❧

Heavenly Father, I thank You for all of the many blessings
You have bestowed upon my life. I praise You especially
as my healer and thank You for all the times You have
healed me in the past and will heal me in the future.
Thank You that even as I praise You now, Your healing
presence is penetrating my life and making me whole.

Pray That Your Faith Will Not Fail

❧ Read and Consider ❧

Luke 22:24-34

"But I have prayed for you, Simon, that your faith may not fail. And when you have turned back, strengthen your brothers" (Luke 22:32).

Jesus prayed that Peter's faith wouldn't fail. And He told Peter this in the middle of their last Passover meal together—the Last Supper—just before revealing that Peter would deny Him. Peter did fail an important test when he denied Jesus, but ultimately his faith did not fail. He could have given up and hid himself in fear and refused to follow God's call. He had denied the very Son of God, after all. But his faith wasn't in works, or perfection, or in himself; it was in Jesus. Peter went on to lead the first-century church even after his failure on the night of Christ's trial.

Jesus' prayer was answered. Peter's faith didn't fail. Jesus' prayer shows us that if our faith doesn't fail, we can endure hardship, face temptation, and even act faithlessly at times, but ultimately we can be God's instruments to do great things. Faith is like the foundation of a house. If the foundation gives way, the house will crumble. Pray that your faith will not fail so your foundation will stay solid.

Pray the same for others as well. When you don't know what to pray for someone—when that person's needs are so great or when you just can't put your finger on the problem—one of the things you can pray for is that his or her faith will not fail. In fact, that's a good prayer to pray for people any time you pray. Who among us doesn't need to have stronger faith?

❧

Father God, I pray my faith will not fail when I am put to the test. Help me to resist doubt and fear so that my foundation will be built solidly in Christ and therefore will not crumble. Enable me to be a person who strengthens the faith of others because my faith in You is so strong.

FATHER, I FORGIVE THEM

*"Jesus said, 'Father, forgive them, for they do not
know what they are doing.' And they divided
up his clothes by casting lots" (Luke 23:34).*

I don't know about you, but when I've just been hurt by someone, the last thing I want to do is pray for that person. Most of us are more interested in focusing on some kind of justice so that the offending person will have to pay for the hurt or damage he or she has inflicted. But not Jesus.

Jesus, who had done nothing wrong, was brutally beaten within an inch of His life. His head was pierced with a crown of long, thick thorns. His skin was slashed. His hands and feet had spikes driven through them. His cross was dropped into a hole in the ground. He hung there, naked and humiliated, for all the world to laugh at and scorn. Some said, "He saved others; let him save himself if he is the Christ of God, the Chosen One" (23:35). The way they crucified Him is horrifying beyond what we can imagine. Yet as Jesus was hanging on the cross and dying in agony, He prayed for the men who were killing Him. "Father, forgive them, for they do not know what they are doing." Such amazing forgiveness and love is hard to fathom.

As we look at the injustices in our lives, how do they compare with what Jesus endured? If He could forgive His torturers, surely we can choose to forgive too. Some of us have very deep wounds that may require time before total forgiveness is worked in us. But in most injustices that we've experienced, we can decide to let go of them quickly and completely and choose to forgive the offenders.

The good news is we can ask God to help us forgive. We can ask Him to show us His perspective in the matter. We can pray for Him to help us remember what Jesus endured and be able to say, "Father, I forgive them whether they knew what they were doing or not. I forgive them, not because they deserve it, but because I want to be like You."

❧

Lord, I pray You would help me to forgive others the way You do. You willingly forgave the unforgivable. I know I can't forgive the unthinkable without You enabling me to do so. Help me to take my focus off whether people deserve to be forgiven or not and instead focus on becoming more like You.

Responding *to* God's Love

❧ Read and Consider ☙
John 3:1-21

*"For God so loved the world that he gave his one
and only Son, that whoever believes in him shall
not perish but have eternal life" (John 3:16).*

God loved us so much that He gave us His Son. Jesus loved us
so much that He gave us His life. He did that so we could
always be close to God and live with Him for eternity. He did that
so we don't ever have to be separated from God. He did it so we
could find healing and wholeness for our body, soul, and spirit.
That's true love.

Jesus told Nicodemus the Old Testament story about the ancient
Israelites wandering in the desert constantly complaining. As a punishment for their complaining, God sent snakes into the camp. But
He also made a provision for those who would trust in Him. "The
LORD said to Moses, 'Make a snake and put it up on a pole; anyone
who is bitten can look at it and live'" (Numbers 21:8). Jesus was
making an analogy referring to His imminent death on the cross.
"The Son of Man must be lifted up, that everyone who believes in
him may have eternal life" (John 3:14-15).

Jesus died to save us not because we earned it, or we were good
enough, or deserved it because of how tough our lives are, but
because He loves us. Jesus did so much for us, yet all He asks in
return is that we look to Him and lift Him up in our hearts and
with our words.

God loves the whole world. He loves you and me. That kind of
love requires a response. That kind of love is an amazing invitation
that we must accept or in some way reject. Rejecting God's love can

take many forms; accepting His love takes only one—believing in His Son, Jesus.

All we have to do to respond to God's great love for us is say, "Jesus, I believe You died on the cross for me in order to give me forgiveness for my sins and eternal life with You. I receive that gift of salvation and redemption today and every day. I will respond to Your great love by lifting You up in praise continually, and loving You with all my heart forever."

❧

Lord Jesus, it is hard to comprehend love so great as Yours.
You laid down Your life for me so that I can live forever
with You. I ask You to help me to lay down my life fully for
You in serving Your purpose here on earth. My response to
Your first loving me is to love You wholeheartedly in return.

GOD ALWAYS HEARS YOU
WHEN YOU PRAY

❧ Read and Consider ❧
<hr>
John 11:1-44

*"Jesus looked up and said, 'Father, I thank you that you
have heard me. I knew that you always hear me, but I
said this for the benefit of the people standing here, that
they may believe that you sent me'" (John 11:41-42).*

J esus showed up for a close friend's funeral—after he had already
been buried. He deliberately missed it all. When Lazarus became
sick, his sisters sent word to Jesus. But Jesus stayed where He was for
two more days, saying to His disciples, "This sickness will not end in
death" (11:4), and then, "Our friend Lazarus has fallen asleep; but
I am going there to wake him up" (11:11). They didn't understand
what He meant, so He finally told them, "Lazarus is dead" (11:14).

By the time Jesus arrived, Lazarus had been in the tomb for four
days. Mary and Martha found it hard not to express their disappointment with Him. They knew He could have healed their brother, but
now they would have to wait until the resurrection to see him again.
In response Jesus said, "I am the resurrection and the life. He who
believes in me will live, even though he dies" (11:25).

When He arrived at the burial site, Jesus asked that the tomb be
opened. When the stone was rolled away, Jesus prayed, "Father, I
thank you that you have heard me." But this sounded like the *end*
of a prayer, not the beginning. Obviously, Jesus had been praying
all along. He had been talking to His Father for days as He always
did, but with full knowledge of this upcoming event.

It surely was difficult for Jesus to *not* be with His friends during
this tragic time. But He talked with God and waited for the right

moment so that God would be glorified in all that happened. He thanked His Father out loud for the benefit of all who were listening, and then He called Lazarus out of the tomb, grave clothes and all.

Jesus knew that His Father always heard Him. He knew days before that Lazarus would be resurrected. What a wonderful thing it is to be so certain that God always hears us when we pray. To trust completely that we are God's very own children and co-heirs with Christ (Romans 8:17).

God wants us to believe that He always listens to our prayers and will answer. He wants us to have an ongoing conversation with Him that keeps us in tune with His will and His purpose. He wants us to remember that Jesus brings life no matter how dead and helpless things seem. We just need to keep praying and believe in His ability and desire to answer.

❦

*Father God, I thank You that I am Your child
and a joint heir with Christ. Because of that, I can
trust that You always hear my prayers. Help me to
maintain ongoing communication with You, just
as Jesus did, so that I may have a deep and abiding
walk with You and You will be glorified by my life.*

REMAINING *in* HIM

"If you remain in me and my words remain in you, ask whatever you wish, and it will be given you " (John 15:7).

Eleven times the word *remain* is used in this short section. Eleven times Jesus chose this term to express the kind of relationship He wants us to have with Him. We are to remain in Christ. We are to remain in His love. If we do that, He will remain in us, His words will remain in us, and our lives will be fruitful.

So what does it mean to remain in Jesus? It means walking with Him and staying close and constantly plugged into Him, just like a branch remains with the vine. When a branch is part of the vine, it bears fruit. Conversely, when a branch is removed from the vine, it dies. Jesus says that if we remain in Him—spend time with Him, learn more about Him, get to know Him, be honest with Him, acknowledge our sins to Him—then we'll bear much fruit.

Jesus wants us to know His Word and allow it to become part of us. That means we need to be reading the Bible so that His words will be woven into the fabric of our being. We must know it so well that it becomes our guide, a source of renewal and knowledge of God's will. We must let it increase our understanding of who God is and who we are in Him.

God says if we remain in Him and let His words remain in us, we can ask of Him whatever we want and He will answer. That doesn't mean we will always get whatever we want. It means that because we are so closely entwined with Christ, we will have His mind and will learn how to pray for what He wants for our lives. When we do that, we end up doing His will and seeing answers to our prayers.

❧

*Lord, help me to walk close to You every day and stay
constantly in communication with You—both by
talking and listening to You speak to my heart. Help me
to stay deeply in Your Word, learning more about You
and getting to know You better. Help me to increase
in the knowledge of Your ways and Your will.*

JESUS' PRAYER *for* YOU

❧ Read and Consider ❧
John 17:20-26

*"My prayer is not for them alone. I pray also for
those who will believe in me through their message,
that all of them may be one, Father, just as you
are in me and I am in you" (John 17:20-21).*

Did you know that Jesus prayed for you and me? In this passage Jesus was interceding for His followers, but He was also speaking ultimately to every believer down through the ages.

We who have come to faith in Jesus can listen back in time to this moment when the Lord prayed for *us*. We were on His mind as He prepared to lay down His life in order to provide forgiveness for our sins, abundant life now, and life with Him for eternity.

Jesus prayed for us to have unity with other believers—across the nations, across cultures, across time, across the street, across the room, across the sanctuary. He also prayed for us to have unity with Him and the Father and the Holy Spirit so that our lives would convince others of who He is. He declared His love for us and promised to share His glory with us. He prayed for our salvation so that we could be with Him forever, and He promised to continue to make Himself known to us so we could experience more and more of His love.

Jesus was thinking of you centuries ago when He was praying. He lives today and every day to "intercede" for you (Hebrews 7:25). His desire is that you become one with Him and one with other believers, so that those who see you will believe in Him. Pray that you will always be one with Him and one with others. Thank Jesus that even way back then, He was already praying for you.

❧

Lord Jesus, just as You prayed for me to be one with You and one with others, I pray You would help me to do just that. Enable me to always be in unity with other believers, no matter what church, race, culture, denomination, city, state, or country they are from. Use this unity I have with You and with others to draw unbelievers to You.

BELIEVING WITHOUT SEEING

"Then Jesus told him, 'Because you have seen me,
you have believed; blessed are those who have not
seen and yet have believed'" (John 20:29).

We've all known people like Thomas. People who are hard to convince, who frequently have doubt, and who are often negative. People who don't believe in what they can't see. Probably all of us have been that way ourselves at one time or another.

Even after all the other disciples believed in the resurrection because they had seen Jesus in person, Thomas still wouldn't believe *them*. He didn't believe it until Jesus appeared in the room where all of them were gathered behind a locked door. One might think that alone would be enough evidence. But Thomas still had to put his fingers on Jesus' hands where the nails had been driven though them and on His side where the spear had pierced it. Jesus told Thomas that he was only believing because he had seen it, but those who believed *without* seeing would be blessed.

Those of us who believe that Jesus died for us and was resurrected from the dead are among the blessed. But God wants to bless us in many ways that require faith. Faith in His Word. Faith in His promises. Faith in His love, power, and goodness. He wants us to believe for things we can't yet see. Thomas needed help to believe. Often we do too. And like the father who brought his son to Jesus for healing, we can cry out to God, "I do believe; help me overcome my unbelief!" (Mark 9:24).

In times of doubt, we must be honest with God. We don't want to be people who won't believe until we see it. Because when it comes to prayer, the truth is we won't see it until we believe.

❧

Lord, I know You want to bless me in countless ways that require believing without seeing. Help me to have the kind of strong faith I need in order to overcome all doubt. Help me to have faith in Your Word and Your promises, and in Your love, goodness, and power. Help me to trust that You are answering my prayers even when I can't see it.

STAYING DEVOTED *to* PRAYER

❧ Read and Consider ❧

Acts 2:42-47

*"They devoted themselves to the apostles'
teaching and to the fellowship, to the breaking
of bread and to prayer" (Acts 2:42).*

When Peter preached the gospel to the crowds, they wanted to know what to do. After they had repented of their sins and been baptized, they devoted themselves to the apostles' teaching, to fellowship with one another, to communion, and to prayer. What was important to the new believers in the first century AD is just as important to believers today. Those four things mentioned above are essential for Christians to learn so they can mature and stay close to God. Studying the Bible, spending time with other believers, and partaking of communion are things that often occur in church but can happen anywhere. And they must be made a priority. Prayer is also something we deliberately need to set aside time for because it often gets set aside for other things.

So how can we be devoted to prayer like those early believers? They surely didn't quit their jobs or leave their family responsibilities in order to pray full-time. They went on with their lives in Christ but with a new focus—they were devoted to communication with God! What an awesome thought! They knew God was listening when they had a need or prayed for the needs of others.

We can be devoted to prayer in that same way as well. From the time we get up in the morning to when we go to bed at night, we always have a direct and open line to God. At any time we want, we can talk to God and He will hear and respond.

Devotion to prayer means that we are ready and willing to talk to God in Jesus' name whenever and wherever we feel the need to approach His throne. If we wake up in the middle of the night, we can ask God if there is someone who needs prayer right then. Wherever we are, at any time of day or night, for whatever needs God brings to mind, we can pray knowing God will hear and answer. That's devotion to prayer. That's how to make talking to God a priority.

❧

Dear God, help me to be diligent to study Your Word.
Teach me from it so that I can understand it perfectly. Help
me to be in communion with other believers so we can be
frequently in prayer together. Enable me to maintain that
direct line to You by praying constantly and devotedly as You
bring things to my mind that need to be covered in prayer.

PRAYING *for* SPIRITUAL
LEADERS *and* SERVANTS

❧ Read and Consider ❧
Acts 6:1-7

"They presented these men to the apostles, who prayed
and laid their hands on them" (Acts 6:6).

People in full-time ministry need our prayer support. In the case of these men who were chosen to handle the food ministry, they were spiritually wise men who would be taking on a huge responsibility. Their job would allow the apostles to focus on preaching and teaching.

Every job within the body of Christ—the church—is important, as signified by the care in which the food-program workers were chosen in the early church. The men chosen to deal with the daily distribution of food had to be men who were "known to be full of the Spirit and wisdom" (6:3). When the apostles prayed for them and laid their hands on them, it signified that they were set apart for special service to God (Numbers 27:22-23; Deuteronomy 34:9).

Carefully choosing and praying for church workers is important because Satan's attacks go first to those who are making a difference for the cause of Christ. Have you ever noticed that when a church is winning souls, attacks seem to come from all sides? Little problems creep in, disagreements arise, temptations sprout like weeds. How do we fight this? By praying for those who minister and serve.

Pray for the Sunday school teacher who has a class full of children. Pray for the pastoral staff who must make decisions that affect the entire congregation. Pray for the administrative staff who carry a heavy load of paperwork each week. Pray for the people who volunteer their time with the youth group. Pray that each of them will be able to stand against every temptation and that none will fall into the traps of the enemy.

Spiritual leadership at all levels is serious business. Be sure to hold up these servants in prayer.

❧

God, I ask You to bless all those in full-time ministry. I pray first of all for my pastor, that You would bless him and his family in every way. I pray for all other pastors and staff members at my church to be blessed by You and led by Your Spirit. Keep them all safe and protect them from any attacks of the enemy. Help them to stand strong against every temptation.

SEEING *in the* DARK

❧ Read and Consider ❧

Acts 9:1-19

*"The Lord told him, 'Go to the house of Judas on
Straight Street and ask for a man from Tarsus
named Saul, for he is praying'" (Acts 9:11).*

S aul had probably grown up doing a lot of praying. He was, after
all, a Pharisee. He was a well-educated Jew who felt that the
Christian movement was heretical and so decided to persecute the
Christians ruthlessly. But on that road to Damascus, a brilliant light
caused him to stop in his tracks. Jesus spoke directly to Saul and
blinded him. As a result, Saul was led into the city of Damascus
where he fasted and prayed as he had never done before.

Why was Saul blinded? It's difficult to do much when you are
suddenly without sight. Saul didn't know if this was a permanent
condition—at least until God spoke to him in a vision that Ananias
would come and restore his sight.

In a terrifying instant, Jesus had made Himself and His holiness
evident to Saul. During those three days that Saul fasted and prayed,
he surely turned his sight inward and examined his life. He believed
he had been doing the right thing by persecuting and arresting
Christians, but now he knew he had been persecuting Jesus. Even as
Paul prayed, God spoke to Ananias to go to him and pray for him
to receive his sight and be filled with the Holy Spirit.

Often God will allow us to get to a dark place in our lives where
we can't see without His help. And He often does that just before
the greatest revelation to us of our purpose and calling.

❧

Lord, just as You appeared to Saul and blinded him in order to get his attention and do a miraculous turnaround in his life, I know You have sometimes allowed me to get to a dark place in my own life where I cannot see without Your help. At those times, help me to do as Saul did and pray fervently, so that my spiritual sight can be restored and Your will be done.

CHANGING *the* WORLD *with* OUR PRAYERS

✤ Read and Consider ✤

Acts 13:1-3

*"While they were worshiping the Lord and fasting, the
Holy Spirit said, 'Set apart for me Barnabas and Saul
for the work to which I have called them'" (Acts 13:2).*

At a prayer meeting in the early church at Antioch, the Lord set
forth a plan that changed the world (Acts 13:1-3). Members of
that congregation recognized that change would involve two things:
their response to the Holy Spirit that brought them to prayer and
fasting, and their sending forth Barnabus and Saul in ministry.

And the world *was* changed. It is an observable fact that history
turned on the basis of that prayer meeting in Antioch, Syria, nearly
two thousand years ago. Any historical analysis shows that the
flow of events that has shaped the world as we know it today—
notably Western civilization—can be directly traced to that prayer
meeting.

People who pray and understand who they have been made to
be in Christ set the direction of history in their world—be it local,
regional, national, or international. Most of the believing church
today thinks of faith in Jesus Christ as an escape. But God says
He wants us to be instruments of redemption through intercessory
prayer, and ministry will flow out of that.

That's why it is so important to have prayer times with other
believers. In fact, *it is impossible to grow and develop to your fullest
potential independently of other believers.* It can't be "just me and
God all the way." We have a mutual dependence upon one another
because we are defined and refined within the context of a local body

of believers. *Building a people to do God's work happens in the local church when we are connected to and grow with the rest of the body of Christ. It is within that context that we find who we are created to be and what we are created to do.*

One of the most important things about being in a spiritual family is finding power in prayer through unity. When believers are in unity, there is a dynamic that adds power to our prayers and the confidence that God will answer in power. Believers praying together can change the world.

❧

*Lord, I know my calling and purpose is revealed in prayer.
I know it is defined within a church body of believers
with whom I can grow. Help me to be in the church body
You want me to be in so that I can pray with others in
unity and power and be refined by Your Spirit. Enable
me to be set apart for the work You have for me to do.*

WHEN WE FACE DECISIONS *and* DIFFICULTIES

"Paul and Barnabas appointed elders for them in each church and, with prayer and fasting, committed them to the Lord, in whom they had put their trust" (Acts 14:23).

Whenever God said something important to His people, or whenever an important decision had to be made, prayer, often accompanied by fasting, preceded it.

When the apostles had to choose a replacement for Judas, they gathered all the believers and "joined together constantly in prayer" (1:14).

When the believers in the church in Jerusalem began to face severe persecution, they prayed for boldness, raising "their voices together in prayer" (4:24).

When it became apparent to the Christians who had converted from Judaism that even Samaritans could be saved, they sent Peter and John to pray for these new followers of Jesus (8:15).

When Saul (Paul) had been struck blind, he fasted and prayed for three days, waiting to see what God would do (9:9).

When God wanted to send His message beyond the borders of Jerusalem, Judea, and Samaria and to "the ends of the earth" (1:8), He sent His message to Peter as he was praying (10:9) and to Cornelius as he was praying (10:30).

When Peter was imprisoned, the church gathered to pray for him (12:12).

God set apart Saul (Paul) and Barnabas while the church at Antioch was worshiping and fasting (13:2).

It comes as no surprise then, that when Paul and Barnabas had to help organize the leadership in the churches they planted, they did so only after prayer and fasting (14:23). They couldn't stay in each church; they had to move on. For a church to continue to thrive, solid Spirit-filled leaders were needed. So Paul and Barnabas sought the Lord and waited for His guidance. As a result the churches grew even after Paul and Barnabas left.

When we face big decisions, difficult circumstances, or hard questions, we should always turn to God first and pray. When we combine prayer with fasting, our prayers gain new power. We are trusting God and only God to be our nourishment and fill our hunger with His Spirit. It is especially powerful when we do that in unity with other believers. So when seeking the Lord's guidance, whether for issues regarding your personal needs, or for the needs of others, in your family, community, nation, or world, don't take a step without seeking God in prayer first.

❧

Lord God, I know when I fast and pray my prayers gain new power. Help me to do that whenever I have to make important decisions and I must have Your guidance. Help me to have the discipline to fast regularly so that I can be prepared when I have to make quick decisions. Make me ready to handle the great opportunities You have ahead for me.

A PARTING PRAYER

❧ Read and Consider ☙
Acts 21:1-16

"But when our time was up, we left and continued
on our way. All the disciples and their wives and
children accompanied us out of the city, and there
on the beach we knelt to pray" (Acts 21:5).

P aul and some believers in Tyre had a chance to meet up as Paul
was passing through and have fellowship for a week. The Holy
Spirit allowed these Christians to foresee the persecution Paul would
endure in Jerusalem (his destination), and they urged him not to go
there. They were worried about his safety and wanted to keep him
from harm. But Paul knew where the Lord wanted him to go, and
he would not be swayed from his purpose. As he departed, all of
the disciples and their families accompanied him to the ship, where
they knelt on the beach to pray before saying goodbye.

What better way to part from someone than to kneel in prayer?
These friends knew the dangers that lay ahead for Paul—and perhaps
eventually for them as persecution clouds began to build. Perhaps
they prayed for safety, but they surely also prayed for guidance and
boldness as they continued to work for the Lord, spreading His
message throughout the land. Perhaps they prayed that God would
bring them back together in fellowship again. And we know that
they prayed for each other when they were apart—Paul says so in
his letters.

We should remember to pray for people whenever we part from
them or they part from us. We can pray for our spouse as he or she
heads off to work. We can pray for our children as they go to school.
We can pray for our friends as they go about their daily business. We

can pray for our guests as they leave our home. Prayer is the most powerful tool we have as believers—our direct link with God. Let's not neglect it as we part from others.

❧

Dear God, help me to remember when I am with people who are about to leave on a journey—no matter how long or short—that I need to pray for them to have safety and guidance. Help me to not forget to pray for my own family members who are leaving the home to start their day, or any guests in my house who are leaving to get about their business or travel home.

WHEN WORDS DON'T COME

❧ Read and Consider ❧
Romans 8:18-30

*"In the same way, the Spirit helps us in our weakness. We
do not know what we ought to pray for, but the Spirit
himself intercedes for us with groans that words cannot
express. And he who searches our hearts knows the mind
of the Spirit, because the Spirit intercedes for the saints
in accordance with God's will" (Romans 8:26-27).*

When we pray, we are talking to God—maybe out loud, or in
a whisper, or silently. Probably most of us try to carefully
choose the words we say. We want to get it just right, to be specific, to
talk to God in a way that is pleasing to Him and that really expresses
our hearts. But sometimes the words won't come. Sometimes the
pain is too deep, the questions too difficult, the situation too con-
fusing or complex, the fear too acute. We want to talk to God, but
we don't know how to express what we feel. What then?

God promises that when we don't have the words, the Holy Spirit
prays *for* us! He searches our hearts and knows what's going on, and
He intercedes. He pleads with God on our behalf.

In times of grief or suffering—when we can barely see past the
pain to communicate with anyone…the Holy Spirit helps us to
pray.

In times of uncertainty—when we are so unsure of the path
ahead that we don't even know what kind of guidance to ask for…
the Holy Spirit helps us to pray.

In times of fear—when we are so frightened that we don't know
where to turn or whom to trust…the Holy Spirit helps us to pray.

In times of feeling overwhelmed—when the crushing weight

349

on our shoulders pushes us to our knees…the Holy Spirit helps us to pray.

When you can't find the words, simply sit with God and invite the Holy Spirit to enable you to communicate to God your deepest thoughts, feelings, fears, and doubts. He will help you pray.

❧

Lord, I don't know how to pray about certain things, but You do. Holy Spirit, help me in my weakness by interceding for me and through me. You know the will of the Father and You know what to pray. Guide me and teach me, especially when I have exhausted all words. Help me to communicate to God my deepest thoughts, feelings, fears, and doubts, so that my prayers are pleasing to God.

BEING FAITHFUL *in* PRAYER

❧ Read and Consider ❧

Romans 12:9-21

"Be joyful in hope, patient in affliction,
faithful in prayer" (Romans 12:12).

A consistent prayer life requires faithfulness. We have to take the time, maintain focus, and commit to not allowing too much time to go in between each prayer. And we need to not grow weary when our prayers seem to go unanswered.

The words Paul wrote to the Romans offer us some insight into the expectations that God places on our prayer lives. God doesn't require eloquence. He doesn't ask that our prayers be a certain length or that we pray a certain number of times every day. God asks that we be "faithful in prayer."

So what does faithfulness in prayer mean? It means making prayer an ongoing, consistent part of our lives. It's being diligent to set aside time for prayer. It's developing a sense of awe and stillness before God. It's praying for someone when we promised we would. It's taking time to sit before God and ask for His direction rather than rushing through each decision. It's seeking out God's purpose in our lives rather than merely reacting to our circumstances. It's continuing to come to Him even when we don't feel that we're getting any answers. When we are faithful to pray—to talk to our heavenly Father—we establish intimacy with Him. That alone is reason enough to be faithful in prayer.

❧

Lord, make me to be a person of powerful prayer. Teach
me how to be a prayer warrior who is always faithful to

pray. I don't want to be someone who prays sporadically, but rather a person so filled with joy and hope that I anticipate great things resulting from each prayer. Help me to have such great faith that I keep praying and never give up.

OVERFLOWING *with* JOY, PEACE, *and* HOPE

❧ Read and Consider ❧
Romans 15:7-13

*"May the God of hope fill you with all joy and peace as
you trust in him, so that you may overflow with hope
by the power of the Holy Spirit" (Romans 15:13).*

We live in a culture that is busy with activities and offers more options than we could ever have time for. We sometimes run on empty more than full, much less overflowing. Yet Paul's prayer for the believers in Rome was that their souls would be so full of joy, peace, and trust that they would overflow with hope. This was to happen not by their own strength or the sheer force of their wills, but "by the power of the Holy Spirit."

Would you like to overflow with hope? Would you like to be a person whose joy seems to light up every room, whose peace can be felt in even the tensest situations? Then by the power of the Holy Spirit, praise God! It's no accident that in this passage Paul quotes from Old Testament passages about praising God, singing hymns to His name, and rejoicing! That's how we find hope in God. Through praise and worship. When we connect to God and honor His presence in our lives, and when we praise Him for His character and the evidences of His works in us, we have so much of Him in us that He spills over. God's gifts in us become our gifts to those around us. That's when we overflow with the joy, peace, and hope that comes only from God.

❧

*Dear God, help me to resist the things that would deplete
my soul or minimize my strength. Fill me instead with Your
hope, peace, and joy, so much so that they overflow from me
to others. I praise You for who You are and thank You that
as I do, Your Holy Spirit pours new life into me. Fill me
afresh with Your Spirit today and take all hopelessness away.*

The IMPORTANCE *of* SPIRITUAL AUTHORITY

❖ Read and Consider ❖

1 Corinthians 11:2-10

*"For this reason, and because of the angels, the
woman ought to have a sign of authority
on her head" (1 Corinthians 11:10).*

Paul wrote that women should have a sign of authority on their heads. This refers to spiritual authority, and it is still very important today. While we may not actually put a covering over our heads, we must submit to divinely appointed authority. It's part of God's order. God won't pour into our lives all He has for us until we are in a right relationship with the proper authority figures He has placed in our lives. They are there for our protection and benefit. God's power is too precious and too powerful to be let loose in an unsubmitted soul.

Women need this spiritual covering. It protects them from the enemy of their soul. When spiritual covering is done right—with strength, humility, kindness, and respect, and not with abuse, arrogance, harshness, or lovelessness—it becomes a place of safety for a woman. It brings a right order to her life.

More and more believing women are being given an open door to become all they were created to be. They are moving out in different areas of expertise and ministry and making important differences in their realms of influence. They are realizing that they are not just an afterthought in the order of God's creation, but were created for a special purpose. More and more they are enabled to fulfill their destiny because more men are rising up to their place of spiritual authority and leadership. This is an answer to the prayers of countless women and something for which everyone must praise God. If a woman will trust God's power to flow through the authorities He has placed over her, she can bloom and grow and change her world by the power of God's Spirit. Pray to be in right order with the spiritual authority in your life.

❦

> *Lord, help me to be in right relationship to the authority figures You have put in my life. I know they are there for my protection. I want my life to be in perfect order so I am submitted in the right way. I don't want to do anything that would delay or prevent my becoming all You created me to be.*

FINDING ORDER *and* PEACE

❧ Read and Consider ❧

1 Corinthians 14:26-40

"For God is not a God of disorder but of peace" (1 Corinthians 14:33).

God is not a God of disorder, He is a God of peace. Just as our households function better when there is some kind of order—you can find what you are looking for and things just make sense—our minds and hearts function better when there is a peaceful order to what we allow to influence us. We have to be careful what TV shows, magazines, and books we look at and what music, radio programs, or CDs we listen to. Those things should fill our minds with godly thoughts and feed our spirits so we are enriched, clear-minded, and peaceful. If, instead, they deplete us and leave us feeling empty, confused, anxious, and fearful, then we must turn them off and get them out of our lives.

It's important to remember that you have a choice about what you will accept into your mind and what you won't. You can choose to take every thought captive and let Christ's mind be in you (Philippians 2:5), or you can allow the devil to feed you lies and manipulate your life. Every sin begins as a thought in the mind (Mark 7:21-22), so if you don't take control of your mind, the devil will. That's why you must be diligent to monitor what you allow into your mind.

It's up to us to fill our minds with God's Word and the words of people in whom God's Spirit resides. It's up to us to fill our hearts and thoughts with praise so that we leave no room for the enemy's propaganda. It's up to us to find order by asking the God of peace to rule our lives. Only then will we know the peace that passes all understanding.

❧

*Heavenly Father, I know You are a God of order, and
order brings peace. Help me to maintain that same
order and peace in my life. Give me the wisdom to
not allow anything that would disturb that order and
peace to influence my life. Help me to fill my mind
with Your Word and my soul with Your Spirit so
that there is no room for the enemy's propaganda.*

PRAYER GROWS LOVE
in YOUR HEART

❧ Read and Consider ❧

2 Corinthians 9:6-15

*"And in their prayers for you their hearts will
go out to you, because of the surpassing grace
God has given you" (2 Corinthians 9:14).*

I t is a powerful thing when we pray for one another. Every time we
pray for someone, we feel more connected to them. It is exactly
as Paul said—your heart goes out to the person you are praying for.
That's because God gives us His heart for them.

That's why praying for our enemies is a good thing. It not only
softens our heart, but it opens a door for them to hear God and for
their heart to be changed. When there are people we are angry with
and don't feel like praying for at all, if we will make ourselves pray
for them, even though we don't feel they deserve it, walls will come
down and forgiveness will happen.

Intercessory prayer is powerful on many levels. It not only influ-
ences situations and people, it changes *us* in the very process. Is there
a difficult person for whom you need to pray? Has someone hurt
you? Ask God to help you pray for them. When you do, He will
work love in your heart for them, which will ultimately be to your
greatest blessing. Only God can cause love to grow in your heart
where there is none. Only God can bring to life love that has died.
It happens as we pray for that person.

❧

Lord, there are certain people I want to pray for because I know You will give me Your heart of love for them. Help me to pray especially for the people who have hurt me. Thank You that praying for others not only changes their lives, but it changes mine as well.

When *the* Failure *of* Others Tests Our Faith

Now we pray to God that you will not do anything wrong. Not that people will see that we have stood the test but that you will do what is right even though we may seem to have failed. For we cannot do anything against the truth, but only for the truth. We are glad whenever we are weak but you are strong; and our prayer is for your perfection" (2 Corinthians 13:7-9).

Paul addressed some criticism that had been spoken against him that had called into question his own faith. This led him to a discussion about passing the test of true faith. He prayed that even if his own faith seemed to fail the test, the faith of the Corinthians would not waver but instead remain strong.

Paul's prayer encouraging the Corinthians to do what was right was not the prayer of a perfectionistic leader who felt that the behavior of those he trained reflected on him. His prayer had to do with urging them on to authentic faith and not being dependent on him. Too often we become so connected to the people who mentor or teach us spiritually that when they fail in our eyes, our faith may fail too. But Paul's prayer was that the faith of these people would be so connected to *God* and to *His* faithfulness that nothing, not even disappointments in their mentors, could shake it.

We all need that kind of faith. People will let us down from time to time—even the best mentors, even our favorite preachers, even the people we need the most will disappoint us. But that won't shake us if the foundation of our faith is in God alone.

To have that kind of faith, we must invest in our relationship with Him. He will never change. We can always depend on Him.

He won't fail us. If we ask Him to, He will strengthen *our* faith so we can lift up others who are struggling with *theirs*.

❧

Lord God, when I see the failure of any servant of Yours, I
pray it will not shake my faith in the least. Help me to
do the right thing and remain strong in You no matter
what I see anyone else doing. Give me faith that is not
dependent on the rise or fall of others. I know You won't
fail, even though others do, and that is all that matters.

MOVING INTO *the* FREEDOM
GOD HAS *for* US

❧ Read and Consider ❧

Galatians 5:1-15

"It is for freedom that Christ has set us free. Stand firm, then, and do not let yourselves be burdened again by a yoke of slavery" (Galatians 5:1).

Did you inherit your mother's eyes or your father's nose? How about your grandmother's talent for art or your grandfather's gift of music?

There are many physical characteristics, gifts, abilities, and talents that we can inherit from our parents and grandparents. Unfortunately, though, we can also inherit character qualities that aren't so enviable—things like a bad temper, a propensity for lying, negativity, unforgiveness, perfectionism, or pride. These and other entrenched characteristics that have a spiritual base can also be passed along from our parents to us, and from us to our children. In a particular family there may be a tendency toward such things as addiction, suicide, depression, rejection, or being accident-prone—all mistakenly accepted as "fate" or "the way I am."

Some of what we accept about ourselves and our lives are actually family bondages, for children can inherit the consequences of their ancestors' sins. "I, the LORD your God, am a jealous God, punishing the children for the sin of the fathers to the third and fourth generation of those who hate me" (Exodus 20:5). This Scripture is referring to people who don't walk in a loving relationship with God, but how many of our ancestors didn't walk with God and how many times have we been less than lovingly obedient to Him?

Galatians warns us not to be burdened again by a yoke of slavery, or bondage. If it is not possible as a believer to become entangled again with a yoke of bondage, why does the Bible warn us about it? The answer is, even though Jesus set us free from sin, we can still make choices that put us back into bondage to it.

Sometimes we accept certain tendencies toward sin in ourselves, without realizing that we don't have to. We can say no to them in our lives. Sometimes we carry on a family tradition that we shouldn't and it affects our children. Unlike physical traits, tendencies toward sin are something we don't have to receive as an inheritance from our parents. That's because these tendencies are nothing more than the unquestioned acceptance of a firmly entrenched lie of the enemy. He wants us to believe that we are not a new creation in Christ and that we have not been set free from our old nature. He wants us to think that because Dad (or Grandpa) drank too much, was a complainer, cheated on his wife, abused his family with his anger, got divorced, or was dishonest in his business dealings, that this is just the way things are done in our family. But we can choose to break away from these old familial habits through prayer and the power of the Holy Spirit. And when we see things we don't like about ourselves reflected in our children, we can pray for them to be set free of that tendency as well. In Jesus' name we can be set free from any family bondage, and by the power of the Holy Spirit we can refuse to allow it any place in our own lives and in the lives of our children.

❧

*Lord, help me to stand firm in the freedom You have
secured for me. Thank You, Jesus, that You gave Your
life so that I could be set free from the yoke of slavery to
the enemy of my soul. Help me to not become entangled
in it again. Make me aware when I am accepting some
bondage in my life for which You died to set me free.*

SEEING *the* POWER *of* GOD *at* WORK

*"I pray also that the eyes of your heart may be
enlightened in order that you may know the hope
to which he has called you, the riches of his glorious
inheritance in the saints, and his incomparably great
power for us who believe" (Ephesians 1:18-19).*

The power of God is at work in our lives and in the world around us wherever He is invited. So if you ever find yourself thinking that you are not seeing His power manifesting in your life as much as you would like, then perhaps you have not invited Him into your situation with as much fervency as *He* would like. The Holy Spirit never forces Himself upon us. He waits for our invitation.

You can only move in the power of God's Spirit if you have first received Jesus as Savior. You need to "know this love that surpasses knowledge—that you may be filled to the measure of all the fullness of God" (3:19). When you have Jesus as ruler of your life, you will come to know Him as the one "who is able to do immeasurably more than all we ask or imagine, according to his power that is at work within us" (3:20). Because of His Holy Spirit in us—His power in us—He can do more in our lives than we can even think to ask for.

Once you receive Jesus and have the Holy Spirit in you, He will begin to work in your life as you pray. The more you pray—or seek God's presence—the more the Holy Spirit will guide and teach you. Jesus said, "The Counselor, the Holy Spirit, whom the Father will send in my name, will teach you all things and will remind you of everything I have said to you" (John 14:26). When you acknowledge the Holy Spirit and then invite Him to move in you freely, He will. You will see His power manifest.

God *wants* us to witness His power at work in the world. He wants us to understand "his incomparably great power for us who believe" (1:19). He desires that we know this power that raised Jesus "from the dead and seated him at his right hand in the heavenly realms, far above all rule and authority, power and dominion, and every title that can be given" (1:20-21). He wants us to understand that Jesus is not weak toward us, but powerful among us (2 Corinthians 13:3). He wants us to understand that though "he was crucified in weakness, yet he lives by God's power," and even though we are also weak, we live by the power of God too (2 Corinthians 13:4). God wants us to see that "we have not received the spirit of the world but the Spirit who is from God, that we may understand what God has freely given us" (1 Corinthians 2:12).

Invite God to open the eyes of your heart and understanding, so that you will be able to see Him and His power at work in you, in your life, and in the world around you.

❧

Dear God, I pray that the eyes of my heart will be opened to see the hope to which You have called me. Help me to understand my true glorious inheritance. Enable me to comprehend the magnitude of Your power on my behalf because I believe in You. I seek more of Your presence and Your power so that I can see them manifested in my life.

GETTING ARMED *for the* BATTLE

❧ Read and Consider ❧

Ephesians 6:10-20

*"Put on the full armor of God so that you can take
your stand against the devil's schemes...Pray in the
Spirit on all occasions with all kinds of prayers and
requests. With this in mind, be alert and always keep
on praying for all the saints" (Ephesians 6:11,18).*

Scripture tells us that we are in a spiritual battle, and we need to be fully covered in the armor of God. From the moment we become believers and align ourselves with God and His purposes, the enemy of our soul wages war against us. Evil may be perpetrated against us by human beings, but we must never forget that it is our ultimate enemy, the devil, who is behind it. "For our struggle is not against flesh and blood, but against the rulers, against the authorities, against the powers of this dark world and against the spiritual forces of evil in the heavenly realms" (6:12).

God's Word, however, tells us how to protect ourselves. First, we are commanded to be strong in the Lord and in His power. Our own human strength is totally inadequate to do battle with our ultimate adversary, but God's power is invincible and His protection is complete.

The way we access that power and protection in this war that the enemy is waging against us is to put on God's armor. Paul tells us of the specific pieces of armor that each believer needs to consciously put on every day: the belt of truth (to fight Satan's lies), the breastplate of righteousness (to protect our hearts), shoes (for firm footing in our walk with Christ), the shield of faith (to repel Satan's accusations), the helmet of salvation (to protect our minds), and the sword of the Spirit—the Word of God (to give us knowledge, instruction, and ever-increasing faith).

Most of all, we must pray! Prayer strengthens us to stand against the enemy. Pray God's covering over yourself and your loved ones daily. Pray that He will reveal to you any place in your protective armor through which the evil one can secure a hook. Pray that any stronghold Satan is trying to erect in your life will be destroyed.

The enemy of our souls will always try to keep us from moving into all God has for us. But we can thwart his plans with prayer, praise, and the sword of the Spirit—which is the Word of God. These are our greatest weapons and the devil cannot stand against them.

❧

Lord, because I have aligned myself with You, the enemy wages war against me. Help me to put on the full spiritual armor You have provided for me. Teach me what that is so I understand how to maintain it. Help me to fully understand the depth of truth, righteousness, faith, a solid walk with Christ, salvation, powerful prayer, and the sword of the Spirit, which is Your Word.

PRAYER *and* THANKSGIVING BRING PEACE

"Do not be anxious about anything, but in everything, by prayer and petition, with thanksgiving, present your requests to God. And the peace of God, which transcends all understanding, will guard your hearts and your minds in Christ Jesus" (Philippians 4:6-7).

These familiar verses remind us to pray and bring all our requests to God so that we can have His peace ruling our hearts. But what we often forget are the two words, "with thanksgiving." We neglect to thank God in the midst of whatever is happening (or *not* happening) to us at the time. We don't remember to praise Him first as the source of all that we will ever need. We don't always remember to worship Him for who He is. And we must do that, because all the things that are true of God are true of Him no matter what is going on inside of us or in our lives.

Just before this verse, Paul tells all of us to rejoice in God. He even says it twice for emphasis. We are instructed to "rejoice in the Lord always" (4:4), to find our joy in Him. So many times we think our fear and anxiety are connected to God. We think we feel that way because of something He didn't do or may not do for us. *What if He doesn't provide for us? What if He doesn't protect us? What if He doesn't give us what we want or need?* But what if we, instead, were to say in the face of these feared problems, "Thank You, Lord, that You will always provide for us." Or, "Thank You, Lord, that You are my protector and You will continue to protect me." Or, "Thank

You, Lord, that You have promised to give us everything we need and give us the desires of our hearts."

Anxiety can come into our souls at any time. It often happens in the middle of the night when the house is quiet but the mind is not. There are pills that promise temporary relief, but when they wear off, the anxiety is still there. The problem has simply been masked. Such anxiety can only be quieted by the peace of God. And the moment we receive Jesus, we have access to peace that "transcends all understanding." When we are fearful, apprehensive, worried, or terrified, the peace of God can restore us to calm, assured confidence.

We have access to that peace every time we praise God and give Him thanks. It's best to do it the moment we sense anxiety over *anything*. And then *continue* to praise and thank Him until all anxiety leaves. Try it and you'll experience greater peace than you have ever known.

❦

Dear God, help me to not be anxious or worried about anything. Help me to pray and intercede instead. Enable me to lift up praise and worship in the face of whatever opposes me. Help me to bring every concern before You and leave it at Your feet. Help me to refuse to think what-if thoughts. Fill me with Your peace that passes all understanding so that my heart and mind will be protected.

The POWER of PRAYING for OTHERS

"For this reason, since the day we heard about you, we
have not stopped praying for you and asking God to
fill you with the knowledge of his will through all
spiritual wisdom and understanding" (Colossians 1:9).

For all the people we care about—parents, children, a spouse, friends, family, neighbors, coworkers, or people in need around the world—one of the best things we can do for them is pray. We may not be able to provide them with good health, financial security, or protection from all harm. But we can pray that *God* will heal them, provide for them, and keep them safe.

The promise to pray for others is one of the finest gifts we can give. Every time we seek the presence of God and the release of His power on behalf of someone else, great things happen. It is the most effective way we can touch others and make a difference in their lives.

The most important thing we can pray about for others is that they will know God better and that He will help them understand His will, grow in spiritual wisdom, and live lives that honor Him. We can pray that they will become more like Him and bear the fruit of His Spirit.

When we pray for others, we are asking God to make His presence known in their lives. We are asking Him to open their heart so they can hear from Him. That doesn't mean there will always be an immediate response. Sometimes it can take days, weeks, months, or even years. But our prayers are never lost or meaningless. If we are praying, something is happening in the lives of those for whom we pray, whether we see it or not. Everything that needs to happen in our lives and in the lives of our loved ones cannot happen without the presence and power of God. Prayer invites and ignites both.

❧

*Lord, I pray for the people You have put in my life and
on my heart. Fill them with wisdom and understanding
and the knowledge of Your will so that they will stay
on the path You have for them. I pray they will learn
to hear Your voice and come to know You better, so
that they can have a closer walk with You.*

How *to* Always Do God's Will

✣ Read and Consider ✣

1 Thessalonians 5:12-28

*"Be joyful always; pray continually; give thanks
in all circumstances, for this is God's will for you
in Christ Jesus" (1 Thessalonians 5:16-18).*

What do you do when you pray and pray about something, and God doesn't seem to answer? For example, what if you've been praying about an important decision, and now time is running out? You have to know what to do right away, but still God seems silent. What do you do then? When that happens, always do what you *know* is God's will. And it is always God's will to be joyful, to *continue* praying, and to give Him thanks regardless of your circumstances (5:16-18). Praise, prayer, and a joyful heart are vital when you need to know God's will for your life.

To "be joyful always" means we have to make a choice. We can't always choose how we feel, but we *can* choose how we respond to our feelings. We can make a decision to be joyful *in spite* of how we feel. The way we do that is to never allow our feelings or our circumstances to interfere with our worship. Whatever the situation is, when we continually acknowledge God's greatness in the midst of whatever is happening, we experience the joy of the Lord.

To "pray continually" means to pray about everything right when you think about it, allowing prayer to become a natural first response to whatever is happening. Imagine how complicated our lives would be if we had to remember to tell our heart to beat and our lungs to breathe. How much time would we spend if we had to schedule all the body repairs that go on around the clock without our conscious attention? The challenge to pray continually is an invitation to develop a prayer life that simply goes on constantly in the background, like our lungs breathing and our heart beating, no matter what is happening in our life.

To "give thanks" is the main reason to pray. It's expressing gratitude for who God is and all He has done. It's deciding to be grateful even in the tough times—times of darkness, sadness, or despair. It's saying "thank you" to God in moments when we can't see the whole picture, knowing He will shed His light on the situation. We need to give thanks "in all circumstances" because something good always happens when we thank God. We become more receptive to God's will. We gain the mind of Christ and the leading of the Holy Spirit. We invite God to work in our situation. That means if we were leaning toward doing something that wasn't actually the will of God, our heart would open up to what He wants for us, and our mind would change.

So when you are waiting to know God's will for your future, do what you know is always God's will right now: Continue praying and praising and letting the joy of the Lord rise in your heart.

❧

God, I know it is always Your will for me to be joyful and pray often and give thanks to You in all circumstances. Help me to remember to do Your will in this regard, even when I don't see answers to my prayers as I would like. No matter what is happening in my life, I know You are greater than anything I face.

PRAYING *for* PEOPLE WHO
NEED GOOD NEWS

❧ Read and Consider ❧
2 Thessalonians 3:1-5

*"Finally, brothers, pray for us that the message of
the Lord may spread rapidly and be honored, just
as it was with you" (2 Thessalonians 3:1).*

D o you remember the first time you heard about Jesus and His message of salvation, when the Good News really penetrated your soul? Do you recall that pivotal moment when your life changed for all eternity? Who brought Jesus' message to you? How did God use that person to reach out and touch your heart?

God is always intensely personal and masterfully creative in the ways He reaches out to us. Each one of us has a unique and wonderful story of our salvation. And all of our stories have one thing in common: Somewhere, somehow, *someone* responded to God's call to spread His love and bring His message. Whether we heard a pastor who preached a message that affected us or listened to a friend who talked to us about Jesus or someone gave us a Bible or a Christian book or a person was praying for us...someone reached out because of a desire to help us discover the truth about God's love.

In this passage, the apostle Paul asked fellow Christians to pray for those who were spreading the message of the Lord, that it would be far-reaching and effective, "just as it was with you." This is a strong reminder to remember how Jesus saved us and all that He has done for us so that we will deeply desire that others experience His love too.

Praying is the most important thing you can do when trying to reach people for the Lord. Whether you feel confident or not about your own efforts to spread the good news, your prayers will pave the way for hearts to open up and receive what God wants to speak to them. Whether you are in the frontlines of evangelism or behind the scenes, as long as you are praying, you are a vital part of God's work here on earth. Along with everything else you are doing for the Lord, don't forget to share your own story about how you came to know Jesus. Tell it often. And let it remind you to pray for those who are searching for truth and need to hear about all the good news Jesus has for them.

> *Lord, use me to bring the good news of salvation through Jesus Christ to others. Just as You have used others powerfully in my life, equip me with the right words at the right time so that those whose hearts are ready will be drawn toward You. I also pray for the men and women who need the good news, that their hearts would be open to receive all You have for them.*

Praying Together *in* Unity

*"I want men everywhere to lift up holy hands in prayer,
without anger or disputing" (1 Timothy 2:8).*

God wants all of us who believe in Him to be in unity. When we are unified, we stand together to glorify Him. Because Jesus "gave himself as a ransom for *all men*" (2:6), we are unified as recipients of His salvation and messengers of His love. That means regardless of how different we are from one another, we are all brought together by His sacrifice. But we have to make a decision to stay in unity. In fact, unity is such an important part of our spiritual foundation that our spiritual growth and the effectiveness of our prayer life depend on us being in unity with one another. God wants us to be unified in our beliefs, unified in our work for Him, and unified in our prayers. That means no arguing or fighting with our brothers and sisters.

Paul urges that "requests, prayers, intercession and thanksgiving be made for everyone," meaning both those who are already followers of Jesus and those who haven't yet met Him (2:1). But sometimes we Christians quarrel among ourselves. We get caught up in unimportant debates and useless arguments. Paul encourages all Christians to pray for others "without anger or disputing" for the common goal of winning people to the Lord (2:8).

When we are selfless in our prayers, increasingly grateful for our salvation, humbled by God's amazing love for us, staunch in our belief in Christ as Savior over all, and unified in prayer with other believers, then our prayers are powerful and will bear fruit beyond measure.

❧

Lord, help me to find other believers who will stand with me in prayer. Bring godly prayer partners into my life with whom I can pray in power. Help us to be so devoted to You that we maintain a oneness of the Spirit, even if we disagree on certain things. I pray we will be unified in our belief in Your Word so that we will be unified in our prayers.

BEING REMEMBERED *in* PRAYER

2 Timothy 1:3-7

"I thank God, whom I serve, as my forefathers did,
with a clear conscience, as night and day I constantly
remember you in my prayers" (2 Timothy 1:3).

We all want to be remembered. We all desire to make a positive and lasting impression on someone's life. None of us wants to be forgotten by the people who are near and dear to us—especially family and friends. And who doesn't want to make a profound impact on the world in some way? But most importantly, we all want to be remembered by others in prayer.

Imagine being remembered day and night in prayer. Think of how loved and cared for you would feel. When we are prayed for, we *feel* those prayers—even if we don't know people are praying, even if we don't fully understand what it is we are feeling. When we lift up each other in prayer, we are not only bound *together* in the love of God, but we also deepen and strengthen our *personal* bond with the Lord. We form a prayer circle with God at the center, and it grows stronger every time we pray. We experience great blessings whether we are the giver or the receiver of prayer.

If you need to be reminded to pray for others, keep a prayer journal with a list of the people who need your prayers and how you want to pray for them. Then pray as the Spirit leads. It's inspiring to think how Paul constantly remembered to pray for Timothy. We can do the same with people in our own lives.

❧

Lord, help me to not forget anyone in my prayers. Especially show me the people who feel forgotten so that I can remember them in intercession. Bring specific people to mind who need a miracle of healing or help. Show me who needs to hear Your voice guiding them. Enable the people I pray for to sense Your love in their lives.

ASK *for* BOLDNESS *to* SHARE YOUR FAITH

❧ Read and Consider ❧
Philemon 1:4-7

"I pray that you may be active in sharing your faith,
so that you will have a full understanding of every
good thing we have in Christ" (Philemon 1:6).

The moment we meet Jesus for the first time, our lives are changed forever. It's a moment we never forget. Why, then, is it so hard to introduce others to Him? After all, we understand the incredible effect knowing Jesus will have on their lives for all eternity. Jesus saves us and transforms our lives, and then He gives us the wonderful privilege of being a part of someone else's salvation and transformation. But when we have an opportunity to speak to others about Him, we can be filled with trepidation. For some of us, the pressure of wanting to be sure we say the right thing causes us to hesitate. We are afraid we might say something wrong, say it insensitively, or turn someone off entirely. We fear we might be rejected and not be a good representative of Christ. That's why prayer in advance of that is crucial!

The apostle Paul's prayer is a model for us as believers and members of the family of God. Sharing our faith is a divine calling and is instrumental in furthering the work of God, but we can't do it without God's power. That's why we need to pray for God's enablement before we share our faith. We need to ask God to open up opportunities to talk about Jesus and to give us the ability to communicate His love in such a way that people can understand it and are attracted to it.

Pray often that you will be able to share your faith whenever the opportunity presents itself and that you will have the perfect words to say. Pray for God to soften the hearts of those you speak to and open their ears and eyes so that their hearts can receive the truth.

❧

God, help me to get over any inhibitions I have about sharing my faith with unbelievers. I know of no greater gift than to give someone Your love and the good news of salvation in Christ, but I always want to be sensitive to Your leading so that I don't come off as insensitive to others. Help me to have a perfect sense of timing and the right words to say.

APPROACH GOD'S THRONE
with CONFIDENCE

❧ Read and Consider ❧
Hebrews 4:14-16

"For we do not have a high priest who is unable to sympathize with our weaknesses, but we have one who has been tempted in every way, just as we are—yet was without sin. Let us then approach the throne of grace with confidence, so that we may receive mercy and find grace to help us in our time of need" (Hebrews 4:15-16).

Jesus understands us completely. That's because He left heaven and came to earth as a human being. He was "in very nature God, [but] did not consider equality with God something to be grasped, but made himself nothing, taking the very nature of a servant, being made in human likeness" (Philippians 2:6-7). He was fully God, yet a human being like us. He suffered heartache, persecution, pain, and suffering, so He is able to sympathize with *our* heartache, persecution, pain, and suffering. He was tempted in every way, so He understands *our* struggle with temptation. Though He never gave in to temptation, He understands that *we* often do.

That's why when we pray—especially in times of weakness, temptation, confusion, or shame—we must pray boldly and with confidence, knowing that Jesus understands us. Knowing that He is right there in the middle of whatever is troubling us, intervening on our behalf. Knowing that because we have aligned ourselves with Him—God's beloved Son who died to save us—God listens to our prayers as His beloved children. We can have confidence before God because of Jesus.

❦

*Thank You, Jesus, that You understand my weaknesses
and my temptations, for You have been tempted in
every way and yet did not sin. Because You understand
my struggles, I know I can come to You and receive
mercy. Help me to approach You with confidence,
knowing You will help me in my time of need.*

ASKING GOD *for* WISDOM

❧ Read and Consider ❧
―――――――――――――――
James 1:2-18

*"If any of you lacks wisdom, he should ask God,
who gives generously to all without finding fault,
and it will be given to him" (James 1:5).*

I f every time we pray for wisdom God will generously give it to us, then we should be praying for wisdom every day and not just when the need is urgent.

The most urgent time that we pray for wisdom is when we are in a difficult and pressing situation and we don't know what to do. We need help. We need to know which way to go. And we usually need to know immediately. In those times it's comforting to know that God is not only available to us and willing to help, but He has *promised* to do so.

However, we don't have to wait until we are in an emergency situation in order to pray for wisdom. We can pray now. How many times have we faced a quick decision or an immediate situation in which our response would have been a lot stronger, better, or more effective if we'd had more of God's wisdom beforehand? King Solomon, when invited to make any request he wanted to God, asked for wisdom early in his reign. And God gladly granted his request (1 Kings 3:5-10). We need to do that too. In other words, we should ask *before* the need arises.

If you don't have God's wisdom, you will try to get through life on your own strength and understanding, and you may end up making bad decisions or doing stupid things. But when you ask God to give you wisdom every day, you will find yourself doing things so wise even *you* may be surprised. You will make a decision that turns out to be so completely right that you will be amazed. You will have insight you never had before. You will be able to give sound advice to someone who asks for it. You will sense danger when it is lurking. You will know when to speak and when not to, and what to say and how to say it. You will have a sense of what to do and what not to do in any situation.

Ask God for wisdom right now. You can trust that He will give it to you because He has promised it in His Word.

❧

God, I ask for wisdom, for I know true wisdom comes only from You. Thank You that Your Word promises You will give wisdom to me when I ask for it. Help me to be wise every day in every decision, especially when I must act quickly. Help me to know what to do and what not to do in any situation.

POWERFUL *and* EFFECTIVE PRAYING

❧ Read and Consider ❧

James 5:13-18

*"Therefore confess your sins to each other and pray for
each other so that you may be healed. The prayer of a
righteous man is powerful and effective" (James 5:16).*

Have you ever wondered, *Are my prayers powerful and effective?
If they aren't, is it because I'm not righteous? After all, James
says the prayers of righteous people are powerful and effective.* If you
ever have doubts about the effectiveness of your prayers because
you haven't seen very many answers to them, then you might be
thinking that you are not good enough to deserve answers. But you
would be mistaken.

Too often when we think about being a righteous person, we
think in terms of our own behavior. The Bible does say that our faith
should work itself out in what we do and the way we live our lives,
but it also teaches that our righteousness comes not because of our
good behavior but because of Christ's sacrifice. The work of Jesus
on the cross and in His resurrection is what gives us righteousness
before God. We are righteous in God's eyes because He sees Jesus'
righteousness in us. We then behave in a righteous manner because
we want to show our love for Jesus by living His way and doing
what He asks us to do.

Too often we think that if our prayers aren't causing sicknesses
to be healed, paralytics to walk, or mountains to be moved, then
they aren't powerful. Too often we think that we have to see such
astounding answers to our prayers in order to prove they are effective.
But the truth is, we often don't get to see the results of our prayers
at all. We don't know the ways in which God is working through

our prayers to touch people or the circumstances of their lives. We don't know how much we have effected or prevented in our own lives through prayer.

Prayer is an act of faith. Our prayers are powerful because we pray them to a powerful God in whom we trust. We just have to pray and trust God to answer in His way and time.

❧

Lord, how grateful I am that my righteousness comes not because I do everything perfectly, but because You have done everything perfectly. I am seen as righteous because of Your great sacrifice on the cross. Help me to confess my sins not only to You, but also to others who may be affected so that healing can come to us all. Thank You for making my prayers powerful and effective.

God Hears Our Prayers
and Sees Our Heart

❧ Read and Consider ❧
1 Peter 3:8-12

*"For the eyes of the Lord are on the righteous and his
ears are attentive to their prayer, but the face of the
Lord is against those who do evil" (1 Peter 3:12).*

Have you ever wondered if God is really listening when you pray? If so, you're not alone. All of us have had that same question in our minds at one time or another. We pray about a specific thing, and if nothing happens we wonder why we are praying at all.

When Peter wrote about God's attentive ears, he was quoting Psalm 34, a psalm written by David after he escaped with his life from the clutches of King Saul. David then traveled to a foreign land to seek asylum, but once he was in the court of the foreign king, he realized he had a reputation as someone who could threaten the king's authority. If this foreign king felt threatened (as Saul had), David would once again be running for his life. To free himself from this situation, David pretended to be crazy until the king literally threw him out of the city (1 Samuel 21). After such a shrewd escape, David wrote the psalm Peter quoted in this New Testament letter. David celebrated the fact that when he cried out to the Lord, God heard him. "I sought the LORD, and he answered me; he delivered me from all my fears…This poor man called, and the LORD heard him; he saved him out of all his troubles…The eyes of the LORD are on the righteous and his ears are attentive to their cry…The righteous cry out, and the LORD hears them; he delivers them from all their troubles. The LORD is close to the brokenhearted and saves those who are crushed in spirit" (Psalm 34:4,6,15,17-18).

David's life was not easy. He went through horrible heartbreak, devastating loss, and extremely troubling situations. But through it all, he knew he was not alone. He knew that in every situation, God was there listening and answering.

We can know that too. We can have the same certainty that God not only hears our requests, He hears our heart. We may say something like, "Lord, help me get this job," but He will hear, "I'm desperate for a change. I feel so unimportant here." We may say, "God, please keep me safe," but He hears, "I am afraid of how dangerous, precarious, and out of control life seems right now." God not only hears what we want, He also knows what we need.

✿

Dear God, I thank You that You see my heart and
hear my prayers. How grateful I am that when You
see me, You see the righteousness of Jesus in me and
not the sinner I was before I received Him into my life.
Thank You that You not only hear my prayers, but You
see my need and will answer the cries of my heart.

FINDING FORGIVENESS
THROUGH CONFESSION

*"If we confess our sins, he is faithful and just
and will forgive us our sins and purify us
from all unrighteousness" (1 John 1:9).*

God offers us three steps for changing our behavior.

The first step is *confession,* which is *admitting* what we did. Everyone makes mistakes, but there is an epidemic in the world today of people who can't admit they did something wrong. God says that all we have to do is confess our sins, and He will forgive us and purify us. Confession means admitting the truth to ourselves first, then to God, and then perhaps to someone else who might have been hurt because of our sin. Sometimes we need to confess to God in front of another person who can pray for us and help us truly get our mistakes off our chest. And confession is not just admitting the truth of what we did, but it is also taking responsibility for it. To own up to wrongdoing can seem like a monumental task, but it is well worth the effort. Confession is one of the best things you can do for yourself. It cleanses your heart by releasing the burden of guilt, and it makes way for God's total forgiveness.

The second step is *repentance,* which means *being sorry* about what we did and wanting to never do it again. We don't confess sin with the intention of clearing the slate and then continuing on with the same sinful behavior, knowing we can just confess it all over again. True repentance means being so sorry before God that we don't ever want to disappoint Him by doing the same thing again.

The third step is *asking for forgiveness* so we can be *cleansed and released* from the consequences of what we did. John didn't say, "If we beg and plead with all of our hearts, then God will forgive us." He said in essence that God's forgiveness flows freely the moment we simply ask for it. God is always waiting and ready to forgive. He doesn't have to be coerced or cajoled. He *wants* us to live free of guilt and shame. He wants us to live in complete forgiveness because only then can we ever find total restoration in our lives.

❧

Lord, I confess my sins before You. Thank You that You are faithful to forgive them and to cleanse me from all the effects of them. If there is sin in my life that I am not seeing, reveal it to me now so that I can confess it before You and be purified of all unrighteousness. I want to live in the wholeness of complete forgiveness.

COMING *to* FATHER GOD *in* CONFIDENCE

❧ Read and Consider ❧
_____
1 John 5:13-21

"This is the confidence we have in approaching God: that if we ask anything according to his will, he hears us. And if we know that he hears us—whatever we ask—we know that we have what we asked of him" (1 John 5:14-15).

The Bible says our relationship to God is like a child's relationship with an adoring father. John spoke of God lavishing His love on us, calling us His own. What a powerful picture of the way we should always approach our heavenly Father. Imagine a small child coming to ask his or her father for something, knowing that it will be given. Would there be any hesitation before the child leaped into the father's arms, relaxed in the safety and security found there? Wouldn't the child be expectant and hopeful as every need is communicated and met?

How does that compare with the way we approach God? Too often we don't bound into His presence as joyfully as a small child. Perhaps we are worried that we're bothering Him with the same old request we've been praying about for years. Or maybe we fear that He is going to deny our request, and we don't want to set ourselves up for disappointment. Or perhaps we feel less than fit to be in His presence because of an area where we feel we are failing.

Whatever the reason we hesitate to come before God with confidence, we know from these verses that He is a good God who hears our requests and cares about our needs. If what we are asking for is wrong for us, He'll let us know. If it's right, He'll make it happen in His way and in His time. We can trust Him enough to run into His

presence like a child who is loved and accepted, who can't imagine
receiving anything but goodness from Father God.

❧

Heavenly Father, it gives me great confidence to know
that if I ask according to Your will, You will hear
me and I will have what I ask for. I come to You
as Your beloved child and ask You to help me pray
according to Your will. I know I will receive only good
things from You because You love and accept me.

PRAYER RISES

*"The smoke of the incense, together with the
prayers of the saints, went up before God from
the angel's hand" (Revelation 8:4).*

You've watched smoke rise from a lighted candle or from the chimney of a fireplace. It naturally goes up and disappears beyond sight. In his wonderful vision of heaven, John saw an angel carrying incense and the prayers of the saints. The aroma and smoke rising up from the angel's hand were offerings to God.

In the Old Testament, the incense that burned on the altar was also symbolic of prayers offered to God by the high priest: God directed the Israelites to place the altar for burning incense "in front of the curtain that is before the ark of the Testimony...where I will meet with you. Aaron must burn fragrant incense on the altar every morning when he tends the lamps. He must burn incense again when he lights the lamps at twilight so incense will burn regularly before the LORD for the generations to come" (Exodus 30:6-8).

This continued into the New Testament worship at the temple. Luke 1 describes the priest Zechariah (the father of John the Baptist) being chosen by lot to "go into the temple of the Lord and burn incense." Incense continued to be burned twice daily at the temple. And when the people saw the smoke rising, they prayed. Both the smoke and their prayers ascended to God's throne.

This is a particularly encouraging picture for us on those days when we feel as if our prayers don't have power enough to make it past the ceiling. As if they just hang there in space or evaporate into thin air. Or worse yet, as if they never even make it off the ground.

At those times, it's wonderful to know that the distance our prayers travel does not depend on the fervency of our prayers or how loud or well we say them. Just as smoke rises, so do our prayers rise to heaven and to the ears of God, because that's what prayers born of faith do.

❧

Lord, how grateful I am that my prayers always rise to You in heaven and You hear each one. Even the quietest prayers of my heart born out of faith are as important as my loudest prayers ignited by fervency. Thank You that You will hear and answer them all. How blessed am I to have You as the center of my life.

Praising God *for the* Future

*"Let us rejoice and be glad and give him glory! For
the wedding of the Lamb has come, and his bride
has made herself ready" (Revelation 19:7).*

We need to praise God for who He *is*. We must praise God for what He has *done*. We should also praise God for what He's *going* to do. The book of Revelation paints a picture of a future world. A world put right side up. It describes a wedding feast to which we are invited, a feast that inaugurates a new world where sadness and fear have no place.

Praising God for what we know is coming doesn't mean that we don't live fully in this day and in this moment. Instead, it means that part of the sweetness of this moment is the anticipation of the moments to come. In fact, knowing what is ahead allows us to better savor what we have, to endure the difficulties, and to continue on with courage.

Most often we praise God for the good things in our lives and the ways He has provided for us. This is right to do. But along with that, let's not forget to praise God that He will one day redeem this world in every possible way. Let's thank Him ahead of time for the feast that He will lay out before us—His beloved children—on the day when He brings all of history to a close and eternity with Him begins.

Let us rejoice in prayer right now that the wedding of the Lamb is coming, and we, as His bride, are being made ready to be with Him. Let us praise Him that our future is secure and good. Let's

worship Him now and thank Him that we are going to have the
privilege of worshiping Him in heaven forever.

❧

*Lord God, I praise You for my future, for You have
promised that it is good. Thank You that my ultimate
end is with You in heaven. I praise You for Your
future redemption of the world and of all things in
my life. As I worship You now, I thank You that one
day I will worship You face-to-face for all eternity.*